THE NAOS OF AMASIS

Sidestone Press

THE NAOS OF AMASIS

A monument for the reawakening of Osiris

Marco Zecchi

PALMA 20

PAPERS ON ARCHAEOLOGY OF THE
LEIDEN MUSEUM OF ANTIQUITIES

PALMA: Papers on Archaeology of the Leiden Museum of Antiquities (volume 20)

Published by Sidestone Press, Leiden
www.sidestone.com

Lay-out & cover design: Sidestone Press
Photographs cover: P.J. Bomhof / A. de Kemp
Volume editor: Maarten J. Raven

ISBN 978-90-8890-795-1 (softcover)
ISBN 978-90-8890-796-8 (hardcover)
ISBN 978-90-8890-797-5 (PDF e-book)

ISSN 2034-550X

Contents

	Preface	7
I	Naos AM 107: from Egypt to Leiden	9
II	Description of the naos	21
	1. The architecture	21
	2. The decoration	21
III	The naoi of Amasis	55
	1. The naoi	55
	2. The *damnatio memoriae*	67
	3. The decorations	69
	4. The recipients: Osiris and the others	73
IV	The role of the naos	87
	1. The recipient of the naos: Osiris Hemag	87
	2. The dedicatory text	109
	3. Great gods, small gods: divine beings in action	112
	4. Naoi at Kom el-Ahmar	138
	List of figures	149
	Abbreviations	153
	Bibliography	155
	Indices	171
	1. Deities	171
	2. Deities (in transliteration)	172
	3. Royal names	173
	4. Egyptian personal names	173
	5. Names of buildings and places	174
	6. Museum collections	175

Preface

This book aims at presenting one of the most peculiar naoi ever produced in Egypt in the Late Period. The naos AM 107 of the Museum of Antiquities in Leiden was made by order of king Amasis in the 6th century BC, a period that saw an intense production of monolithic shrines. Despite its unimpressive dimensions, the naos of Leiden stands out for its originality. What is particularly interesting about this monument is that its distinctiveness is strictly connected to the nature of its recipient. Amasis dedicated the naos to Osiris Hemag, one of the most important and enigmatic Osirian forms of the first millennium BC. Osiris Hemag represents Osiris at a crucial moment of his existence: his reawakening. It was precisely this aspect of the god that strongly influenced both the shape and the decoration of the naos, creating a unique effect. This naos is not only a shrine housing a statue of Osiris Hemag, but also a monument conveying a new definition of the god and new ideas concerning his rebirth.

Some interpretations remain uncertain, and hopefully future archaeological research will provide answers to a series of questions related to the original location and use of the naos. I hope, however, to have contributed to the understanding of one of the most intriguing monuments left by king Amasis.

I would like to thank those people who have contributed to the project in many different ways. I am indebted to the entire staff of the Museum of Leiden. I wish to express to Maarten Raven my deep and sincere gratitude for his remarks and contributions towards the completion of this book and for allowing me to study and publish this interesting monument.

I am heartily grateful to Giuliano Carapia for the drawings. I would also like to thank Valentina Gasperini (British Museum, London), Christian Greco (Museo Egizio, Turin), Daniela Picchi (Museo Civico Archeologico, Bologna), and Joanne Rowland (University of Edinburgh) for their cooperation in various ways.

I would like to acknowledge the following scholars and institutions for their kind permission to reproduce their photos: Penny Wilson (Director of the Delta Survey Projects); Vincent Rondot (Musée du Louvre, Paris); Nicky Nielsen (Field Director of the Tell Nabasha Survey Project); Claudio Parisi Presicce (Director of the Musei Capitolini, Rome); Luc Delvaux (Museés Royaux d'Art et d'Histoire, Brussels); Alice Stevenson (Petrie Museum of Archaeology, London); the Egypt Exploration Society, London; the Walters Art Museum, Baltimore; Laurent Coulon (EPHE Egypte ancienne); and the Institut Français d'Archeologie Orientale, Cairo.

Chapter I

Naos AM 107: from Egypt to Leiden

The Rijksmuseum van Oudheden in Leiden, located in a monumental building at the Rapenburg 28, houses what is arguably one of the finest and most important Egyptian collections in the world. Not only it spans every period of Egyptian history, from the Predynastic to the Graeco-Roman era and beyond, but also its extent and quality are notably impressive. Among its objects, there is a magnificent naos in red granite registered under the inventory number AM 107 and dated to the reign of king Amasis (570-526 B.C.) of the 26th Dynasty. The monument is undoubtedly one of the most remarkable naoi of the whole Late Period. It shows a certain amount of originality in shape and decorations and, as such, has drawn the attention, over the years, of many Egyptologists.

The first to give notice of the presence of this naos in the Rijksmuseum van Oudheden in Leiden was Conrad Leemans, museum director from 1839 to 1891. In his Letter to Francesco Salvolini,[1] published in 1838, he mentioned 'un beau temple monolithe en granit rouge ... d'une conservation parfaite, mais il ne parait jamais avoir été achevé. Témoin le côté gauche qui ne présente que des sculptures imparfaits'. The volume also included a plate with a drawing of the royal *serekh* on one of the roof sides. Two years later, in 1840, Leemans published the first catalogue of the museum's Egyptian collection, the *Description raisonnée des monumens égyptiens du Musée d'antiquités des Pays-Bas à Leide*,[2] in which he presented a more detailed description of the naos. He recognized the figures of the Four Sons of Horus on the front, and of the goddesses Isis and Nephthys and of the three images of Osiris on the left side, while all the other deities on the surfaces of the shrine were just recorded as being depicted under different human and animal guises. The concomitant plates of the monument – a drawing of the monument from the front and drawings of the roof, front, and outer walls – appeared five years later, as folio-sized lithographs with the text and figures of the gods, in his *Aegyptische Monumenten* (Figs. I.1-5).[3] Despite a few inaccuracies, the divine images and the inscriptions of the roof, front, and left side were fairly accurate. In the following years, the naos was mentioned by Alfred Wiedemann[4] and Flinders Petrie[5] in volumes on Egyptian history.

1 Leemans 1838, 134-135, pl. XXVI no. 267.
2 Leemans 1840, 42-43 (C 9).
3 Leemans 1839, livraison 7 (1845), 73-75, pl. XXXV.9a, d; XXXVI.9b, c, e.
4 Wiedemann 1880, 190; Wiedemann 1884, 656.
5 Petrie 1905, 349.

Figs. I.1-5. The Leiden naos, as drawn and lithographed by the museum's assistant T. Hooiberg for Leemans 1839-, livraison 7 (1845), pls. XXXV-XXXVI.

I. 1. general view (= pl. XXXV.9a).

I. 2. front (= pl. XXXVI.9b).

I. 3. left side (= pl. XXXVI.9c).

I. 4. right side (= pl. XXXVI.9e).

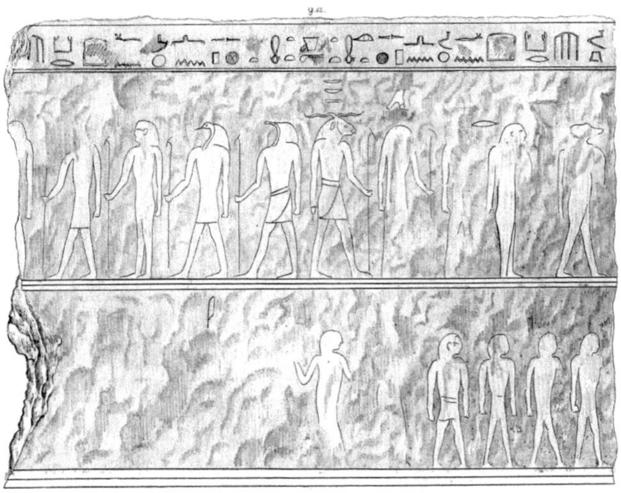

I. 5. rear (= pl. XXXV.9d).

The first attempt to identify the names of the divine figures was made by the vice-director Pieter Adriaan Aart Boeser, who in 1907 included the monument in his general catalogue of the Egyptian collection.[6] Boeser offered a more detailed description of the naos a few years later, when, in one volume of his *Beschreibung der aegyptischen Sammlung* published in 1915, he presented the reading of the names of a few deities. The volume also contained five plates with photographs of the monument (Figs. I.6-10).[7] Since then, the naos has appeared in the catalogues[8] of the Leiden Egyptian collection and has been described, or simply mentioned, by many scholars,[9] without receiving, however, the due attention that it deserves.

An important contribution to the knowledge of the origin of the monument is due to Jean Yoyotte. Until quite recently, its exact provenance was unknown and it was usually suggested that it could come from Sais, mainly because of its dedication to Osiris Hemag. But in an article published in 2001, Jean Yoyotte[10] was able to establish, on the basis of archival research, that the naos of Leiden originally came from Kom el-Ahmar,[11] a site near Shiben el-Kom, in the Minufiyeh province in the Delta. In particular, he showed that the discovery of the monument was strictly linked to the presence in Egypt of two French travellers from Marseilles, Pascal-Xavier Coste (1787-1879) and Jean-Jacques Rifaud (1786-1852).

Pascal Coste[12] arrived in Egypt on November 1st, 1817, when he was thirty, destined to become, within three years, the chief architect of the Ottoman viceroy and pasha

6 Boeser 1907, 75-77 no. 146.

7 Boeser 1915, 1, pls. I-V. These photographs were taken from impressions in gypsum plaster, as the best means to get a perfect lighting of the reliefs and also to improve their legibility by evading the mottled aspect of the original granite.

8 Schneider/Raven 1981, no. 123; Schneider 1992, 80-82.

9 See, for example, Leclant 1962, 109; Baines 1973, 9-10; El-Sayed 1975, 209; El-Sayed 1982, 415; Baines 1983, 147; Lloyd 1986, 216; Myśliwiec 1988, 49, 62, pl. LIXb; Zecchi 1996, 12-15 doc. 8; Blöbaum 2006, 32, 163; Spencer 2006, 1, 9, 15, 17, 21-22; Leclère 2008, 176; Rowland/Billing 2009, 7; Lucarelli 2010, 90; Meijer 2010, 15-19; Jansen-Winkeln 2014, 423-424.

10 Yoyotte 2001, 54-83.

11 PM IV, 67.

12 On Pascal Coste, see Hill 1991 and Jacobi 1998.

Figs. I.6-10. The Leiden naos, as represented in Boeser 1915, pls. I-V.

I.6. general view (= pl. I).

I.7. roof and front (= pl. II).

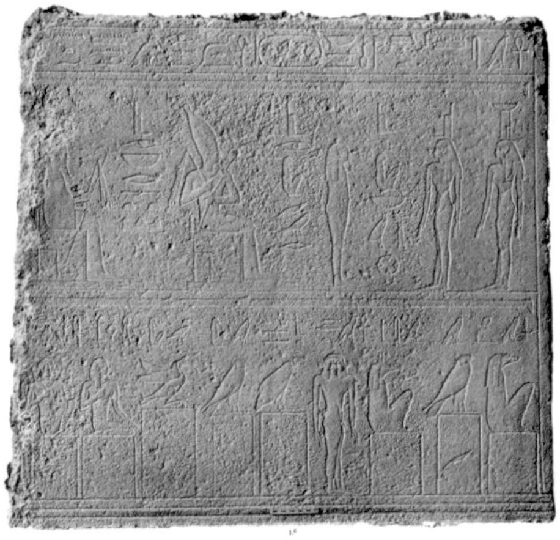

I.8. left side (= pl. III).

Mohammed Ali. During his first three years in Egypt, Coste worked more as an engineer than as an architect, but in 1820, just when he was finishing the work on the Mahmudiyya canal in Alexandria, he was commissioned three important buildings in the same city. Mohammed Ali required Coste to work on a new pavilion at the seaside in the old port and on an Italianate villa for Boghos Bey Yusufian, his interpreter and minister of foreign affairs. Moreover, the British consul asked Coste to design a villa

I.9. right side (= pl. IV).

I.10. rear (= pl. V).

along the Mahmudiyya canal, which had to serve as his own private home and as the British consulate. The year 1820 represented a very active period in Coste's life. He was not only summoned by Mohammed Ali in Cairo, where he was asked to design two other palaces, but obtained numerous other commissions, which included a network of canals and designs for telegraph towers which stretched from Alexandria to the Cairo citadel. Thanks to these new projects, in the following years Coste was able to travel all over the Delta. During his voyages, he kept a detailed diary in which he included sketches of the landscapes, people, and ruins of the localities he visited.

It was during one of these journeys in the Delta that, in late 1821, Coste arrived at Kom el-Ahmar in the Minufiyeh province, an area with which he was already familiar. Indeed, in 1817-1818, when he was working on the construction of a saltpetre factory, he had the opportunity to make many excursions, one of which was 'aux environs de Téraneh, aux ruines de Terunthes et à Menouf, ville au centre du Delta'.[13] On November 26th, 1821, about four years after his arrival in Egypt, Coste drew a sketch of the site (Fig. I.11).[14] The picture shows the locality from the north, with the hill and the modern town in the background and palm trees on the right. At the foot of the hill, there are seven blocks of stone, scattered on the ground. On at least three of them, Coste outlined figures and hieroglyphic inscriptions. Of the seven blocks represented, two can be identified with some degree of certainty. Among the monuments seen by the French architect there were very likely two important naoi connected by a similar destiny and now kept in two different European museums.

In his sketch drawn in 1821, just at the foot of the hill, he represented a monument resembling a naos with a curved roof, which might be the naos subsequently in the possession of Bernardino Drovetti (1776-1852) and that Coste himself drew in Alexandria a few months after his visit to Kom el-Ahmar. The painting in question has a caption reading: 'Alexandrie février 1822 Monument monolite en granite rouge trouvé au village

13 Yoyotte 2001, 76.

14 Zivie 1998, 165, 178; Yoyotte 2001, 62-64.

Fig. I.11. Drawing by Pascal Coste, labelled *Basse Egypte / Province de Menoufie / Ruines d'une ville égyptienne / actuellement village de Coum-Larma / du 26 novembre 1821 / P.C.* Reproduced from Yoyotte 2001, 63, fig. 2.

Coum Larmar dans la Province de Menoufie enlevé par [or perhaps 'pour'] M. Drovetti consul general de France P.C.'.[15] This monument has quite recently been identified as the naos of Amasis with a curved roof that arrived in Paris in 1826, donated by consul Drovetti to the king of France, Charles X, and now at the Louvre Museum under the inventory number D 29.[16]

But in Coste's drawing, precisely at the centre of the monuments spread on the ground, there is another big block with figures and hieroglyphs, which looks like an intact naos with a pyramidal roof and can now be identified with the naos in granite in the Rijksmuseum van Oudheden in Leiden.

Whereas Pascal Coste was the first European to record the existence of this monument, further confirmation of the correctness of this identification is offered by another Frenchman from Marseilles, Jean-Jacques Rifaud,[17] who spent over forty years in Egypt, carrying out numerous excavations for Bernardino Drovetti. Documents about Rifaud's presence in Egypt contribute to following, even though rather vaguely, the stages of the monument's journey from Kom el-Ahmar to Leiden. It took this monolithic naos a little more time to find its permanent location than that in the Louvre. Indeed, when the naos now at the Louvre reached Paris in 1826, the one now in Leiden was certainly still in Egypt. Moreover, in 1822, when the naos of the Louvre was in the possession of Drovetti and could be drawn by Pascal Coste in Alexandria, the naos of Leiden was surely still at Kom el-Ahmar, where it remained for at least another three years.

15 Yoyotte 2001, 66, 68.

16 Zivie 1998, 187; Yoyotte 2001, 66-70. For this naos, see Piankoff 1933, 161-169, pl. VIII; Jansen-Winkeln 2014, 420-423.

17 On Jean-Jacques Rifaud, see Bruwier 1998; Yoyotte 1998; Yoyotte 2001; Yoyotte 2003, 87-97; Bruwier/Claes/Quertinmont 2014.

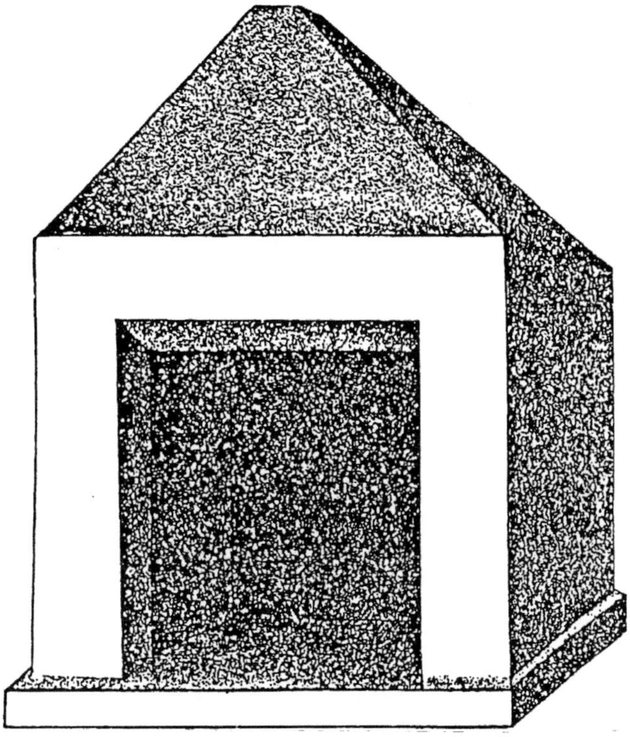

Fig. I.12. Drawing by Jean-Jacques Rifaud, as lithographed for Rifaud 1830, pl. 109, fig. 2. Reproduced from Yoyotte 2001, 71.

In 1825, after a period of digging in Karnak, Jean-Jacques Rifaud began to travel in the Delta, also going to Kom el-Ahmar, where he made a drawing of the modern site from the same point of view as Coste, but clearly with a different perspective. Although in his picture there is no trace of ancient monuments and when he arrived at Kom el-Ahmar the naos of the Louvre was no longer there, Rifaud saw the other large naos and drew it. His *Voyage*[18] contains two lithographs representing the same naos with minor differences. In plate 109, fig. 2 the naos is simply named 'un monolite' (Fig. I.12),[19] while plate 188, fig. 13 shows the same monument together with four other Egyptian antiquities with the caption 'divers sujets d'antiquités égyptiennes'. However, Jean Yoyotte has pointed out that the Bibliothèque Publique et Universitaire of Geneva holds a preliminary design for the same plate where the naos is called 'monolite en granit rose au Com Larmar Deltha 1825'.[20] Despite the fact that the naos drawn by Rifaud does not present any decorations or inscriptions, there can be little doubt, as suggested by Yoyotte, that Rifaud's naos and the large naos at the centre of Coste's landscape of 1821 are the same monument and that this must be identified with the naos in Leiden. Both naoi depicted by the two Frenchmen were seen at Kom el-Ahmar and have a pyramidal roof. Coste's naos presents figures and hieroglyphs; Rifaud's has *granit rose* as material and possesses a peculiar shape (short relative to its width, with a large central cavity and a base which surpasses the width of the side walls), both corresponding to the material and the shape of the Leiden naos. Moreover, this last monument was dedicated, as was the naos at the Louvre, to one specific Osirian form by king Amasis, whose name is attested at Kom el-Ahmar thanks to other objects.

18 Rifaud 1830.
19 Yoyotte 2001, 71, fig. 7; Bruwier/Claes/Quertinmont 2014, 87.
20 Yoyotte 2001, 73, fig. 8.

Figs. I.13-17. The Leiden naos, as displayed today in the galleries of the National Museum of Antiquities in Leiden (photographs by Robbert-Jan Looman).

I.13. front.

At present, there is no way to know whether Rifaud was personally involved in the transport of the naos from Kom el-Ahmar. However, its presence among the ruins of the site could no longer go unnoticed, as the following year the monument was already in the possession of Jean Anastasi (1780-1857), a Greek merchant residing in Alexandria. In a letter to Drovetti dated 16 May 1826, Rifaud mentions two visits to Anastasi, the first one 'pour lui presenter mes respects et lui parler de son monolythe', and indeed it is tempting to identify this *monolythe*, the only one sent by the merchant to the Netherlands, with the naos seen and drawn by Rifaud himself the previous year at Kom el-Ahmar.[21] But before reaching Leiden, it stopped off in Italy. In 1827, the naos in granite arrived in Livorno, together with all the other items of Anastasi's collection waiting for a purchaser.

In the meantime, in 1818 in the Netherlands, king Willem I had established the Rijksmuseum van Oudheden in Leiden. The founding director of the Museum, Caspar Jacob Reuvens (1793-1835), started, thanks to government support, to gather various collections, with an interest also in Egyptian artefacts. A few years later, in 1821, a small number of Egyptian antiquities came to the museum from the university collection and, in the period from 1826 to 1828, these were supplemented by purchases from an auction of objects from the collection of Jean-Baptiste de Lescluze (1780-1858), a merchant and ship owner from the Netherlands. Nevertheless, the first important acquisition was made in 1827, when the Dutch lieutenant-colonel Jean Emile Humbert (1771-1839),

21 Yoyotte 2001, 75-76.

I.14. left side.

I.15. right side.

I.16. rear.

I.17. roof.

who acted as agent for the Dutch government, acquired the antiquities of Signora Maria Cimba, the widow of a personal physician of Henry Salt's in Cairo. After the death of her husband and children, in 1824, Maria Cimba left Egypt to return to her native Livorno. Here, she offered for sale her late husband's collection, consisting of 335 pieces at the price of 14,000 guilders. In 1826, Humbert arrived in Livorno and sent Reuvens a catalogue of the objects. But in the Netherlands the price was regarded as too high and Humbert was asked to bid 8,000 guilders for the whole collection. Moreover, owing to the offer made by another, English, purchaser, the transaction seemed doomed to fail. Nonetheless, it started again when it turned out that the Englishman had not been able to collect all the money and, after a short negotiation between the two parties, the deal was concluded in 1827, with the collection being sold for 5,000 guilders.[22]

In the same year, Humbert sent news to Holland that a new and more impressive collection of Egyptian antiquities had been put on the market at the price of 400,000 francs (about 200,000 Dutch guilders) by Costantino Tossizza, a Greek merchant of the firm Fratelli Tossizza, who acted on behalf of Anastasi. In Livorno, Humbert was able to inspect the collection, which included over 5,600 objects, scattered in various storehouses in the city. The negotiations started in August 1827 and lasted more than a year, partly because of the careful valuations by Reuvens, who, at least at the beginning, showed a certain degree of mistrust towards both the reliability of the vendors and the actual importance of the collection, which was carefully compared to the Drovetti and Salt collections. However, due to the importance of the sum involved, the bargaining was put under the supervision of the Ministry of Foreign Affairs, represented by the ambassador in Rome, Johann Reinhold. Humbert was helped by the merchant Giuseppe Terreni, who acted as his intermediary. On the other side, together with Tossizza, Jean Anastasi was aided by the American Francis Barthow[23] and by the Italian Francesco de Castiglione in their capacity of negotiators. The Dutch ministry suggested to king Willem I to offer 300,000 francs for the entire collection, a sum which was regarded by the king as too high. Eventually, in 1828, and with a certain amount of pessimism regarding the outcome of the transaction, a final bid of 230,000 francs was offered, which was accepted by Anastasi, perhaps also because of the absence of other possible buyers. In the following months, Humbert busied himself in packing the antiquities and in facing the problems arising from both the fragility and the heavy weight of many objects, among which, of course, the large granite naos. Finally, in October 1828, a ship with the entire collection left the harbour of Livorno for the Netherlands, where it arrived on 1 December in the harbour of Hellevoetsluis, to be delivered one month later, on 1 January 1829, in Leiden.[24]

When the Anastasi collection arrived in Leiden, Reuvens had to face the urgent and complicated task of finding a building for the more than 5,600 Egyptian objects. It was decided to build a wooden barn in the botanical gardens for the largest and heaviest pieces, and to put the mummies and other delicate objects in the museum. Although this was supposed to be just a temporary solution, it took a few years to find a more suitable location. In 1835, after Reuvens's death, Conrad Leemans was appointed as first curator; in the same year, the university bought a building in Breestraat, a central street, to house the whole archaeological collection. The moving of the heavy objects from the botanical gardens to the new location started in January 1837 and had to be carefully arranged. It was decided to transport the heaviest pieces on boats via the canals of the city. But this was not without danger. The monolithic naos turned out to be the most problematic object, to the point that it risked being lost forever. Indeed, it was so heavy that it fell into the water. In a letter to the Ministry of Interior dated 20 January,[25] Leemans describes this event: 'We have started the transportation of heavy objects to the new building,

22 Halbertsma 2003, 98-99.

23 On Francis Barthow, see Vivian 2012, 56-72.

24 Halbertsma 2003, 99-106. See also Zago 2010, 50-52; Vivian 2012, 69-70.

25 Letter in Halbertsma 2003, 146.

but this enterprise was interrupted two days ago by a most disagreeable incident. The most difficult object, a granite temple of about 25,000 pounds, had been transported with much difficulty half way from the shed to the vessel when it overbalanced and fell into the water of the canal'. The mud at the bottom of the canal presented a great danger to such an object, since it risked sinking deeper and deeper. Leemans decided to consult the engineers of the Royal Navy in Rotterdam for help: 'The means to lift it from the sludgy bottom were totally unavailable in Leiden, so I had to go to Rotterdam today, to find a solution to safeguard this object and to prevent further misfortunes'. The Royal Navy sent some men and the naos was rescued. Finally, the naos, together with the rest of the Anastasi collection, arrived at its new destination and, on 7 August 1838 – the same year Leemans was promoted director – the museum opened to the public.

Over the years, new acquisitions were made and the museum started suffering from lack of space. The situation was definitely solved in 1918, when the National Museum of Natural History left its Rapenburg 28 address, and two years later the Rijksmuseum van Oudheden could move to precisely the same location where it had first been established by king Willem I in 1818. The naos from Kom el-Ahmar is now visible to the public in one of the rooms of this beautiful building (Figs. I.13-17).

Chapter II

Description of the naos

1. The architecture

The naos of Leiden AM 107 is hewn from a single piece of red granite and measures 137 cm in depth and 194 cm in height. The width at the front is 175 cm at the base and 164 cm at the lintel level. This difference of 11 cm is due to the slightly battered walls, an architectural element not unusual in naoi of the Late Period. The base of the naos – that is the part below the cavity – consists of a socle wider than the rest of the monument, which has been left undecorated but polished. The presence of a similar socle is found in other naoi of the 26th or 30th Dynasties.[26] In the Leiden naos, it juts out 3.1-3.5 cm all around the central body of the structure and measures 32.5 cm in height at the corners, with the exception of the left corner at the rear, which is a little higher (33 cm). The central part of the naos is also higher at the rear than in front, with a difference of nearly 2 cm (from a measurement of 114.5-115 cm at the front to about 116.5 cm at the rear). The naos has a decorated pyramidal roof, whose height is roughly 45 cm, but no cavetto cornices or torus moulding.

The left jamb of the cavity is 115 cm high and 30.2 cm wide at the base, the right jamb is 114.8 cm high and 30.1 cm wide at the base, while the lintel measures 26.5 cm in height. All around the cavity there is an additional indentation, serving as casing for the door, of 4.4 cm in height and 4.5 cm in width. The interior cavity is wider than it is deep, being 99 cm in width, 69 cm in depth and 79.2 cm in height. The four corners of the indentation, on the base and at the top, have cylindrical holes of about 3.2 cm in diameter, which served to accommodate door-pivots. Nothing can be said of the door-leaves, with the exception that they opened outwards. They were very likely made of bronze or wood inlaid with precious metals and costly stones.

2. The decoration

2.1. Technique and preservation

There is no evidence of unfinished carvings upon the naos. A close examination confirms that the decorative program was completed on all the surfaces of the monument. The apparent incompleteness of some of its parts, in particular the rear and the right outer wall, is due to the present state of preservation of the naos, which is probably the result

26 See, for example, the naoi Cairo CG 70008 of Apries (Roeder 1914, pl. 11) and Louvre D 29 of Amasis (Piankoff 1933, pl. VIII), and the naoi Cairo CG 70019 and 70022 of Nekhtnebef and CG 70013 of Nekhthorheb (Roeder 1914, pls. 13, 15, 16b).

Fig. II.1. Detail of front, centre of lintel: shrine with row of uraei. Author's photograph.

of the way it remained exposed and abandoned at the site. As confirmed by the 1820 drawing by Pascal Coste, before arriving at Leiden the monument must have been for centuries in a state of neglect that caused some damage, above all on the right outer wall, the rear (particularly along the edges), and parts of the roof, while the front and the left outer wall are in very good condition.

All the exterior surfaces have been decorated: the two jambs and the lintel on the front of the naos, the two lateral outer walls, the rear as well as the roof are covered with figures in sunk relief and incised texts of excellent quality. Instead, the interior is polished but undecorated.

There is no evidence of ancient paint upon the naos. In the 20th century, red paint was added on the gods' figures and hieroglyphs with the evident intent to improve their legibility. Nevertheless, this had the opposite effect, since some of the figures and captions are now so damaged that the presence of the red paint is often misleading and does not help to identify the names or other details of the deities.

2.2. Roof

One of the peculiarities of the naos of Leiden, and which is not to be found in any other shrine of Amasis' reign, is that all the surfaces forming the pyramidal roof are fully decorated. On each of the four sides of the roof, at the centre, there is a column of hieroglyphs:

di ꜥnḫ wꜣs nb ḏd nb ꜣwt-ib nb mi rꜥ

'giving all the life and power, all the stability and all the joy, like Ra'.

Fig. II.2. Detail of front, lintel, right of centre: Anubis and lion. Author's photograph.

Fig. II.3. Detail of front, lintel, left of centre: Anubis and lion. Author's photograph.

At each side is the inscription, *ỉmy-wt*, below which is the *ỉmy-wt* fetish, an animal-hide hanging from a pole in a small vessel. Facing it is a hawk on a *serekh*, containing the partially erased Horus-name (*smn-mꜣʿt*) of king Amasis. From the beak of the hawk departs an *ankh*-sign, whose loop surrounds the head of a long *was*-staff which is inserted in the vessel. Behind the *serekh* is an inscription in five vertical lines of hieroglyphs:

ḥr smn-mꜣʿt nṯr nfr ḫnty pr ʿꜣ ʿnḫ ḏd mỉ rʿ ḏt

'Horus Semen-maat, the beautiful god, foremost of the *per-aa*, living and stable like Ra, forever'.

2.3. Front

The front is very well preserved. Almost all the figures here represented are clearly recognizable. They are disposed in registers and look towards the entrance of the naos. The lintel is slightly uneven in height; it measures 27.4 cm on the left and 26.8 cm on the right. In the centre, a shrine adorned with a row of *uraei* is depicted (Fig. II.1). On each side:

I.1) , *ỉnpw*, Anubis is represented in the form of a canid lying on a shrine or a high pedestal, with his ears erected, his legs stretched out before him, and his tail hanging down.

I.2) A lion, called , *ỉwʿ nṯr*,[27] 'Heir of the god', is represented as if it was inside or next to each pedestal (Figs. II.2-3). This deity always appears under an iconography very

27 Leitz 2002, I, 178-179.

Fig. II.4. Detail of front, lintel, right side: Seherdju, Isis, and Maaitef. Author's photograph.

Fig. II.5. Detail of front, lintel, left side: Dewenhor, Sekhem, and Horus. Author's photograph.

similar to the one of the Leiden naos. He is attested for the first time in the 21st Dynasty, when he appears both on the granite outer sarcophagus originally for Merenptah and later usurped by Psusennes I (Cairo JE 87297)[28] and in a papyrus;[29] he is also known thanks to a statuette[30] from the tomb of Montuemhat (TT 34), the sarcophagus of the 'overseer of the army' (*ỉmy-r mšʿ*) Iahmes,[31] son of king Amasis and the king's wife Nekhtbastetru, and the tomb of Mutirdis (TT 410)[32] of the 26th Dynasty, while in the Graeco-Roman Period he is present on the sarcophagi of Ankhhapi son of Tefnakht (Cairo CG 29303) and Djedhor son of Iahmes (Cairo CG 29304).[33]

On each side of this group, there is a row of three deities (Fig. II.4). On the right:

I.3) , *sḥr-ḏw*,[34] 'He who drives away evil': male deity, squatting on a low base. Images of this deity are rather rare. The first known examples go back to the New Kingdom, when he appears inside the Theban tombs TT 58 and 158,[35] as a manifestation of the sun god and Amun-Ra, respectively. The first example of *sḥr-ḏw* as an independent deity is the statuette from the tomb of Montuemhat,[36] depicting him as a human-headed deity squatting on a base and together with an image of the lion *ỉwʿ nṯr*. He occurs once again in the company of *ỉwʿ nṯr* on the sarcophagus of the 'overseer of the army' Iahmes[37] and in the tomb of Mutirdis[38] of the Saite period and, in the Graeco-Roman Period, on the sarcophagi of Ankhhapi son of Tefnakht (CG 29303) and Djedhor son of Iahmes (CG

28 Montet 1961, pl. 88.
29 Nelson 1986, 14 and fig. 3.
30 Statue Athens A 112: Leclant 1961, 116.
31 On the sarcophagus, Hermitage, St. Petersburg 766, from tomb LG 83 in Giza, see PM III^2, 289; LD III, 276 (f-h); Leclant 1962, 111, fig. 17; El-Sadeek 1984, 123-125; Bolshakov 2010, 45-53; Jansen-Winkeln 2014, 479-482.
32 Assmann 1977, 94, pl. 45.
33 Maspero 1908-1914, 101, 109, 144-145, pl. 11.
34 Leitz 2002, VI, 459, who does not include the Leiden naos among the sources of this deity.
35 Assmann 1983, 80, 6 and 156, 14.
36 Statue Athens A 112: Leclant 1961, 116.
37 Hermitage 766: Leclant 1962, 111, fig. 17.
38 Assmann 1977, 94, pl. 45.

29304).[39] In the third eastern Osirian chapel of the temple of Dendera, he is portrayed as an ibis-headed mummified deity seated on a throne.[40]

I.4) Isis, represented anthropomorphically in the form of a woman wearing a long dress and crowned with the sign of the 'throne'. Unlike all the other divine images of the front, this figure is not accompanied by its name, evidently regarded as superfluous.

I.5) , *mꜣꜣ-i͗[t=f]*, 'He who sees his father': falcon on a *nb* basket. This name is attested from the Middle Kingdom to the Graeco-Roman Period and is associated with a variety of human, falcon, ram and baboon deities.[41] *Mꜣꜣ-i͗t=f* was portrayed for the first time as a falcon on a *nb* basket in the 26th Dynasty, inside the tomb of Mutirdis[42] and also on the sarcophagus of the 'overseer of the army' Iahmes son of king Amasis,[43] and subsequently, in the Graeco-Roman period, on the sarcophagi of Ankhhapi son of Tefnakht (CG 29303) and Djedhor son of Iahmes (CG 29304).[44] On the north-west wall of the third eastern Osirian chapel at Dendera, Maaitef is depicted as a falcon on the sign of gold, placed on a pedestal, while on the north-east wall of the same chapel, he appears just before *sḥr-ḏw*, but in the guise of a man holding two vases.[45] Moreover, one of the statuettes from the tomb of Montuemhat represents this falcon deity next to a squatting canine-headed guardian deity called *wr-nrw*.[46]

On the left, behind Anubis and *i͗wꜥ nṯr* (Fig. II.5):

I.3) , *dwn-ḥr*,[47] 'Extended of face': standing ibis-headed deity, holding a *was*-staff in one hand and an *ankh*-sign in the other. He appears for the first time in the 26th Dynasty: as well as on the Leiden naos, he is represented as a squatting ibis-headed deity on the sarcophagus of the 'overseer of the army' Iahmes, son of king Amasis.[48] Subsequently, he is to be seen again only on the sarcophagi of Ankhhapi son of Tefnakht (CG 29303), and Djedhor son of Iahmes (CG 29304),[49] both of the Graeco-Roman Period. The sarcophagus of Khaf, where the deities are accompanied by a text usually constructed on a pun or alliteration between the deity's name and the verb expressing his action for the deceased's benefit, presents the annotation: *dwn=i͗ ḥr(=i͗) r mꜣꜣ i͗i͗ r=k*, 'I raise (my) face to see the one who comes to you'.[50]

39 Maspero 1908-1914, 101, 144, pl. 11.
40 *Dendera* X 194, 12, pl. 94.
41 Leitz 2002, III, 199-200, who does not include the naos of Leiden among the known examples of this deity. See also Leitz 2011, 28, 30, 36.
42 Assmann 1977, 94, pl. 45.
43 Leclant 1962, fig. 17.
44 Maspero 1908-1914, 101, 144, pl. 11.
45 *Dendera* X 197, pls. 94-95.
46 Clère 1986, 100-101, pl. III.
47 Leitz 2002, VII, 527.
48 Hermitage, St. Petersburg 766: Leclant 1962, fig. 17.
49 Maspero 1908-1914, 106, 109, 127, 146, pl. 11.
50 Daressy 1917, 11.

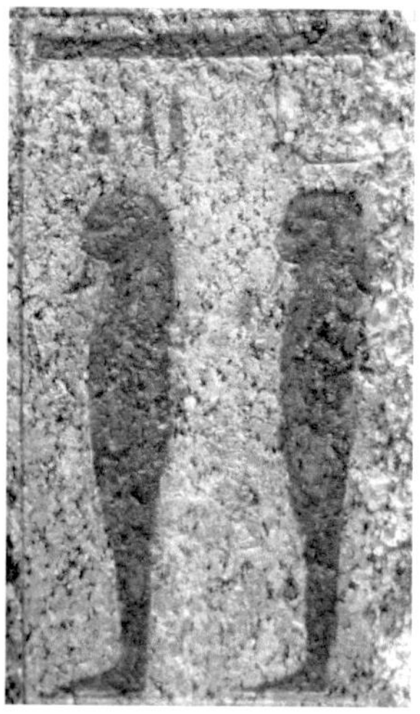

Fig. II.6. Detail of front, right jamb, upper register: Hapy and Qebehsenuef. Author's photograph.

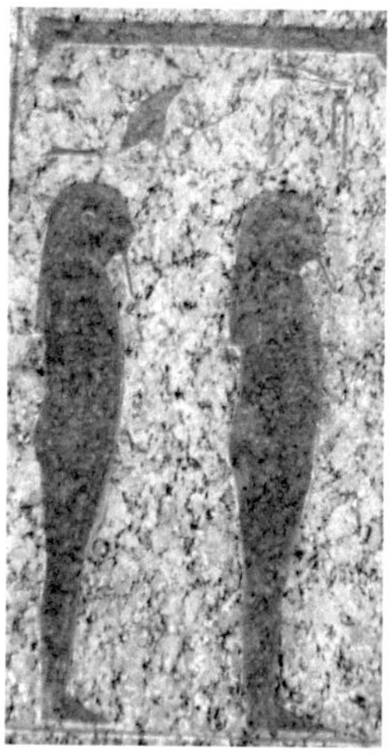

Fig. II.7. Detail of front, left jamb, upper register: Imsety and Duamutef. Author's photograph.

Fig. II.8. Detail of front, right jamb, lower register: Muyt. Author's photograph.

Fig. II.9. Detail of front, left jamb, lower register: Nekhbet. Author's photograph.

I.4) , *sḫm*,[51] 'The powerful': a *sekhem*-sceptre. *Sḫm* is both used as an epithet for many important gods and as a name for an independent deity. Apart from the Leiden naos, images of Sekhem in the guise of a *sekhem*-sceptre occur starting from the 21st Dynasty and, with the exception of the Leiden naos and a statuette in the Museum of Bologna (EG 347), only on sarcophagi: the sarcophagus usurped by Psusennes I (JE 87297),[52] of Iahmes son of Amasis[53] of the 26th Dynasty, of Tjahorpta (CG 29306)[54] of the Late Period, and of Djedhor son of Iahmes (CG 29304) of the Graeco-Roman Period.[55]

I.5) , *ḥr*, Horus: hawk-headed god, swathed and squatting on a low dais. The group of three deities composed by *dwn-ḥr*, *sḫm* and *ḥr* is certainly to be identified with the group of three guardian deities represented in the aforementioned granite statuette of the 25th-26th Dynasty in the Archaeological Museum of Bologna (EG 347), showing a falcon-headed figure squatting on a base between a *sekhem*-sceptre on the left and another squatting ibis-headed god on the right.[56]

Both doorjambs of the naos feature two registers of gods, surmounted by the *pt*-sign of heaven. The two top registers measure 40.4 cm in height and show the Four Sons of Horus, represented as human-headed mummiform figures.

51 Waitkus 1987, 55; Leitz 2002, VI, 523-525.
52 Montet 1951, pl. 88.
53 Hermitage 766: Leclant 1962, fig. 17.
54 Maspero 1908-1914, 235, pl. 21.
55 Maspero 1908-1914, 146.
56 According to Pernigotti 1980, 56-57, pl. LXXV, one of the squatting gods has a falcon head and the other a jackal head and, as such, might be identified with Qebehsenuef and Duamutef. Even though the statuette has no inscription, it is not possible to rule out that it was part of the group of granite sculptures of guardian demons from the tomb of Montuemhat. See also Etienne 2009, 157 n. 123; Picchi 2011, 199, 209, 324.

On the right (Fig. II.6):

II.1) , Hapy;

II.2) , Qebehsenuef.

On the left (Fig. II.7):

II.1) , Imsety;

II.2) , Duamutef.

The lower register on the right measures 40.9 cm in height and shows:

III.1) , *mwyt*,[57] a female figure offering a plateau with a *was*-sign between two *hes*-vases and two hanging *ankh*-signs; she wears a long and voluminous garment and leans slightly forward (Fig. II.8).

The lower register on the left measures 40.7 cm in height and shows:

III.1) , *nḫbt*,[58] represented identically to *mwyt* (Fig. II.9).

2.4. Left

The other three exterior sides of the naos present the same decorative design. At the top is a horizontal line of hieroglyphs, containing part of the dedicatory text, which is repeated twice, being read both on the right and left sides, starting from the front of the shrine and ending in the centre of the back side. The band of hieroglyphs with the dedicatory text measures 10 cm all around the naos.

From the left:

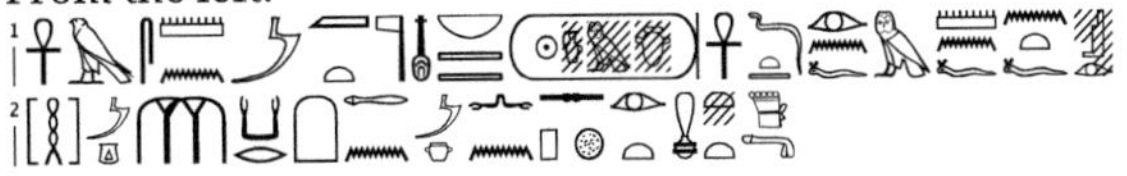

From the right:

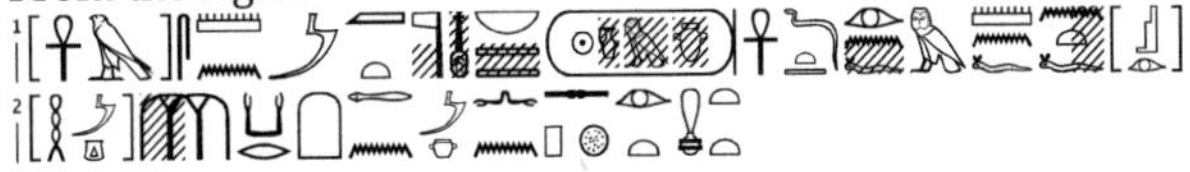

ʿnḫ ḥr smn mꜣʿt nṯr nfr nb tꜣwy [ḫnm-ỉb-]rʿ ʿnḫ ḏt ỉr.n=f m mnw=f n ỉt=f wsỉr ḥmꜣg kꜣr ʿꜣ n mꜣṯ nn sp ỉrt mỉtt ḏr-bꜣḥ

'The living Horus, He-who-establishes-*Maat*, the beautiful god, lord of the two lands [Khnemib]ra, living forever. He made as his monument for his father Osiris Hemag a great shrine in granite. Never had the like been done before'.

57 Leitz 2002, III, 251.

58 On these two figures, appearing also on the naos Louvre D 29 of Amasis (Piankoff 1933, figs. 2-3, pl. 8), see Baines 1973, 9-14; Baines 1983, 110-111, 147.

Fig. II.10. Detail of left side, upper register: Isis and Nephthys. Author's photograph.

Fig. II.11. Detail of left side, upper register: Osiris, lord of Djedu. Author's photograph.

Fig. II.12. Detail of left side, upper register: Osiris, the Great Saw. Author's photograph.

Fig. II.13. Detail of left side, upper register: Osiris, lord of Ra-setjau. Author's photograph.

The direction of the dedicatory text here adopted seem to have been particularly appreciated during Amasis' reign, since it is found on two other shrines of the king: on the naos from Kom el-Ahmar at the Louvre, and on a naos from Athribis.[59] Beneath the dedicatory text are two registers, each surmounted by an extended *pt*-sign, containing a row of divine images, most of them accompanied by their name in hieroglyphs, but which are, in many cases, no longer readable.

The left outer wall (from the viewpoint of someone approaching the naos from the front) is in pretty good condition and all the gods here represented are recognizable. In the upper register, which measures 50 cm in height, there are five gods. The first two deities (Fig. II.10), starting from the front of the naos, look towards the back of the monument and, although they are not accompanied by their names, can be easily identified as:

I.1) Nephthys: female standing figure, with arms hanging down the body and with her hieroglyphic headdress on her head.

I.2) Isis: female standing figure, with arms hanging down the body and with her hieroglyphic headdress on her head.

They actually face three different forms of the god Osiris, with their names written, unlike the other images of the naos, in a single column of hieroglyphs in front of them:

I.3) , *wsir nb ḏdw*, 'Osiris, lord of Djedu': mummiform figure, with curved beard and standing on a low pedestal (Fig. II.11).

59 Cairo CG 70011: Roeder 1914, 38; Habachi 1982, 227.

I.4) , *wsỉr ỉtfꜣ wr*, 'Osiris, the Great Saw': seated on a curved-back throne placed on a pedestal. He wears an enveloping garment, the white crown, a curved beard and a broad collar; the arms are held at different levels – one over the breast and the other over the stomach – with the left hand holding the *heqa*-sceptre and the right hand the flail (Fig. II.12).

I.5) , *wsỉr nb rꜣ-sṯꜣw*, 'Osiris, lord of Ra-setjau': seated on a curved-back throne on a pedestal and wearing a cloak, a curved beard and a broad collar. His crown is damaged and his hands come out of his garment to grasp, in front of him, the *heqa*-sceptre and flail (Fig. II.13).

The lower register is slightly higher on the left (48.5 cm) than on the right (47.1 cm). It presents a row of nine deities, all looking towards the front of the naos and provided with short captions above:

II.1) , *ḥsf-m-tp-ʿ*,[60] 'He who repels at the beginning': a crocodile-headed swathed deity, squatting on a pedestal. He usually appears in rows of deities and is known for the first time thanks to the sarcophagus of Merenptah usurped by Psusennes I (JE 87297);[61] then he is attested during the 25th Dynasty – in the sarcophagus of Ankhefenkhonsu (CG 41001bis)[62] and in a statuette from the tomb of Montuemhat (CG 38274)[63] – and in the Saite period, when he appears, besides the Leiden naos, on the sarcophagus of Iahmes,[64] son of king Amasis, and in the tomb of Mutirdis.[65] In the Graeco-Roman Period he is present on some sarcophagi – of Ankhhapi son of Ta-net-ba-anepet (CG 29301),[66] Ankhhapi son of Tefnakht (CG 29303),[67] Djedhor son of Iahmes (CG 29304)[68] – and on the east wall of the third eastern Osirian chapel of Dendera,[69] where he is portrayed as a standing god whose face is not longer recognizable, holding a knife. On the sarcophagus of Khaf[70] the god's name is accompanied by the text: *ḥsf.n(=ỉ) n=k ḫmyw nw ỉḫḫ* (?), 'I have repelled for you the enemies of darkness (?)'.

II.2) , *ḥr*, Horus: a falcon on a pedestal, on which a knife is represented. A precedent of this image is shown on the sarcophagus usurped by Psusennes I (Fig. II.14).[71]

60 Leitz 2002, V, 955.
61 Montet 1951, pl. 86.
62 Moret 1913, 24, pl. III.
63 Leclant 1961, 120.
64 Leclant 1962, 111, fig. 17I.
65 Assmann 1977, 94, pl. 45.
66 Maspero 1908-1914, 53, pl. 4.
67 Maspero 1908-1914, 106, pl. 11.
68 Maspero 1908-1914, 137.
69 *Dendera* X 195, 8, pl. 94.
70 Daressy 1917, 7.
71 Montet 1951, pl. 88.

Fig. II.14. Detail of left side, lower register: Khesefemtepa and Horus. Author's photograph.

Fig. II.15. Detail of left side, lower register: Aseb and Ankhemfedet. Author's photograph.

Fig. II.16. Detail of left side, lower register: Isis and Horus. Author's photograph.

Fig. II.17. Detail of left side, lower register: Akh, Inher, and Seqedher. Author's photograph.

II.3) , *ꜣsb*,[72] 'Radiant one': a canine-headed swathed deity, crouched on a pedestal. This deity, who is usually a member of rows of gods, is known from the Coffin Texts[73] onwards and can be depicted as a canid, donkey, serpent, bull, and human god. In the New Kingdom, he occurs in Chapters 69,[74] 144,[75] and 147[76] of the Book of the Dead and on the second shrine of Tutankhamun.[77] He appears for the first time in canine form in Chapter 147 of the Book of the Dead, then on the sarcophagus usurped by Psusennes I, where he is followed by the god Horus represented as a falcon on a knife,[78] and, for the last time, on the Leiden naos. He will still be included in Chapter 144 of the Book of the Dead in the Saite[79] and in the Graeco-Roman[80] Periods, when he is also depicted on a pair of sarcophagi.[81]

II.4) , *ꜥnḫ-m-fdt*, 'He who lives on sweat':[82] male standing deity with Bes-like features, naked (though the hem of a garment is indicated at the ankles) and with face and shoulders shown in full frontal aspect,[83] but with legs in profile (Fig. II.15). This otherwise unattested god is very likely a variant of an identical deity called *ꜥnḫ-m-fnṯw*, 'He who lives on worms',[84]

72 On this god, see Altenmüller 1975, 12; Munro 1987, 215, 232; Leitz 2002, I, 79; Abdelrahiem 2006, 6.
73 CT III, 260d; IV, 39j; VI, 32d; VII, 215e, 288c, 499h.
74 Ratié 1968, pl. 8.
75 Lapp 1997, 26.
76 Budge 1913, 11.
77 Piankoff 1955, pl. 39.
78 Montet 1951, pl. 88.
79 Verhoeven 1993, col. 70 b, 4.
80 Lepsius 1842, pl. 60.
81 Sarcophagi of Panehemisis (Vienna ÄS 4: Leitz 2011, 273, 365) and Horemheb (Leitz 2011, 410).
82 Leitz 2002, II, 143.
83 For this feature, see Volokhine 2000.
84 Munro 1987, 215, 232-233; Leitz 2002, II, 142-143; Abdelrahiem 2006, 8-9.

known from the Middle Kingdom onwards and who appears in Chapter 144 of the Book of the Dead[85] and in many other sources together with other deities of the Leiden naos.[86]

II.5) , *ꜣst ḥnwt tꜣwy*, 'Isis, mistress of the two lands': a vulture on a pedestal. This is the only case on the naos in which the goddess does not appear in human form and her figure is accompanied by name and title.

II.6) , *ḥr*, Horus: a falcon on a pedestal, but without knife (Fig. II.16).

II.7) , *ꜣḫ*,[87] Akh: a crested ibis alighting on a pedestal. Akh denotes both a manifestation of various Egyptian main gods and an independent deity. He certainly is the same god portrayed in a similar manner in a row of divine images between *ꜥnḫ-m-fnṯw* and a deity named *sḫd-ḥr,* both on the sarcophagus usurped by Psusennes I and in his tomb at Tanis.[88] The Leiden naos is the only source of the Saite period featuring an image of this deity.

II.8) , *in-ḥr*, 'He who brings the face' (?).[89] This is another guardian-deity attested for the first time in the Coffin Texts,[90] then in Chapters 144[91] and 147[92] of the Book of the Dead, and on the third shrine of Tutankhamun.[93] He can appear as a ram or crocodile deity, usually holding a knife and an ear of corn, but in the Leiden naos he is portrayed differently, that is as a human figure kneeling on a pedestal, with his right hand on his chest clenched to a fist, and his left hand on his knees. Like *ꜣsb*, in the Saite and Graeco-Roman Periods he is also known thanks to Chapter 144 of the Book of the Dead,[94] but he does not appear in any other sources of the period.

II.9) , *sḳd-ḥr*, 'watchful of face':[95] a male deity, squatting on a pedestal, with both hands on his chest and grasping a knife; his face is shown in full frontal aspect (Fig. II.17). Also this guardian-deity, who can take different guises (human, baboon, ram, crocodile), is known from the Coffin Texts[96] and Chapters 144[97] and 147[98] of the

85 Lepsius 1842, pl. 61; Verhoeven 1993, 70; Munro 1995, 206; Lapp 1997, 26. See also Thausing/Goedicke 1971, pl. 78.

86 See the sarcophagus usurped by Psusennes I (Montet 1951, pl. 84) and the sarcophagi of Iahmes (Hermitage 766: Leclant 1962, 111, fig. 17), Panehemisis (Leitz 2011, 117), Khaf (Daressy 1917, 10) and Cairo CG 41001bis (Moret 1913, 27, pl. 3), 29301, 29303, 29304 (Maspero 1908-1914, 16, 42, 99, 112, 131, 146, pls. 2, 11, 13), and the tomb of Mutirdis (Assmann 1977, 93, pl. 44).

87 On Akh, see Leitz 2002, I, 35. However, the naos of Leiden is regarded as the only example of the god 'Der Schopfibis' by Leitz 2002, I, 23.

88 Montet 1951, pls. 14, 84.

89 Munro 1987, 215, 235; Leitz 2002, I, 377-378. Another possible reading of this name is *in-ḥr-sḏt*, 'He who brings to the fire', as translated by Piankoff 1955, 78. See also *Wb.* IV, 376 and Abdelrahiem 2006, 9-10, who translates the name 'He who looks to and fro'.

90 CT VII, 291d.

91 Davis 1908, pl. 20; Munro 1995, 202; Lapp 1997, 26.

92 Budge 1913, 11.

93 Piankoff 1955, pl. 29.

94 Verhoeven 1993, col. 70 f, 3; Lepsius 1842, pl. 61.

95 Munro 1987, 215, 231-232; Leitz 2002, VI, 660.

96 CT VII, 296g: Lesko 1972, 49.

97 Munro 1995, 210; Lapp 1997, 26.

98 Budge 1913, 11.

Fig. II.18. Detail of right side, upper register: Shu and Tefnet. Author's photograph.

Fig. II.19. Detail of right side, upper register: ram-headed god. Author's photograph.

Fig. II.20. Detail of right side, upper register: canine-headed god and Isdes. Author's photograph.

Book of the Dead and from the second shrine of Tutankhamun.[99] In the following periods, he also occurs in the tomb and sarcophagus usurped by Psusennes I (JE 87297) in a similar iconography as on the Leiden naos,[100] and in Chapter 144 of the Book of the Dead of the 26th Dynasty,[101] in the sarcophagi of Ankhhapi son of Tefnakht (CG 29303) and Djedhor son of Iahmes (CG 29304),[102] and, as a standing baboon-headed god holding a flabellum, in the temple of Edfu[103] and on the south-east wall of the third eastern Osirian chapel at Dendera.[104] Some sources of the Saite Period[105] and Graeco-Roman Period[106] show a female hippopotamus goddess named *sḳdt-ḥr*. It is should be noted that, in the New Kingdom, the male version of the name, *sḳd-ḥr*, appears connected with a lion-headed goddess in the tomb of Nefertari.[107]

2.5. Right

The decoration of the right outer wall is not as well preserved as the one on the left side. The dedicatory text is only partially readable, since the very beginning and the last part of the line of hieroglyphs are missing. The first register is slightly uneven in height; it measures 48.4 cm on the left and 49.5 cm on the right. It contains five figures of deities, all facing left, towards the front of the shrine:

99 Piankoff 1955, 101, pl. 39.
100 Montet 1951, pls. 14, 84.
101 Verhoeven 1993, col. 70 b, 3.
102 Maspero 1908-1914, 105, 145, pl. 11.
103 *Edfu* I 195, 14; IX, pl. 24a.
104 *Dendera* X 196, 4, pl. 94.
105 Sarcophagus Hermitage 766 of Iahmes (Leclant 1962, 111, fig. 17) and tomb of Mutirdis (Assmann 1977, 93, pl. 44).
106 Sarcophagi of Khaf (Daressy 1917, 10), Ankhhapi son of Tefnakht (CG 29303), and Djedhor son of Iahmes (CG 29304); see Maspero 1908-1914, 99, 131, pl. 13.
107 Thausing/Goedicke 1971, pls. 74-75.

I.1) , Shu, seated on a curved-back throne placed on a low pedestal. Both his stretched out hands are empty; his name is written in front of him. He is followed by a group of three deities whose captions are no longer readable. Shu appears also on the naos Louvre D 29 from Kom el-Ahmar[108] and on the naos of Nekhtnebef of Saft el-Henna (CG 70021).[109] The same king dedicated a naos in the same locality to Shu 'lord of *pr-wr*, who is in *ḥwt-nbs*'.[110]

I.2) Lioness-headed goddess seated, in the same posture as Shu, on a curved-back throne placed on a low pedestal (Fig. II.18). Her name is lost and her identity is therefore uncertain. Many goddesses could indeed be shown in this guise. Nevertheless, it seems plausible that this female deity is an image of Tefnet, who could be often listed or represented in rows of gods behind her brother-husband Shu. Similarly to her companion Shu, her presence on monolithic shrines is restricted to the naos Louvre D 29[111] and the naos CG 70021[112] of Nekhtnebef. This king was very likely also responsible for the creation of another naos dedicated to Tefnet 'lady of *pr-nsr*, who is in *ḥwt-nbs*'.[113]

I.3) An enthroned ram-headed god, with horizontal, undulating horns and in the same posture as Shu and Tefnet (Fig. II.19). Only a single hieroglyph of his name is still visible – the gaming-board sign *mn* – and one might suggest that he is either an image of Montu,[114] who could occasionally be represented as a ram, or of Amun, who is represented three times on the Louvre naos.[115]

I.4) A standing canine-headed male deity, with his arms hanging down by his sides, empty-handed. Unfortunately, his name is completely lost and, therefore, his identity remains unknown.

I.5) Although the right edge of the upper register is very badly damaged, the right foot, arm and hand of a figure are still visible. Equally visible is the beginning of his name, consisting of two surviving signs, the hieroglyph of the reed followed by that of the folded cloth, *ỉs*[...] (Fig. II.20). The identification of this god seems to be restricted to two deities, who in the Late Period tend to merge with each other. His fragmentary name might be restored as *ỉsdn*, a god who appeared for the very first time, as a seated male baboon, on the naos of king Amasis from Athribis (CG 70011),[116] or, most likely, as *ỉsds*, who is attested since the Middle Kingdom and was mostly represented in the guise of a canine-headed god.[117] During the 26th Dynasty, he also appears on a naos of king Apries,[118] in

108 Piankoff 1933, 170.
109 Roeder 1914, 84, 87, 91.
110 Cairo JE 25774 (now in the Alexandria Graeco-Roman Museum) and Louvre D 37: Clère 1950; Leitz 1995, 3-57, pls. 1-23; von Bomhard 2008.
111 Piankoff 1933, 170.
112 Roeder 1914, 87, 91.
113 The present location is unknown: Yoyotte 1954, 81-82, fig. 1; Davoli 2001, 46, 64, 99, 110, fig. 16.
114 Montu and Montu-Ra are represented on the naos of Nekhtnebef (CG 70021): Roeder 1914, 65, 78.
115 Piankoff 1933, 165-168.
116 Habachi 1982, 226, fig. 6. On this god, see Leitz 2002, I, 558-560.
117 Leitz 2002, I, 560-561; Roberson 2013, 28.
118 Cairo CG 70008: Roeder 1914, 29.

Fig. II.21. Detail of right side, lower register: Horus and Sha. Author's photograph.

Fig. II.22. Detail of right side, lower register: turtle-headed god. Author's photograph.

Fig. II.23. Detail of right side, lower register: antelope-headed god. Author's photograph.

Fig. II.24. Detail of right side, lower register: hippopotamus-headed goddess. Author's photograph.

the tomb of Mutirdis,[119] and on the sarcophagi of Iahmes,[120] of the divine adoratress of Amun Ankhnesneferibra,[121] and of Anlamani and Aspelta.[122] His name became much more widespread in the Graeco-Roman Period, in particular in the temples of Edfu and Dendera – where it is often associated with the king – and on a few sarcophagi showing other deities of the Leiden naos.[123] On the sarcophagus of Khaf, one reads: *sd ꜥwy iwꜥ n sb(b)*, 'May the two arms of the heir celebrate on behalf of the traveller'.[124]

The lower register is less high than the upper one, since it measures 47 cm on the left (the right edge of the naos is lost). It included at least six figures of deities, all facing left:

II.1) , *ḥr nṯr ꜥꜣ*, 'Horus, the great god': a standing falcon-headed Horus, with his arms hanging down by his sides. His hands are empty.

II.2) , *šꜥ*, 'He who cuts to pieces': a lion-headed deity, with his right hand raised towards the shoulder of Horus (Fig. II.21). His name is written with two one-consonant signs, rendering *šꜥ*, followed by the hieroglyph of the knife. This group of signs might be simply read as *šꜥ*, 'He who cuts to pieces', a god attested in the 'Book of Gates'[125] of the New Kingdom, where he is depicted in human form. But it seems more likely that

119 Assmann 1977, 93, pl. 41.
120 Hermitage 766: Leclant 1962, 111, fig. 17.
121 British Museum EA 32: Sander-Hansen 1937, VIId, 262.
122 Khartum 1868 and Boston MFA 23729: Soukiassian 1982, 337.
123 Sarcophagi of Panehemisis (Leitz 2011, 325), Horemheb (Leitz 2011, 396, 410), Cairo CG 29303 and 29304 (Maspero 1908-1914, 101, 135, pl. 13).
124 Daressy 1917, 10.
125 Hornung 1979-1980, 374. See also Leitz 2002, VII, 28, who included also the naos of Leiden.

he is meant to be a variant of *šʿ-tb* or *šʿ-bṯw*, 'He who cuts the serpent to pieces',[126] a god always represented standing and lion-headed and who appears in rows and lists of gods that include numerous other deities present on the naos of Leiden: the cenotaph of Sety I in the New Kingdom,[127] the sarcophagus and tomb of Psusennes I[128] and that of Sheshonq III[129] in the Third Intermediate Period, the sarcophagus of Iahmes[130] and the tomb of Mutirdis[131] in the 26th Dynasty, and the sarcophagus of Ankhhapi son of Tefnakht (CG 29303)[132] in the Graeco-Roman Period. The sarcophagus of Khaf[133] shows the text: *šꜣʿ iw(t=i) r=k*, 'I shall be the first to come to you'.

II.3) A damaged figure of a turtle-headed[134] deity, squatting on a pedestal (Fig. II.22). He raises his right arm in front of him, while the left one is on his breast, with the hand clenched into a fist. Of his names, only the one-consonant sign of the twisted wick *ḥ* and the hieroglyph of the lasso *wꜣ* remain, [...]*ḥwꜣ*[*t*], to be restored [*wnm*]-*ḥwꜣ*[*t*], 'eater of excrements', attested for the first time in the Coffin Texts[135] under the variant *wnm-ḥwꜣt-nt-pḥwy.fy*.[136] The shortest version of his name started being used for the very first time on the sarcophagus of Merenptah usurped by Psusennes I[137] and was preferred to the longer one during the whole Late Period. This god is constantly part of rows of deities. During the 26th Dynasty, *wnm-ḥwꜣt* is represented, besides on the Leiden naos, only on the sarcophagus of the 'overseer of the army' Iahmes,[138] in the tomb of Mutirdis,[139] and (under the longest and most ancient version of his name) in Chapter 144 of the Book of the Dead.[140] In the Graeco-Roman Period, his presence was restricted to a few sarcophagi[141] and to the west wall of the third eastern Osirian chapel at Dendera.[142] The sarcophagus of Khaf adds the annotation: *wnm.n(=i) ḥʿw n(w) sbyw iyw r=k*, 'I have eaten the limbs of the enemies who come to you'.[143]

II.4) An antelope-headed deity in the same pose as *wnm-ḥwꜣt* (Fig. II.23). His identity is not recognizable with certainty, since of his name only the lower part of the hieroglyph of the quail chick survives. However, it should be restored either as [*ʿꜣ-ẖr*]*w* or, more likely, as [*nfr-nfr*]*w*. Like the god on the Leiden naos, both these deities share similar

126 Leitz 2002, VII, 20, who suggests the translation 'Der die Bewegung abschneidet'. See also Roberson 2013, 33.
127 Frankfort/De Buck/Gunn 1939, pl. 74.
128 Montet 1952, pls. 12, 92.
129 Montet 1960, pl. 30.
130 Leclant 1962, fig. 17.
131 Assmann 1977, 93, pl. 41.
132 Maspero 1908-1914, 101, pl. 13.
133 Daressy 1917, 10.
134 On the turtle in the Egyptian religion, see Van de Walle 1953, 177-178.
135 CT VII, 423b.
136 Pantalacci 1983, 297-311; Leitz 2002, II, 408-409; Abdelrahiem 2006, 7.
137 Cairo JE 87297: Montet 1951, pl. 86.
138 Leclant 1962, 111, fig. 17.
139 Assmann 1977, 94, pl. 45. See also the sarcophagus V.O. 1000 at the Museo del Vicino Oriente, La Sapienza, Rome, dated to the 25th-26th Dynasty: Sist 2013, 76-77.
140 Verhoeven 1993, 70c.
141 Sarcophagi of Panehemisis (Leitz 2011, 282), Ankhhapi son of Ta-net-ba-anepet (CG 29301), Ankhhapi son of Tefnakht (CG 29303), Djedhor son of Iahmes (CG 29304) (Maspero 1908-1914, 15, 53, 105, 106, 137, 145, pls. 2, 4, 11), and Wennefer (CG 29310: Maspero/Gauthier 1939, 54, pl. 15).
142 *Dendera* X 193, 13, pl. 95.
143 Daressy 1917, 7.

iconographies, have names ending with the quail chick *w*-sign, and can appear behind the turtle-headed *wnm-ḥwꜣt*.

The god *ꜥꜣ-ḫrw*,[144] 'loud of voice', is attested since the Coffin Texts[145] and, as well as other guardian-deities on the naos, appears in Chapters 144[146] and 147[147] of the Book of the Dead, on one of the shrines of Tutankhamun,[148] and, just behind *wnm-ḥwꜣt*, on the sarcophagus of Psusennes I (JE 87297)[149] of the 21th Dynasty. He vanishes from the sources of the Late Period, to show himself again in the Graeco-Roman Period in Chapter 144 of the Book of the Dead,[150] on the sarcophagi of Ankhhapi son of Ta-net-ba-anepet (CG 29301)[151] and of Djedhor son of Iahmes (CG 29304),[152] in a papyrus containing a ritual for the protection of Osiris,[153] in the temple of Edfu[154] as a baboon-headed deity, and inside the third eastern Osirian chapel at Dendera.[155]

Alternatively, the god *nfr-nfrw*,[156] 'the one with a beautiful beauty', who might perhaps be regarded as a variant of *ꜥꜣ-ḫrw*, is known for the first time thanks to the statue of the fourth *hem-netjer* priest of Amun Djedkhonsefankh of the 23rd Dynasty found in the Karnak cachette.[157] Starting from the 25th Dynasty,[158] he seems to take the place of *ꜥꜣ-ḫrw* in rows of deities, being almost constantly represented behind *wnm-ḥwꜣt*, as in the case of the sarcophagus of the 'overseer of the army' Iahmes, during the 26th Dynasty.[159] In the tomb of Mutirdis,[160] they constitute a unity, since they are depicted inside the same chapel. In the Graeco-Roman Period he is included in five sarcophagi[161] and in the third Osirian chapel of the eastern group at Dendera.[162]

II.5) A hippopotamus goddess with pendulous breasts, squatting on a pedestal. She is shown with her mouth open, the tongue jutting out, and with a knife in her hands (Fig. II.24). Of her name, only the hieroglyph of the owl followed by that of the bread, *m* + *t*, are still readable. One might suggest[163] that it should be restored as *[s]mt*, a deity represented as a standing hippopotamus-headed goddess in the tomb of queen

144 Munro 1987, 215, 236; Leitz 2002, II, 41; Abdelrahiem 2006, 10.
145 CT III, 393a; VII, 147j, 148c, 292a, 501j.
146 Munro 1995, 200; Lapp 1997, 26.
147 Budge 1913, 11.
148 Piankoff 1955, pl. 29.
149 Montet 1951, pl. 86.
150 Lepsius 1842, pl. 61.
151 Maspero 1908-1914, 16, pl. 2.
152 Maspero 1908-1914, 127.
153 Papyrus New York 35.9.21: Goyon 1975, 399.
154 *Edfu* I 195, 14; IX, pl. 24c.
155 *Dendera* X 196, 6, pl. 94.
156 Leitz 2002, IV, 212.
157 Cairo CG 42211: Jansen-Winkeln 1985, 88, 474.
158 Sarcophagus Cairo CG 41001bis: Moret 1913, 24, pl. III.
159 Leclant 1962, fig. 17. See also the sarcophagus Rome, V.O. 1000, where he is just behind a ram-headed deity: Sist 2001, 537; Sist 2013, 77.
160 Assmann 1977, 94, pl. 45.
161 Sarcophagi of Khaf (Daressy 1917, 7), Ankhhapi son of Ta-net-ba-anepet (CG 29301), Ankhhapi son of Tefnakht (CG 29303), Djedhor son of Iahmes (CG 29304) (Maspero 1908-1914, 53, 106, 137, pls. 4, 11), and Wennefer (CG 29310: Maspero/Gauthier 1939, 54, pl. 15).
162 *Dendera* X 195, 8, pl. 94.
163 As in Leitz 2002, IV, 212.

Nefertari.[164] However, *smt*[165] is usually the name of a male deity attested from the Pyramid Texts until the Graeco-Roman Period, not rarely in company with other deities of the Leiden naos.[166] This god may be represented behind *wnm-ḥwꜣt* and *ꜥꜣ-ḫrw*,[167] or from the 25th Dynasty onwards *wnm-ḥwꜣt* and *nfr-nfrw*,[168] as a squatting divinity holding a goat, gazelle or antelope in his hands. Very often, he is portrayed as a crocodile-headed god.[169]

Another solution also seems possible. The deity's name on the Leiden naos might be restored as [*nḥm*]*mt*,[170] who appears on a few coffins dating from the 25th Dynasty onwards;[171] in particular, in the Ptolemaic sarcophagus of Khaf, she is accompanied by the text *nḥm=i ḏt=k swḏꜣ.n(=i) ḥꜥw=k*, 'I save your body, I healed your limbs'.[172] In one of her most ancient sources, the sarcophagus and tomb of Psusennes I,[173] she is represented as a hippopotamus goddess with pendulous breasts and knives, placed next to an architectonic structure with a *khekeru* frieze and a vulture named *mwt*. But in two other Saite documents – the sarcophagus of king Amasis' son Iahmes[174] and the tomb of Mutirdis[175] – she appears as a vulture in front of a structure with *khekeru* and followed by another hippopotamus with pendulous breasts and knives called *sḳd ḥr*. The Leiden naos might have moved away from this tradition, placing behind *wnm-ḥwꜣt* and *nfr-nfrw*, instead of *smt*, the goddess *nḥmmt*, adopting however her most ancient iconography, but discarding the images of the structure and vulture.

II.6) A rather damaged recumbent lion on a tall pedestal. Unfortunately, no sign of his name survives. An image of a recumbent lion, named Amun, on a tall pedestal also occurs on the right outer wall of the other naos of Amasis from Kom el-Ahmar.[176]

The right edge of the lower register is lost. However, there is sufficient space for a further figure of a deity to have been included.

---

164 Thausing/Goedicke 1971, pls. 73-74.

165 Leitz 2002, VI, 358.

166 Cenotaph of Sety I (Frankfort/de Buck/Gunn 1939, pl. 74); sarcophagi of Psusennes I (Montet 1951, pls. 86, 92), Cairo CG 41001bis (Moret 1913, 24, pl. III), Iahmes (Leclant 1962, 111, fig. 17), Khaf (Daressy 1917, 7), Panehemesis (Leitz 2011, 143-144), Cairo CG 29303, 29304 (Maspero 1908-1914, 106, 108, 138, pls. 11, 12), and CG 29319 (Maspero/Gauthier 1939, 54, pl. 15); tombs of Sheshonq III (Montet 1960, pl. 30) and Mutirdis (Assmann 1977, 93, pl. 41).

167 Sarcophagus of Psusennes I (JE 87297): Montet 1951, pl. 86.

168 For the 25th Dynasty: sarcophagus CG 41001bis (Moret 1913, 24, pl. III); for the Saitic period: sarcophagus of Iahmes (Leclant 1962, 111) and tomb of Mutirdis (Assmann 1977, 94, pl. 45); for the Graeco-Roman Period: sarcophagi CG 29301, 29303, 29304 (Maspero 1908-1914, 53, 106, 138, pls. 4, 11), CG 29310 (Maspero/Gauthier 1939, 54, pl. 15), and sarcophagus of Khaf (Daressy 1917, 7).

169 Cenotaph of Sety I (Frankfort/de Buck/Gunn 1939, pl. 74); tomb of Sheshonq III (Montet 1960, pl. 30); sarcophagus of Iahmes (Leclant 1962, fig. 17); tomb of Mutirdis (Assmann 1977, pl. 41); sarcophagus of Khaf (Daressy 1917, 7); sarcophagi Cairo CG 29303 and 29304 (Maspero 1908-1914, 108, 142, pl. 12).

170 Waitkus 1987, 52-53; Leitz 2002, IV, 286.

171 Sarcophagi Cairo CG 41001bis (Moret 1913, 27, pl. III), CG 29303, 29304 (Maspero 1908-1914, 99, 130, pl. 13), and CG 29310 (Maspero/Gauthier 1939, 51, pl. 15).

172 Daressy 1917, 10.

173 Montet 1951, pls. 14 and 84.

174 Leclant 1962, fig. 17.

175 Assmann 1977, 93, pl. 44.

176 Louvre D 29: Piankoff 1933, 165.

Fig. II.25. Detail of rear, upper register, right half: Khesesi. Author's photograph.

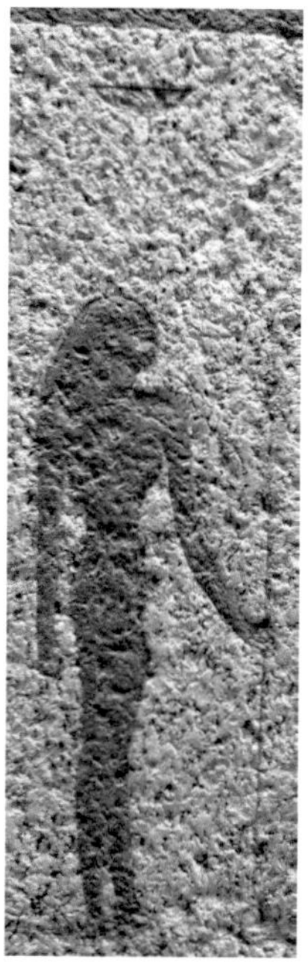

Fig. II.26. Detail of rear, upper register, right half: Nephthys. Author's photograph.

Fig. II.27. Detail of rear, upper register, right half: Pehrer. Author's photograph.

Fig. II.28. Detail of rear, upper register, right half: Heremhunet and Keku. Author's photograph.

2.6. Rear

The dedicatory text at the top is in pretty good condition. Below, the first register is slightly higher on the right (49.7 cm) than on the left (49.3 cm). It contained the figures of ten standing deities, five facing right and five facing left, so that all the gods seem to look towards the niche. With the exception of the first god on the left, whose name is only partially preserved, they are all recognizable.

Group facing right:

I.1) , *ḫssỉ*, 'Fish-man': a crocodile-headed god, represented holding a *was*-staff and an *ankh*-sign (Fig. II.25). This divine name,[177] known from the New Kingdom, occurs also in the variant *ỉḫssỉ* and describes a variety of human-,[178] cat-fish-,[179] ichneumon-,[180] canine-,[181] lion-,[182] ram-,[183] and above-all crocodile-headed[184] gods. He appears also,

177 On this god, see Leitz 2002, I, 550; Roberson 2013, 31-32. For his connections with Sobek and the Fayum region, see Beinlich 1991, 320-322; Zecchi 2010, 125-126.

178 Small temple of Medinet Habu, Graeco-Roman Period: LD III, 37b.

179 Manassa 2007, 32; Werning 2011, 50-51, 110-111.

180 *Tôd* II 248, II, 8.

181 Tomb and sarcophagus of Psusennes I (Montet 1951, pls. 12, 92) and sarcophagus of Iahmes (Hermitage 766: Leclant 1961, fig. 17).

182 Du Bourguet/Gabolde 2008, § 76.

183 *Dendera* X 196, 10, pl. 95.

184 Tomb of Ramses VI (Piankoff 1954, fig. 142); cenotaph of Sety I (Frankfort/de Buck/Gunn 1939, pl. 74); tomb of Sheshonq III (Montet 1960, pl. 30); tomb of Mutirdis (Assmann 1977, 93, pl. 41); temple of Hibis (Davies 1953, pl. XXI); sarcophagi of Khaf (Daressy 1917, 10) and Cairo CG 29303 and 29304 (Maspero 1908-1914, 101, 135, pl. 13).

together with other deities of the upper register of the rear, in scenes describing the awakening of Osiris by his son Horus: the cenotaph of Sety I, the tombs of Ramses VI, Sheshonq III and Mutirdis, the sarcophagi of Merenptah/Psusennes I, Iahmes and Khaf. The sarcophagus of Khaf adds the text: *ẖsf.n(=ỉ) ẖftyw=k*, 'I have repelled your enemies'.

I.2) A goddess with the *was*-staff and *ankh*-sign (Fig. II.26). The text is damaged; of her name only the first sign – the hieroglyph of the basket – survives. The names of several goddesses begin with the double consonant *nb* and also her iconography is not useful to disclose her identity. However, a comparison with the temple of Ramses II at Abydos[185] and the tombs of Sheshonq III[186] and Mutirdis,[187] which include a sequence of gods similar to the one present on the naos – that is *nbt-ḥt, ẖꜣbs, kkw* and *ḥr=f-m-ẖꜣẖ* – makes it clear that the goddess on the naos is an image of Nephthys, who is therefore represented twice on the Leiden monument.[188]

I.3) , *pḥ*[…]*r*; the reading of this name is uncertain. It might perhaps be restored as *pḥrr*,[189] 'The runner'. He is depicted as a canine-headed deity, holding a *was*-staff in one hand and an *ankh*-sign, no longer visible (but it is still visible in the photo of the plaster cast in Boeser's Beschreibung), in the other (Fig. II.27). The name *pḥrr* is known from the Coffin Texts to the Graeco-Roman Period and is prevalently used as an epithet for important gods, such as Ra, Amun-Ra, and Horus. In the Saite period, the name *pḥrr* occurs only in association with the solar god in Chapter 162 of the Book of the Dead, where he is invoked as 'the great runner, swift of strides' (*pḥrr ꜥꜣ ẖꜣẖ nmtt*),[190] and on the sarcophagus of the divine adoratress of Amun Ankhnesneferibra (BM EA 32),[191] where Ra is said to be *pḥrr wbn m nwn*, 'the runner who rises in the Nun'. However, it should be noted that *pḥrr* does not appear in any other monument together with the other guardian-deities of the naos. If the identification with *pḥrr* is correct, the Leiden naos would be the only source to present an image of this god. Moreover, the traces of the sign above the *r* seem to belong to a small sign, such as *t* or *g*. But neither *pḥtr* nor *pḥgr* are deities otherwise attested.

I.4) A female lioness-headed (or cat-headed with pointed ears) deity, holding a *was*-staff and an *ankh*-sign. Her identity is not easily recognizable. The name is written in two lines, with *m* + *ḥ* above the hieroglyph of the hare, followed by the one-consonant sign *t*, which might be read as *mḥwnt*, a goddess who is not elsewhere attested.[192] But before the hieroglyph of the owl, there is a small sign, which might very likely be the hieroglyph of the face, *ḥr*, or perhaps the sign of the heart, *ib*. So, the name of this goddess might actually be *ḥr-m-ḥwnt*, or, less likely, *ib-m-ḥwnt*, which might be variants

185 Mariette 1880, pl. 19b.
186 Montet 1960, pl. III.
187 Assmann 1977, 91, pl. 41.
188 In the awakening tableau of the sarcophagus of Khaf, her figure is omitted, but it is represented with Anubis in another group of deities: Daressy 1917, 6.
189 Leitz 2002, III, 101-102.
190 Verhoeven 1993, 135.
191 Sander-Hansen 1937, IXg, 448-449.
192 Leitz 2002, III, 383 quotes only the Leiden naos as example of this goddess.

Fig. II.29. Detail of rear, upper register, left half: Abuy and Maat. Author's photograph.

Fig. II.30. Detail of rear, upper register, left half: Khabes and Herefemkhakh. Author's photograph.

(or mistakes) of the name of two other lioness-headed deities, *ḥr-m-ḥwrt*, 'Face as a poor woman',[193] or *ib-m-ḥwrt*. However, the presence of the hieroglyph of the hare in the name [*ḥr-*]*m-ḥwnt* is intriguing and, indeed, there is also a lioness-headed goddess named *ḥwnt*, the 'Young one', 'Kitten',[194] seen for the first time in the Coffin Texts. As well as other gods represented on the Leiden naos, *ḥwnt* also appears in the cenotaph of Sety I,[195] and, together with *ḥr-m-ḥwrt*,[196] in the tomb and sarcophagus of Psusennes I[197] and in the tomb of Mutirdis,[198] and, together with *ib-m-ḥwrt*, in the tomb of Sheshonq III,[199] while her name and image are lost in the sequence of gods of the tomb of Ramses VI. In the sarcophagus of Khaf, *ḥr-m-ḥwrt* has been replaced by a deity named *rs-ḥr=i*, 'my face is awake/vigilant', while *ḥwnt* is accompanied by the text *ḥwn(=i) ḏt=k r ꜥꜣ pḥty=k*, 'I shall made your body young, so that your strength might be great'.[200] Very likely, the Saite engravers of the Leiden naos merged the names of at least two different lioness-headed deities, *ḥr-m-ḥwrt* and *ḥwnt*, creating an otherwise unknown goddess [*ḥr-*]*m-ḥwnt*, 'Face as a young girl'.

193 Leitz 2002, V, 303. Translation of the name suggested by Roberson 2013, 38.
194 Leitz 2002, V, 102-103.
195 Franfort/de Buck/Gunn 1939, pl. 74.
196 In the cenotaph of Sety I her name is present, but her image is lost; they both survive in the tomb of Ramses VI.
197 Montet 1951, pls. 11, 12, 92.
198 Assmann 1977, pl. 41.
199 Montet 1960, pl. 30.
200 Daressy 1917, 7. For the figure of *rs-ḥr=i*, Khaf adds the annotation: *rs ḥr=k ḏr kkw*, 'Your face shall awaken, after darkness has been dispelled'.

I.5) , *kkw*,[201] 'Darkness': a ram-headed deity, holding a *was*-staff and an *ankh*-sign (Fig. II.28). This god is known for the first time thanks to a passage in the Coffin Texts.[202] Starting from the New Kingdom, he often appears in Egyptian sources, prevalently as a member of the Ogdoad or, occasionally, together with other deities of the Leiden naos: in the temple of Ramses II at Abydos,[203] on the sarcophagus of Merenptah/Psusennes I[204] and in the tomb of Sheshonq III,[205] in the tomb of Mutiridis,[206] and on the sarcophagi of Panehemisis,[207] Ankhhapi son of Tefnakht (CG 29303)[208] and Djedhor son of Iahmes (CG 29304).[209] He is also depicted, as a frog-headed deity and member of the Ogdoad of Hermopolis, in the upper register of the rear of the naos Louvre D 29[210] from Kom el-Ahmar. The sarcophagus of Khaf[211] adds the annotation: *kk.n ḥr=ỉ sn(=ỉ) r=k*, 'My face has become dark, so that I might resemble you'.

Group facing left:

I.1) The left edge is lost. Of the first figure of the group of gods facing left only parts of his head, left shoulder, arm and hand with an *ankh*-sign survive. The text is almost completely lost, but traces of the hieroglyph of the swallow and of the one-consonant *r* are still visible: [...]*wr*. His identity remains unknown.

I.2) , *ꜥbwy*, 'He with two horns':[212] an antelope-headed god with the *was*-staff and *ankh*-sign. This god, who is mentioned for the first time in the 'Book of Amduat'[213] and subsequently in the Third Intermediate Period,[214] will not be seen again in Egyptian sources. However, since the naos of Leiden contains the only example of *ꜥbwy* as an antelope-headed god, one might assume that he is just a variant or short name of *ꜥnn-ꜥbwy*,[215] 'He who averts the horns', attested for the first time in the Third Intermediate Period. In the 26th Dynasty he could be represented antelope-headed in the tomb of Mutirdis[216] and on the sarcophagi of Iahmes son of king Amasis,[217] and in the Graeco-Roman Period on the sarcophagi of Panehemisis,[218] Khaf, and Ankhhapi son of Tefnakht (CG 29303).[219] He could also appear as a ram-headed deity on the sarcophagus of

201 Leitz 2002, VII, 296-297.
202 CT II, 4d.
203 Mariette 1880, pl. 19b. His name and figure are lost in the cenotaph of Sety I and in the tomb of Ramses VI: Roberson 2014, 53.
204 Montet 1952, pl. 92.
205 Montet 1960, pl. 30.
206 Assmann 1977, 93, pl. 41.
207 Leitz 2011, 138-139.
208 Maspero 1908-1914, 108, pl. 12.
209 Maspero 1908-1914, 117, 143.
210 Piankoff 1933, 167.
211 Daressy 1917, 7.
212 Leitz 2002, II, 81.
213 Hornung 1987-1994, 413 no. 352.
214 Piankoff 1942a, 153; Piankoff 1957, no. 19.
215 Leitz 2002, II, 116; Roberson 2013, 50.
216 Assmann 1977, 93, pl. 41.
217 Leclant 1962, fig. 17.
218 Leitz 2011, 133-134.
219 Maspero 1908-1914, 108, pl. 12.

Psusennes I,[220] and subsequently in other sources such as the tomb of Sheshonq III,[221] or as a human-headed deity in the third eastern Osirian chapel at Dendera.[222] In the cenotaph of Sety I[223] his figure is damaged, while his name and image are both lost in the tomb of Ramses VI.[224] The sarcophagus of Khaf[225] adds the text *sḥn ỉw r=k*, 'Let the one who comes toward you retreat'.

I.3) , Maat (*mꜣꜥt*): a woman with the *was*-staff and *ankh*-sign (Fig. II.29). Maat quite often appears in rows of gods in scenes of the awakening of Osiris and together with many other deities of the Leiden naos, such as in the cenotaph of Sety I,[226] the sarcophagus of Psusennes I,[227] and the tombs of Sheshonq III[228] and Mutirdis,[229] but her name and image have disappeared in the tomb of Ramses VI.[230] In the Ptolemaic sarcophagus of Khaf,[231] her text runs as follows: *smꜣꜥ=k m wsḫ(t) mꜣꜥty*, 'You have been praised in the Hall of the Two Truths'. It is worth noticing that Maat is not represented on any other naos of the Saite or Late Period.

I.4) , *ẖꜣbs*:[232] a deity with the head of an ibis or heron, holding the *was*-staff and *ankh*-sign. The name *ẖꜣbs* is attested since the Coffin Texts,[233] where the deceased is said to become *ẖꜣbs* as the *ẖꜣbs*-bird, translated by Faulkner as the 'glitter bird'.[234] In the New Kingdom, he started to appear as an ibis/heron-headed god in some scenes featuring the awakening of Osiris. In the cenotaph of Sety I and in the tomb of Ramses VI[235] his name and figure are lost, but he is present in the temple of Ramses II at Abydos,[236] on the sarcophagus of Merenptah/Psusennes I,[237] and in the tombs of Sheshonq III[238] and Mutirdis,[239] while on the sarcophagus of Ankhhapi son of Ta-net-ba-anepet (CG 29301)[240] he appears as a lion-headed deity. He is not included on the sarcophagus of Iahmes (Hermitage 766) of the 26th Dynasty, and on the sarcophagus of Khaf he is replaced by another ibis god, called *rs-wsrt*, 'He who watches the powerful one'.[241]

220 Montet 1951, pl. 92.
221 Montet 1960, pl. 30.
222 *Dendera* X 197, 7, pl. 95.
223 Franfort/de Buck/Gunn 1939, pl. 74.
224 Piankoff 1954, fig. 142.
225 Daressy 1907, 7.
226 Franfort/de Buck/Gunn 1939, pl. 74.
227 Montet 1951, pl. 92.
228 Montet 1960, pl. 30.
229 Assmann 1977, 93, pl. 41.
230 Piankoff 1954, fig. 12.
231 Daressy 1917, 7.
232 Leitz 2002, V, 628; Roberson 2013, 52-53.
233 CT IV, 26d, 27f; VI, 16e-I, 196k, 285b; VII, 11j.
234 Faulkner 1973-1978, I, 210; II, 184; III, 5.
235 Franfort/de Buck/Gunn 1939, pl. 74; Piankoff 1954, fig. 142.
236 Mariette 1880, pl. 19b.
237 Montet 1951, pl. 92.
238 Montet 1960, pl. 30.
239 Assmann 1977, 93, pl. 41.
240 Maspero 1908-1914, 16, pl. 2.
241 Daressy 1917, 7.

Fig. II.31. Detail of rear, lower register, right half: hippopotamus goddess and frontal face male. Author's photograph.

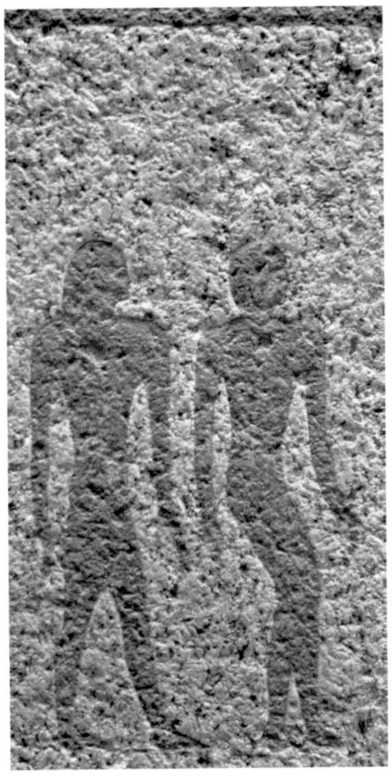

Fig. II.32. Detail of rear, lower register, right half: Medes and standing male. Author's photograph.

Fig. II.33. Detail of rear, lower register, right half: semi-sitting male and Irrenefdjesef. Author's photograph.

I.5) , *ḥr=f-m-ḫ3ḫ*, 'His face is in haste':[242] a serpent-headed god, with the *was*-staff and *ankh*-sign (Fig. II.30). He is known only thanks to four sources, of which the naos of Amasis is the most recent one. Besides the tomb of Mutirdis,[243] his name and figure, like in the case of *ḫ3bs*, are lost both in the cenotaph of Sety I and in the tomb of Ramses VI,[244] but he occurs in the temple of Ramses II at Abydos,[245] and subsequently on the sarcophagus usurped by Psusennes I[246] and in the tomb of Sheshonq III.[247] On the sarcophagus of Khaf, he is replaced by another serpent-headed deity named *isbt-im(y)-ḥtpwy*.[248]

The lower register of the rear is very badly damaged and is less tall than the upper one, since it is 48.5 cm high. Here, as in the upper register, there are two rows of deities, one facing right and one facing left. The first row is composed by six divine figures, of which the last five are on a low base:

II.1) a hippopotamus-goddess with open mouth and pendulous breast and squatting on a pedestal. Of her name only a hieroglyph of a bird, very likely an owl, survives. Is this another image of the goddess *nḥmmt*?

242 Leitz 2002, V, 304; Roberson 2013, 54-55.
243 Assmann 1977, pl. 41.
244 Franfort/de Buck/Gunn 1939, pl. 74; Piankoff 1954, fig. 142.
245 Mariette 1880, pl. 19b.
246 Montet 1951, pl. 90.
247 Montet 1960, pl. 30.
248 Daressy 1917, 9.

II.2) a standing male figure with full frontal face. Its caption is completely lost (Fig. II.31).

II.3) , *md*[...], a naked male figure in a semi-sitting posture, with both his arms by his sides. His name might be restored *mds*, 'the knife carrier' or 'the sharp one', a deity known from the Pyramid Texts to the Graeco-Roman Period.[249] On the sarcophagi of Ankhhapi son of Tefnakht (CG 29303) and Djedhor son of Iahmes Medes appears as a standing god with both his arms by his sides.[250]

II.4) a naked male standing figure, with empty hands and arms hanging by his sides. Traces of a caption above, with the surviving one-consonant *n* (Fig. II.32).

II.5) a naked deity in a semi-sitting position with legs slightly bent at the knee, but without seat, and with upraised arms presumably holding lizards. The figure is very damaged: hands, head and name are no longer visible.

II.6) 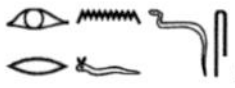, *ỉr-rn=f-ḏs*[*=f*], 'He who makes his own name':[251] a naked deity in a semi-sitting position with legs slightly bent at the knee, but without seat, and with upraised arms holding lizards (Fig. II.33). He is the only deity of the lower register of the rear that can be recognized with certainty. This god, who appears for the first time in the Coffin Texts,[252] can take different aspects and is represented in numerous sources, above all in groups or rows of gods on sarcophagi.[253] On the sarcophagus of Khaf his name is accompanied by the text: *nỉs(=ỉ) rn=k m wsỉr*, 'I shall invoke your name as Osiris'.[254]

On the Leiden naos, traces of a lizard held up by its tail are still visible in his left hand. Similar reptiles were probably also held in his right hand and by the identical deity before him. As in the Leiden naos, gods holding lizards usually appear in pairs.[255] But the naos moves away from the norm, since *ỉr-rn=f-ḏs=f*, when holding lizards,[256] is always the first of the two. In the other examples showing Ir-ren-ef-djes-ef holding lizards, he is followed by *mꜣꜣ-ỉt=f*, as in the tomb and on the sarcophagus of Psusennes I,[257] or by *sḫm-ḥr*, 'Powerful of face',[258] on the sarcophagus of Ankhefenkhonsu (CG 41001bis)[259] of the 25th Dynasty. To these sources, one should add a statuette from the tomb of Montuemhat that is the only three-dimensional image of this god, portrayed with a lizard in one of his hands and

249 Leitz 2002, III, 469-470.

250 Maspero 1908-1914, 100, 132-133, pl. 13.

251 See Berlandini 1995, 39-40; Egberts 1995, 126; Leitz 2002, I, 471-472, who however does not include the Leiden naos among the known examples of this deity.

252 CT IV, 192e, 206e; VII, 457h.

253 For example, the sarcophagi of Psusennes I (Montet 1951, pl. 84), Cairo CG 41001bis (Moret 1913, 27, pl. III), Iahmes (Leclant 1962, fig. 17), Cairo CG 29301, 29303, 29304 and 29319 (Maspero 1908-1914, 21, 42, 51, 111, 157, pls. 2, 12, 15), Cairo TR 21/11/14/6 (LD III, 279e; Buhl 1959, 23), Panehemisis (Leitz 2011, 24, 30, 36-37), and Horemheb (Leitz 2011, 402-403).

254 Daressy 1917, 11.

255 On lizards in ancient Egypt, see Guilhou 2009.

256 When represented under other guises or holding knives, he can be either the first or the second of the two: Leitz 2002, I, 471-471.

257 Montet 1951, pls. 14, 84.

258 Leitz 2002, VI, 538-539.

259 Moret 1913, 27, pl. III.

next to the guardian-deity *nrw* in the guise of a bird.[260] The god *mꜣꜣ-ỉt=f* is depicted on the front of the naos as a falcon; therefore, unless he appears twice on the same monument, one might suggest that the deity before *ỉr-rn=f-ḏs=f* should be identified as *sḫm-ḥr*, even though one should also remember that other deities can be portrayed with lizards in their hands, such as *ḥꜣḳw*, 'Plunderer',[261] and *ḫnfꜣ*[262] or *ḫnfꜣ-ḥr*,[263] who on the sarcophagus of Wennefer (CG 29310)[264] is depicted holding lizards just behind *ỉr-rn=f-ḏs=f*, represented as a standing god with arms at his sides. Like a few other deities of the Leiden naos, Ir-ren-ef-djes-ef is also depicted, holding a knife, in the third eastern Osirian chapel at Dendera.[265]

The number of gods of the row facing left is no longer determinable, even though one could assume that it was the same as in the row facing right. Unfortunately, the first part of this group of gods is completely lost. Between the left edge and the first visible pair of gods, there is space enough for the figure of one or more divine images.

II.x+1) Of the first surviving image, there are only traces of the body and knees of a deity squatting on a pedestal, which has disappeared. The name is lost.

II.x+2) A deity squatting on a pedestal, which is clearly visible. The name is lost (Fig. II.34).

II.x+3-5) These two deities are followed by another group of gods squatting on a tall pedestal and whose names have disappeared. The last one is in the guise of a baboon (Fig. II.35). Before him, there are traces of what appears to be, very likely, another baboon, of which only the back and part of the muzzle remain, and perhaps traces of another figure, which was not placed on the pedestal. In spite of the damages, it is possible to make an attempt to identify the names of these two or three deities. Groups of three baboons can indeed be represented in funerary contexts, above all coffins, and in the company of other gods depicted on the Leiden naos. In the sarcophagus of Pasherihoraawasheb (BM EA 6666) of the 22nd Dynasty, these three gods have no name.[266] There is also a three-dimensional example of this group: a statuette (Berlin 23729) from the tomb of Montuemhat represents one standing and two squatting baboons.[267] A standing baboon followed by two baboons on a pedestal appears also on a granite block from Kom el-Ahmar, probably part of another naos of Amasis. In this case, only traces of the name of the last baboon survive: [...]*nt*, preceded

---

260 Clère 1986, 103, pl. III.

261 For the 25th Dynasty, see the sarcophagus Cairo CG 41001bis (Montet 1913, 27, pl. III); for the Saite period, the sarcophagus of Iahmes (Leclant 1962, 111, fig.17) and the tomb of Mutirdis (Assmann 1977, 93, pl. 43); for the Graeco-Roman Period, the sarcophagi of Khaf (Daressy 1917, 11), Cairo CG 29303 and 29394 (Maspero 1908-1914, 100, 132, pl. 13), and *Dendera* X 194, 9, pl. 94. The meaning of the name of this deity is uncertain. Leitz 2002, V, 26-27 suggests 'Der Behaarte (?)', that is 'The hairy one'; Roberson 2013, 33 suggests 'He-who-is-arrogant'.

262 For the 26th Dynasty, see the sarcophagus of Iahmes (Leclant 1962, fig. 17); for the Graeco-Roman Period, the sarcophagi of Khaf (Daressy 1917, 8) and Cairo CG 29303 (Maspero 1908-1914, 107, pl. 17). See also Leitz 2002, V, 751.

263 Leitz 2002, V, 751.

264 Maspero/Gauthier 1939, 52, pl. 15.

265 *Dendera* X 194, 9, pl. 94.

266 Taylor 2010, 202-203. See also the sarcophagus of Rome V.O. 1000: Sist 2001, 538.

267 Leclant 1961, 121-123.

Fig. II.34 (left). Detail of rear, lower register, left half: two squatting deities. Author's photograph.

Fig. II.35 (right). Detail of rear, lower register, left half: two baboons. Author's photograph.

by part of a bird hieroglyph.[268] In the majority of the cases, however, the first standing baboon, represented with its arms at its sides, is called *ỉf*, 'Flesh'.[269] Behind him, there are two other baboons, either on separate pedestals, as on the sarcophagus of Psusennes I[270] and on the sarcophagus of Ankhefenkhonsu (CG 41001bis)[271] of the 26th Dynasty, or with both the animals on the same pedestal or naos, as on the sarcophagi of Iahmes,[272] Khaf,[273] and Ankhhapi son of Tefnakht (CG 29303),[274] and probably in the tomb of Mutirdis. In the first case, the two baboons are differentiated by their names: *sẖd-ḥr*, 'He with an upside down face',[275] and *db-ḥr-k*;[276] but in the second case, when they are placed on the same pedestal, they seem to form a unity, defined by the single name *sẖd-ḥr*, while the name *db-ḥr-k* is ascribed to a ram-headed guardian-deity following them. The two squatting baboons, *sẖd-ḥr* and *db-ḥr-k*, each on his own pedestal, are represented also in a row of divine images in the third eastern Osirian chapel of Dendera,[277] but the standing baboon *ỉf*

268 Rowland/Billing 2009, 7-8; Billing/Rowland 2015, 105-106, fig. 4. Perhaps to be read *bnty* or *bntywy*, 'baboon' or 'two baboons' (Leitz 2002, II, 807).

269 Leitz 2002, I, 222-223, where another reading of his name is suggested: *ỉwf*, 'Der zujubelt (?)'. In Leitz 2011, 284 the deity's name is read 'Der Jubelnde'. Very likely, this deity is to be identified with the baboon-headed god *ỉf* represented in the cenotaph of Sety I (Franfort/de Buck/Gunn 1939, pl. 74), the tombs of Ramses VI (Piankoff 1954, fig. 142) and Sheshonq III (Montet 1960, pl. 30), the sarcophagus usurped by Psusennes I (Montet 1951, pl. 92), the tomb of Mutirdis (Assmann 1977, pl. 41), and the sarcophagus of Khaf (Daressy 1917, 10). See also Waitkus 1987, 54.

270 Montet 1951, pl. 86.

271 Moret 1913, 24, pl. III.

272 Leclant 1962, fig. 17.

273 Daressy 1917, 8.

274 Maspero 1908-1914, 106, pl. 12.

275 Leitz 2002, VI, 592.

276 Leitz 2002, VII, 528. The reading of this name is uncertain.

277 *Dendera* X 197, 13, pl. 95.

is not included in this sequence of deities. Although highly hypothetical, it is plausible that the same iconography, or a very similar one, was also included on the Leiden naos; indeed, before the squatting baboons there is enough room for the presence of a third image, which might have been the deity *ỉf*, while the two baboons sharing the same pedestal might have been labelled *sẖd-ḥr*.

2.7. Some palaeographic and stylistic observations

The workmanship of the Leiden naos is excellent and the figures and hieroglyphs have been skilfully worked out. As we have seen, unlike the other naoi of Amasis with rows of gods, this monument has the particularity to have divine images of a rather large size, which occupy three registers on the front and only two registers on the rear and side walls.

It is unfortunately impossible to know where the monument was carved and decorated, whether in Memphis or in another locality, or, more specifically, at Kom el-Ahmar. The latter seems however the most plausible solution, since the monument shares with the other naos from the site (Louvre D 29) some peculiarities that might be ascribed to a local trend or tradition. For example, some divine images appear only on these two monuments; moreover their dedicatory inscriptions are very similar, sharing the same phraseology, analogous royal epithets, and identical graphic forms. But it is equally impossible to know whether this local trend was able to influence, at least partially, the style and content of the decoration.

A certain degree of flexibility in the choice of the represented subjects was very likely allowed. For example, the new guardian-deity Ankh-em-fedet, naked and with shoulders and face shown frontally, is to be understood as a variant of the more conventional Ankh-em-fenetju, 'created' due to local initiative. The same principle might be valid for other deities, such as in the case of the goddess *ḥr-m-ḥwnt* in the upper register of the rear, who seems to have been created by merging two more ancient goddesses with similar names.

Like the divine figures, the hieroglyphs are rather elegant, characterized by clear-cut and elongated lines. This is particularly evident with the vertical and horizontal signs, as for example the *nṯr*-sign (Gardiner sign-list R8): tall and with a small pennant in top; the sign of the hand (D46): long and slightly undulated, above all in the trapezium; or the sign of the mouth (D21): long and flat. The upper line of the eye-sign (D4) is also elongated, as if the cosmetic line has been extended. A few particularities should be noted. The sign of the cloth (S29) is folded over for more than half of its height; in the sign of the face (D2), the head is slightly dolichocephalic, with a round top and protruding ears. The stool sign (Q3) also has an elongated form, rather common during the Late Period.[278] In the sign of the arms in the gesture of negation (D35), the point of junction of the two arms is quite high and pointed. In the unclassified sign Aa1, consisting of a circle with internal lines, these are always horizontal. The sign of the seat (Q1) is constantly high-backed. The signs of the water (N35) and of the board game (Y5) are both rather long; the former presents from nine to eleven undulations, the latter

278 Engsheden 2014, 103.

Fig. II.36. Detail of left wall, dedication text: *mnw*. Author's photograph.

Fig. II.38. Detail of rear, dedication text: *ḥmꜣg*. Author's photograph.

Fig. II.37. Detail of rear, dedication text: *kꜣr* and *mꜣṯ*. Author's photograph.

shows from eight to eleven playing pieces, which are aligned with the two extremities of the sign.

The animal hieroglyphs do not present particularities worthy of note. The hare sign (E34) has large ears and an upraised short tail; the horned viper (I9) shows an undulated body; the bird signs – the Egyptian vulture (G1), the falcon (G5), the vulture (G14), the owl (G17), the crested ibis (G25) and the swallow (G35) – are clearly differentiated from each other, with very well carved tails and wings; the only exception is the sign of the quail chick (G43), which does not present any detailed anatomical details.

A few words of the dedicatory text show unusual writings. The word *mnw*, 'monument', is written with just two signs, the biliteral *mn* followed by the *n* as phonetic complement (Fig. II.36); the word *kꜣr*, 'naos', has a determinative consisting of a simple structure with an arched roof, while the word *mꜣṯ*, 'granite', is written just with the biliteral *mꜣ* and the sign of the granite bowl (W7) as determinative (Fig. II.37). Identical writings are also found on the naos Louvre D 29.

However, one of the most interesting palaeographical aspects of the Leiden naos is perhaps the writing of the epithet *hemag*, of which the sources present several graphic variations.[279] Here, the fully written form is used, composed of the *ḥ*-sign, the biliteral *mꜣ* and the *g*-sign, rendering the reading *ḥmꜣg*. Starting from the 26th Dynasty, this was the most common way of rendering the Osirian epithet, and in many cases it could be followed by different kinds of determinatives, such as the seated god, the *nṯr*-sign, or

279 Zecchi 1996, 63-64.

more specifically the sign of the fist, which in a few examples holds an object, very likely to indicate the activities involved in the creation of the *hemag*. But in the Leiden naos the engravers chose as determinative a hieroglyph showing the façade of an architectonic structure with arched roof, characterized by two vertical lines in front or inside it (Fig. II.38) and probably representing columns or poles of the temple of *hemag*. This peculiar sign is found for the very first time in room XV of the tomb of Pediamenopet in el-Assasif in the Theban necropolis (TT 33),[280] and then in the Delta, at Sais, where it seems strictly linked to the local temple of *hemag*. It is used as determinative in the epithet of an image of 'Osiris Hemag, the great god, foremost of the *hut-bit*'[281] on a block from Sa el-Hagar of the Saite period. A variant of this determinative, showing a door in the centre of the structure, appears in the epithet *ḥmꜣg* on a statue originally from Sais and dated from the end of the 26th Dynasty to the early 27th Dynasty.[282] Then, the hieroglyph occurs again on a statue of the end of the 30th Dynasty or early Ptolemaic Period discovered at Delos,[283] but originally from Sais, belonging to the musician Nesnephthys, daughter of an 'administrator of the mansions of Neith'; unlike the previous examples, here it is used as determinative for the *ḥwt-ḥmꜣḳ*: '... may you receive the *snw*-breads at the gate of the temple of *hemag* on the shore of this lake, for ever, in the temple of Neith...', probably a reference to the sacred lake in the vicinity of the temple of *hemag* in the complex of the temple of Neith. At present, the Leiden naos and the Theban Tomb TT 33 are the only monuments where this determinative is not used in a context directly associated with Sais. If this sign was a privileged way to specifically determine, at a local level, Osiris Hemag and his temple, its presence on the Leiden naos might be due to the importance of this Osirian form at Sais during the 26th Dynasty, rather than to a Saite origin of the monument or of Osiris Hemag himself, and might evoke the façade of the local *ḥwt-ḥmꜣg*.

There is another aspect that should be pointed out. Even though the king is not represented, the divine figures were carved according to a trend or style of the royal art of Amasis' reign. Some of the figures show, indeed, characteristics and iconographic details of the king's portraiture found in other contexts, both in Lower and in Upper Egypt.[284] This is particularly observable on the left outer wall, which, besides being very well preserved, presents many anthropomorphic deities. For example, the eighth deity in the lower register, called *ỉn-ḥr*, is depicted with rather slim and elongated limbs, and a narrow, almond-shaped eye bordered by an eyebrow in relief (Fig. II.39); a deep furrow starts from the wings of the nostrils towards the small chin, separating the prominent cheeks from the mouth, which is also small, but with thick lips and corners lifted in a slight smile. Similar features are also found in the faces of Osiris 'lord of Ra-setjau' and

280 Traunecker 2014, 226, fig. 10.8.

281 Wilson 1998, 4, pl. I.4; Leclère 2003, 34; Wilson 2006, 219-220, pl. 31e; Jansen-Winkeln 2014, 759.

282 Statue Florence 1522, found in 1858 in the house of the Tranquilli, near the apse of Santa Maria Sopra Minerva, in Rome: Schiaparelli 1887, 222-223; PM VII, 413; Roullet 1972, 112, pl. CLIV, fig. 217; Zecchi 1996, 15-16 doc. 9.

283 Statue Delos A 379: Leclant/De Meulenaere 1957, 33-42; Zecchi 1996, 31-33 doc. 22; Wilson 2006, 25. This fragmentary statue, made of green stone, represents a walking woman and was very likely moved to Delos when it became a Ptolemaic colony; the back-pillar preserves an autobiographical text in three columns of hieroglyphs.

284 Mysliwiec 1988, 60-65.

Fig. II.39. Detail of right side, lower registre: face of Inher. Author's photograph.

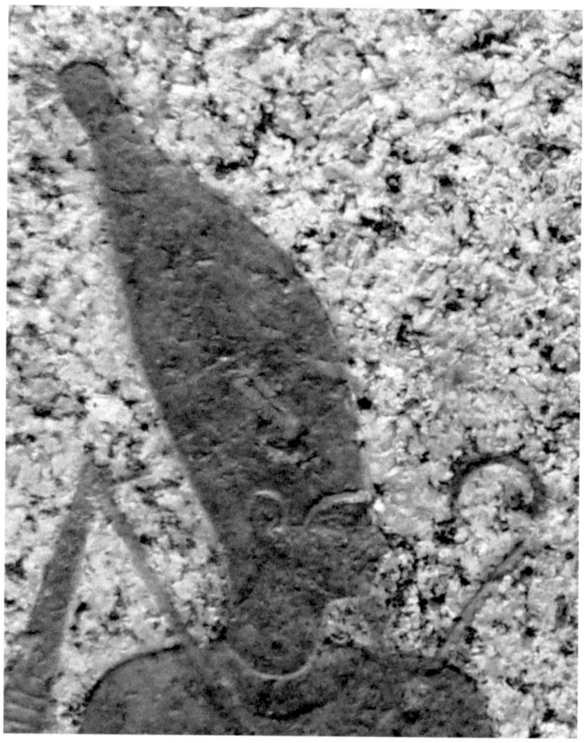

Fig. II.40. Detail of right side, upper registre: face of Osiris the Great Saw. Author's photograph.

Osiris *ỉtfꜣ wr*, represented in the upper register. In particular the figure of Osiris *ỉtfꜣ wr* (Fig. II.40), with his rather long and thin neck, and above all the extremely elongated proportions of his white crown, recalls an image of Amasis on a relief from Memphis.[285]

Because of its visual heaviness and compactness and the plainness of its design, lacking all architectonic decoration on the front, the Leiden naos may seem a rather austere and sober monument. However, the adoption of the royal portrait-type of the period and the high quality of its carving, besides the religious themes expressed, indicate the great attention paid to its execution.

285 Jamb of granite in the University of Memphis, Tennessee, Collection of the Institute of Egyptian Art and Archaeology: Freed 1983, 51; Mysliwiec 1988, 48-49, pl. LXII.

Fig. II.41. Line drawing of front including roof (drawn by Giuliano Carapia).

2.8. List of deities on the naos (Figs. II.41-44)

Front – left

I.1.	Anubis	(canid on naos)
I.2.	*ỉwꜥ nṯr*	(recumbent lion)
I.3.	*dwn-ḥr*	(ibis-headed, standing)
I.4.	Sekhem	(*sekhem*-sceptre)
I.5.	Horus	(falcon-headed, squatting)
II.1.	Imsety	(mummiform)
II.2.	Duamutef	(mummiform)
III.1.	*nḫbt*	(female figure)

Front – right

I.1.	Anubis	(canid on naos)
I.2.	*ỉwꜥ nṯr*	(recumbent lion)
I.3.	*sḥr-ḏw*	(squatting)
I.4.	Isis	(standing)
I.5.	*mꜣꜣ-ỉt=f*	(falcon on *nb*-basket)
II.1.	Hapy	(mummiform)
II.2.	Qebehsenuef	(mummiform)
III.1.	*mwyt*	(female figure)

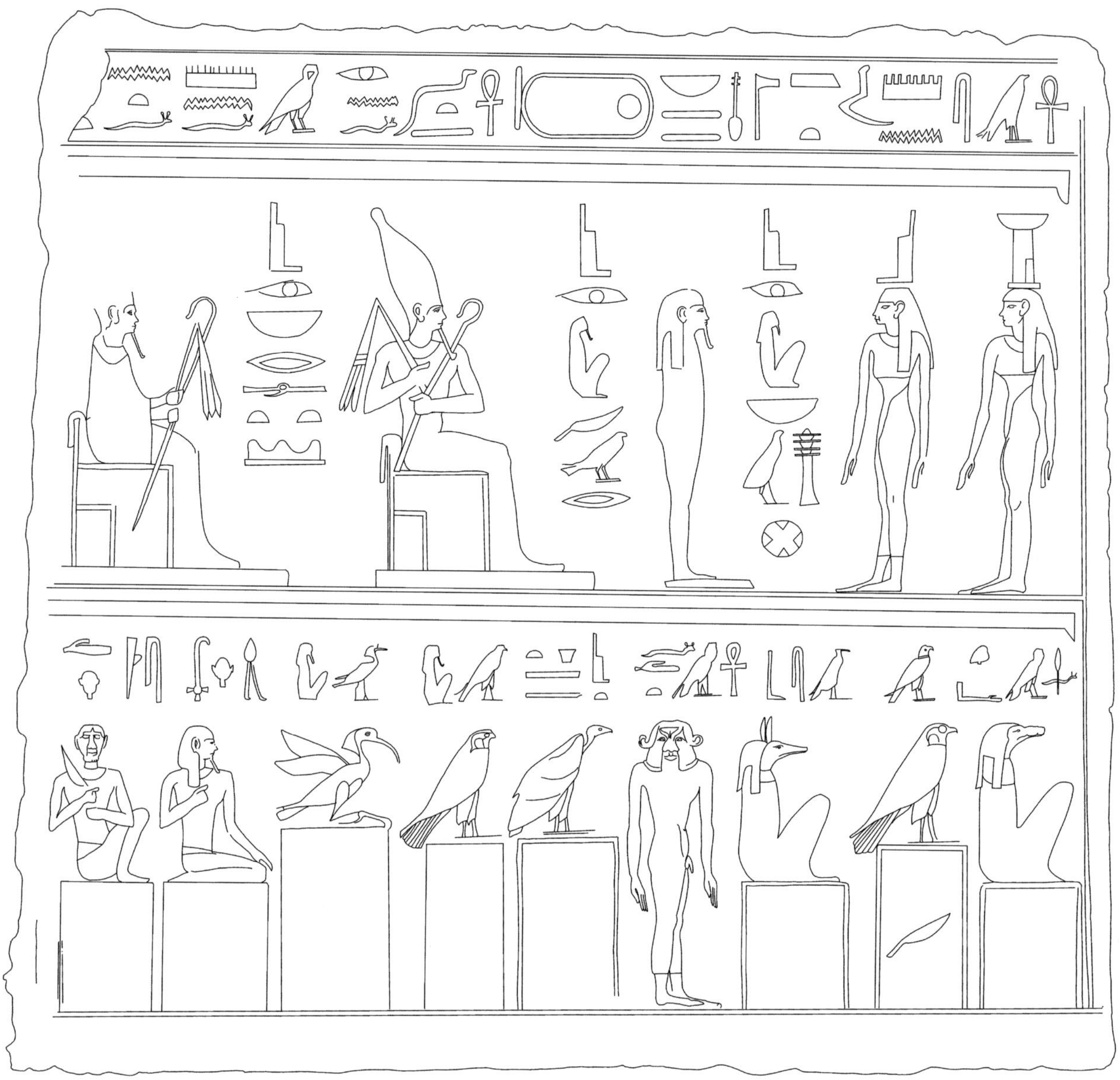

Fig. II.42. Line drawing of left side (drawn by Giuliano Carapia).

Left – upper register

I.1.	Nephthys	(standing)
I.2.	Isis	(standing)
I.3.	Osiris lord of Busiris	(mummiform, standing)
I.4.	Osiris *ỉtfꜣ wr*	(seated)
I.5.	Osiris lord of Ra-setjau	(seated)

Left – lower register

II.1.	*ḫsf-m-tp-ꜥ*	(crocodile-headed, squatting)
II.2.	Horus	(falcon on pedestal)
II.3.	*ꜣsb*	(canine-headed, squatting)
II.4.	*ꜥnḫ-m-fdt*	(full frontal figure)
II.5.	Isis *nbt tꜣwy*	(vulture on pedestal)
II.6.	Horus	(falcon on pedestal)
II.7.	Akh	(ibis on pedestal)
II.8.	*ỉn-ḥr*	(kneeling)
II.9.	*sḳd-ḥr*	(full frontal face, squatting)

Fig. II.43. Line drawing of right side (drawn by Giuliano Carapia).

Right – upper register

I.1.	Shu	(seated)
I.2.	Tefnet (?)	(lioness-headed, seated)
I.3.	Montu/Amun (?)	(ram-headed, seated)
I.4.	[?]	(canine-headed, standing)
I.5.	*ỉs*[*ds*]	[?]

Right – lower register

II.1.	Horus 'the great god'	(falcon-headed, standing)
II.2.	*šʿ*	(lion-headed, standing)
II.3.	*wnm-ḥwꜣt*	(turtle-headed, squatting on pedestal)
II.4.	*ʿꜣ-ḫrw / nfr-nfrw* (?)	(antelope-headed, squatting on pedestal)
II.5.	[?]	(hippopotamus goddess, squatting on pedestal)
II.5.	[?]	(recumbent lion or sphinx on pedestal)
II.6.	[?]	[?]

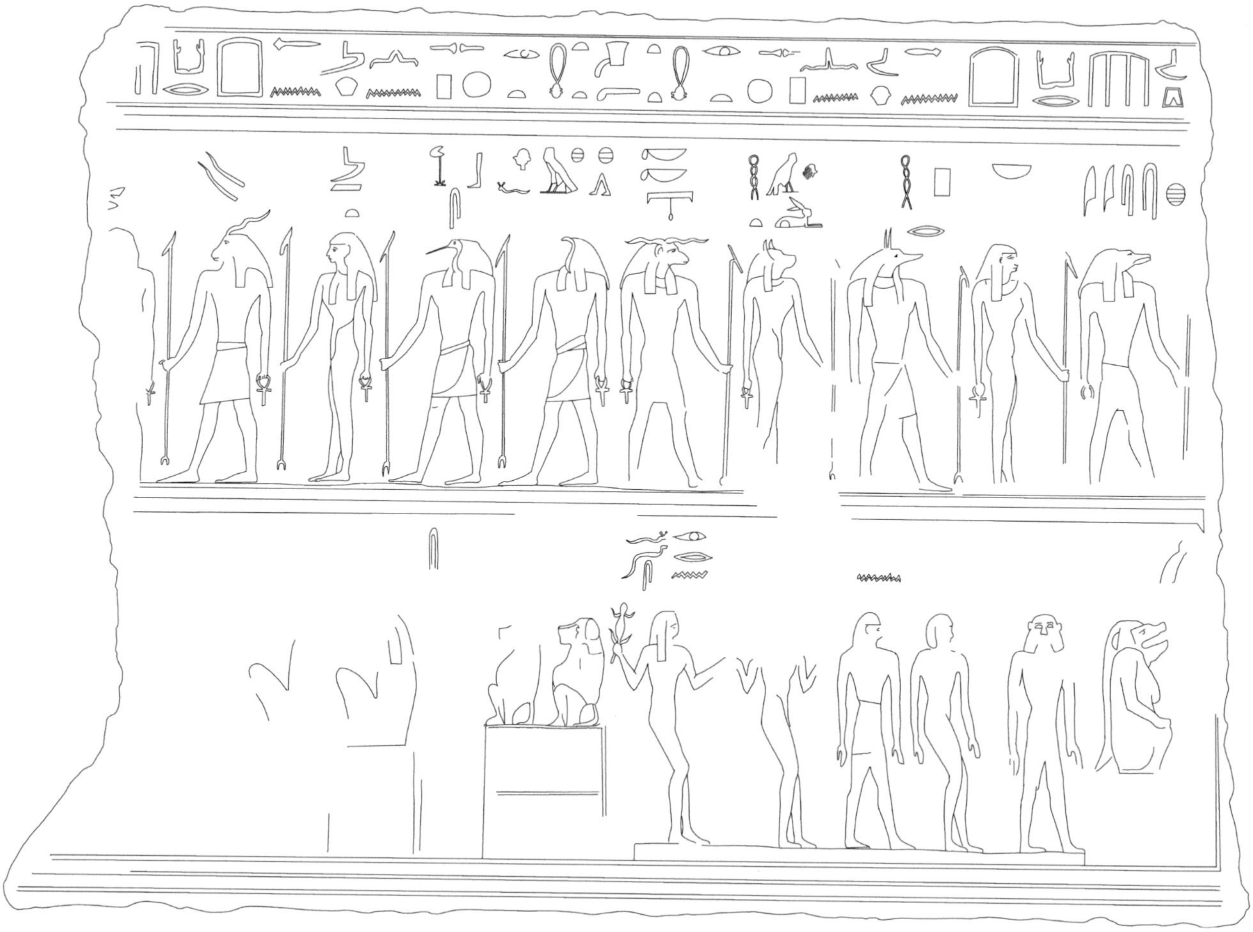

Fig. II.44. Line drawing of rear (drawn by Giuliano Carapia).

Rear – upper register, looking left

I.1.	[...]*wr* (?)	[?, standing]
I.2.	*ꜥbwy*	(antelope-headed, standing)
I.3.	Maat	(standing)
I.4.	*ḫꜣbs*	(ibis- or heron-headed, standing)
I.5.	*ḥr=f-m-ḫꜣḫ*	(serpent-headed, standing)

Rear – upper register, looking right

I.1.	*ḫssỉ*	(crocodile-headed, standing)
I.2.	Nephthys	(standing)
I.3.	*pḥ*[...]*r*	(canine-headed, standing)
I.4.	*ḥr-m-ḥwnt*	(lioness-headed, standing)
I.5.	*kkw*	(ram-headed, standing)

Rear – lower register, looking left

II.x.	[?]	[?]
II.x+1.	[?]	(squatting deity)
II.x+2.	[?]	(squatting deity)
II.x+3	[?]	[baboon?]
II.x+4	[?]	(squatting baboon on pedestal)
II.x+5	[?]	(squatting baboon on pedestal)

Rear – lower register, looking right

II.1.	[?]	(hippopotamus-goddess, squatting on pedestal)
II.2.	[?]	(male figure, full frontal face)
II.3.	*mds* (?)	(male figure, semi-sitting position)
II.4.	[?]	(male standing figure)
II.5.	[?]	(male figure,semi-sitting position with lizards)
II.6.	*ỉr-rn=f-ḏs=f*	(male figure, semi-sitting position with lizards)

Chapter III

The naoi of Amasis

1. The naoi

Amasis was one of the most prolific builders of the Late Period. His monuments are present in the Delta, in the Nile valley, and in the western oases:[286]

- In the area of Saqqara and Memphis, his building programme was rather intense and concentrated above all in the temple of Ptah.[287] Along the east-west axis of this building, Petrie found some blocks in quartzite and one in granite with the names of Amasis.[288] At Mit Rahina also two quartzite doorjambs with his image were brought to light.[289] At Kom el-Nawa Petrie discovered a granite block belonging to the king,[290] while another block in quartzite with his names has more recently been found at Kom el-Qalʿa.[291]
- In the north area of Athribis, in 1956-1957 the Polish Mission discovered, north-east of kom A, a foundation pit in mud bricks of a temple of about 15 x 30 m, orientated towards the South and with foundation deposits dated to the reign of Amasis.[292]
- An intense building activity was also carried out in Mendes, with the construction of a sanctuary with an impressive naos-court, housing four huge monolithic shrines.[293]
- The Late Period temple of Buto (Tell el-Fara'in) was presumably erected during the reign of Amasis, since fragments of mortar with his cartouches were found in the destruction layer of the building.[294]
- Also the smaller stone temple in the sacred enclosure of ancient Imet (Tell Nabasha) has been attributed to Amasis, on the basis of plaques with his cartouches found in its foundation deposits.[295] Besides, in this locality, Petrie discovered a fragment of a naos and some granite blocks[296] with the names of Amasis and of the god Min, identified

286 On the monuments of Amasis, see: Bresciani 1967, 277 n. a; De Meulenaere 1968, 183-184 n. 30; Arnold 1999, 83-91; Graefe 2011, 159-164; Jansen-Winkeln 2014, 415-478.

287 Mysliwiec 1988, 48-49; Arnold 1999, 86-87; Leclère 2008, 61-72.

288 Petrie 1910, 39, pls. XXIX (4-5), XXXIII (4-7); PM III/2, 840; Jansen-Winkeln 2014, 436-437.

289 Memphis, Tennessee, Institute of Egyptian Art and Archaeology of Memphis State University: Mysliwiec 1988, pl. 72; Jansen-Winkeln 2014, 436.

290 Petrie 1909, 14, pl. XXIII; PM III/2, 851; Jansen-Winkeln 2014, 438.

291 Moussa 1987, 147-148; Jansen-Winkeln 2014, 436. For other objects belonging to Amasis from the territory of Memphis, see Jansen-Winkeln 2014, 437-444.

292 Ruszczyc 1976, 117-127; Vernus 1978, 89; Habachi 1982, 223; Leclère 2008, 245-246.

293 De Meulenaere/MacKay 1976; Bothmer 1988, 205-209; Leclère 2008, 324-326; Redford 2010, 157-158.

294 Seton-Williams 1969, 7; Faltings *et al.* 2000, 164-166, figs. 13-15; Leclère 2008, 206, 208, 212, 236, 619.

295 Petrie 1888, 14, pl. V; Arnold 1999, 86; Leclère 2008, 493-494.

296 Petrie 1888, 33-35, pl. IX.4.

with Horus 'chief of the deserts' (*ḥry-tp ḫ3swt*). These have recently been interpreted as doorjambs of the temple erected by the king, perhaps for Min himself.[297]

- Even though little evidence survives of Amasis' buildings at Sais (modern Sa el-Hagar), the inscriptions of private individuals give notice of works ordered by the king in the temple of Neith and in a local lake.[298] According to Herodotus (II, 175), the king built a gateway to the sanctuary of Neith, where he also erected statues, man-headed sphinxes, and a huge monolithic granite naos.[299] Moreover, in Rosetta and el-Nahhariya Labib Habachi found some blocks[300] in quartzite, which were very likely connected with a *sed*-festival construction of Amasis at Sa el-Hagar.
- At Philae, about three-hundred reused blocks from a small temple of Amasis were recovered in the foundations of the second pylon and hypostyle hall of the Ptolemaic temple.[301] According to the inscriptions and representations of these blocks, the goddess Isis played a preeminent role inside Amasis' building, which consisted of three aligned rooms. The cartouches of Amasis were also found on the neighbouring islands of Biggeh and Sehel. On the former, a rock-cut text presents the king as 'beloved of Khnum lord of Biggeh' (*mry ẖnmw nb snmt*),[302] on the latter as 'beloved of Khnum, Satet, and Anuket'.[303]
- In the Siwa Oasis, Amasis ordered the construction of the temple of Agurmi, the Ammoneion,[304] while at Ayn el-Muftella, in the Bahariya Oasis, there are four chapels which were part of a wider cult area erected during the king's reign.[305]

Objects belonging to Amasis were discovered in various sites of the Delta, such as, for example, Tanis,[306] Naukratis,[307] Kom Firin,[308] Tanta,[309] Tell Defenneh,[310] Bubastis,[311] Tell el-Maskhuta,[312] and Heliopolis,[313] but also at Edfu,[314] Hermopolis,[315] Elkab,[316] Thebes,[317] Elephantine,[318] and in the Wadi el-Hammamat.[319]

---

297 Razanajao 2009, 103-108. See, however, Defernez 2011, 123, where the temple is said to be dedicated to the goddess Wadjet. For the site of Tell Nabasha, see Nielsen/Gasperini/Mamedow 2016, 65-74.

298 Leclère 2008, 175-176; Spencer 2010a, 449-452. For objects belonging to the king, see Jansen-Winkeln 2014, 416-419.

299 El-Sayed 1982, 35; Arnold 1999, 84-85; Leclère 2008, 172-173, 180-181.

300 Habachi 1943, 384-385, fig. 105, 398-399, pl. XXVIIb; Habachi 1982, 231; Wilson 2006, 312, 314.

301 Farag/Wahbah/Farid 1977, 315-324; Farid 1980, 81-103. See also Haeny 1985, 202.

302 LD III, 274 (p); PM V, 256; Jansen-Winkeln 2014, 457.

303 PM V, 252; Jansen-Winkeln 2014, 457.

304 Colin 1998, 329-356; Bruhn 2010.

305 Fakhry 1942, 152-171; Colin/Labrique 2002, 45-78; Labrique 2004, 327-357.

306 Leclère 2008, 430; Jansen-Winkeln 2014, 432.

307 Leclère 2008, 118, 127, 131.

308 PM IV, 51; Spencer 2008, 26, 34, pl. 92. See also Spencer 2010, 519.

309 Gauthier 1923, 71-72; PM IV, 45-46; Jansen-Winkeln 2014, 426.

310 Petrie 1888, 72, 77, pls. XXXVI (5), XLI (76), XLIV; Jansen-Winkeln 2014, 434.

311 PM IV, 33; Leclère 2008, 377; Jansen-Winkeln 2014, 433-434.

312 Leclère 2008, 554; Jansen-Winkeln 2014, 435.

313 Leahy 1984a, 66; Jansen-Winkeln 2014, 435.

314 Alliot 1932, 26, pl. XXIII; Bianchi 1979, 18, pls. 4-5; Jansen-Winkeln 2014, 448.

315 Jansen-Winkeln 2014, 444.

316 Jansen-Winkeln 2014, 448.

317 Jansen-Winkeln 2014, 447-448.

318 Junge 1987, 67-68; Leahy 1988, 190-191; Jansen-Winkeln 2014, 448-452.

319 Bas-relief showing Amasis kneeling before Min of Coptos: *LD* III, 275c; PM VII, 335; Mysliwiec 1988, 49.

The reign of Amasis was characterized by a widespread production of monolithic naoi in hard stone that had never been matched during the 26th Dynasty:[320]

1) Naos of Leiden AM 107

Provenance: Kom el-Ahmar.

Material: red granite.

Size: height 1.94 m; width 1.75; depth 1.37 m.

Beneficiary: Osiris Hemag (dedicatory text).

King's titulary: ḥr smn-mꜣꜥt; nṯr nfr nb tꜣwy ẖnm-ib-rꜥ.

Damnatio memoriae: yes.

Roof type: pyramidal.

Decoration: dedicatory text and registers with rows of gods; decorated roof.

Bibliography (selected): Leemans 1840, 42-43; Schneider/Raven 1981, 124-125; Schneider 1992, 80-82; Zecchi 1996, 12-14; Yoyotte 2001, 54-83; Spencer 2006, 21-22; Jansen-Winkeln 2014, 423-426.

2) Naos Louvre D 29

Provenance: Kom el-Ahmar.

Material: red granite.

Size: height about 2.55 m; width 1.61 m; depth 1.50 m.

Beneficiary: Osiris Merty 'the great god, foremost of Fekat' (*wsir mryt nṯr ꜥꜣ ḫnty fkꜣt*) (dedicatory text).

King's titulary: ḥr smn-mꜣꜥt; nbty sꜣ-nt-spd-tꜣwy; ḥr nbw stp-nṯrw; nṯr nfr nb tꜣwy ẖnm-ib-rꜥ; sꜣ rꜥ iꜥḥ-ms-sꜣ-nt.

Damnatio memoriae: yes.

Roof type: curved.

Architecture: cavetto cornice, torus moulding, frieze of uraei.

Decoration: dedicatory text and registers with rows of gods.

Bibliography: Piankoff 1933, 161-179; PM IV, 5; Vernus 1978, 87-88; Yoyotte 2001, 54-83; Spencer 2006, 11, 17, 21-22, 33; Jansen-Winkeln 2014, 420-423.

3) Fragment (corner of a naos?)

Provenance: Kom el-Ahmar.

Material: red granite.

Size: unknown.

Beneficiary: unknown.

King's titulary: [...] *nsw-bity iꜥḥ-ms-sꜣ-nt* [...].

Damnatio memoriae: ?

Roof type: unknown.

Architecture: unknown.

320 For a list of the known Egyptian monolithic naoi from the Old Kingdom onwards, see: Thiers 1997, 259-265; Thiers 2012, 983 n. 7.

Decoration: unknown. The fragment preserves part of the shoulder of a figure, perhaps an offering bearer.

Bibliography: Rowland/Wilson 2006, 13; Jansen-Winkeln 2014, 426; Billing/Rowland 2015, 164.

4) Fragment (upper corner)

Provenance: Kom el-Ahmar.

Material: red granite.

Size: unknown.

Beneficiary: Hathor 'who resides in the *set-weret* (*ḥry-ib st-wrt*) and the gods who are in the Upper Mansion (*nṯrw imyw ḥwt-ḥry-tp*)' (dedicatory text).

King's titulary: (?), the attribution of the naos to Amasis is based on the comparison with the other naoi from Kom el-Ahmar.

Damnation memoriae: ?

Roof type: unknown.

Architecture: unknown.

Decoration: dedicatory text and register with rows of gods.

Bibliography: Rowland 2007, 70; Rowland/Billing 2009, 7-8; Jansen-Winkeln 2014, 761; Billing/Rowland 2015, 107.

5) Naos of Mendes

Provenance: Mendes (still *in situ*).

Material: granite.

Size: height about 8 m; width 4 m; depth: 3.3 m.

Beneficiary: Shu (king is 'beloved' of the god in the texts of doorjambs and lintel).

King's titulary (preserved): ḥr smn-mꜣꜥt; nsw-bity ẖnm-ib-rꜥ.

Damnatio memoriae: no.

Roof type: low-pitched pyramidal.

Architecture: plain sides.

Decoration: inscriptions on doorjambs and lintel.

Bibliography: Burton 1825, pl. XLI; Gauthier 1915, 123-124 (XLVI); Hansen 1967, 6-8, pls. VI-VIII, XVI; Soghor 1967, 16-18; PM IV, 35; De Meulenaere/MacKay 1976, 191, pls. 2-3, 5, 8a; Bothmer 1988, 205-220; Leclère 2008, 324-327; Redford 2010, 157-158; Jansen-Winkeln 2014, 426-427.

6) Naos of Mendes

Provenance: Mendes.

Material: granite.

Size: the reconstructed height corresponds to the height of the Shu naos.[321]

Beneficiary: Osiris (king is 'beloved' of the god in the texts of doorjambs and lintel).

King's titulary: ḥr smn-mꜣꜥt; nbty sꜣ-nt-spd-tꜣwy; ḥr nbw stp-nṯrw; nsw-bity ẖnm-ib-rꜥ (var. *ẖnm-ib-rꜥ*); *sꜣ rꜥ iꜥḥ-ms-sꜣ-nt* (var. *nsw-bity iꜥḥ-ms-sꜣ-nt*).

Damnatio memoriae: no.

321 Soghor 1967, 20.

Roof type: flat.[322]

Architecture: plain sides (?).

Decoration: inscriptions on doorjambs and lintel, decorated lintel. Small fragments survive.

Bibliography: Hansen 1967, 6, pls. VIII, XVI; Soghor 1967, 18-23; Leclère 2008, 324-327; Redford 2010, 157-158; Jansen-Winkeln 2014, 427.

7) Naos of Mendes

Provenance: Mendes.

Material: granite.

Size: unknown, but probably identical in scale to the naos of Shu.

Beneficiary: Geb (king is 'beloved' of the god in the texts of doorjambs and lintel).

King's titulary (preserved): ḥr smn-mꜣꜥt; nsw-bity ḫnm-ib-rꜥ.

Damnatio memoriae: no.

Roof type: low-pitched pyramidal.

Architecture: plain sides (?).

Decoration: inscriptions on doorjambs and lintel. Small fragments survive.

Bibliography: Hansen 1967, 6; Soghor 1967, 20-21; Leclère 2008, 324-327; Redford 2010, 157-158; Jansen-Winkeln 2014, 427-428.

8) Naos of Mendes

Provenance: Mendes.

Material: granite.

Size: unknown, but probably identical in scale to the naos of Shu.

Beneficiary: Ra (god mentioned on the doorjambs).

King's titulary (preserved): ḥr smn-mꜣꜥt; nbty sꜣ-nt-spd-tꜣwy; ḥr nbw stp-nṯrw; ḥr nbw stp-nṯrw; sꜣ rꜥ iꜥḥ-ms-sꜣ-nt (var. *nsw-bity iꜥḥ-ms-sꜣ-nt*).

Damnatio memoriae: no.

Roof type: no trace of the lintel or of any other upper part of the shrine has been found, therefore it remains uncertain whether it had a flat or low-pitched pyramidal roof.

Architecture: plain sides (?).

Decoration: inscriptions on doorjambs. Small fragments survive.

Bibliography: Hansen 1967, 6, pl. XVI; Soghor 1967, 20, 22; Leclère 2008, 324-327; Redford 2010, 157-158; Jansen-Winkeln 2014, 428.

9) Naos of Sais (Fig. IV.10)

Provenance: Sais ('Sa el-Hagar, in front of the house of Hussein al-Shabawy, transferred to Office in 1992'[323]).

Material: quartzite.

Size: preserved height 1 m, restored height 1.075 m; width 1.05 m; depth 0.685 m.

Beneficiary: Osiris 'in the House of Sekhmet' (*wsir m ḥwt-sḫmt*) (king is 'beloved' of the god in the text of the right doorjamb).

322 According to the reconstruction of Soghor 1967, 18.

323 Wilson 2006, 212.

Fig. III.1. Naos Cairo CG 70010. Reproduced from Roeder 1914, pl. 8.

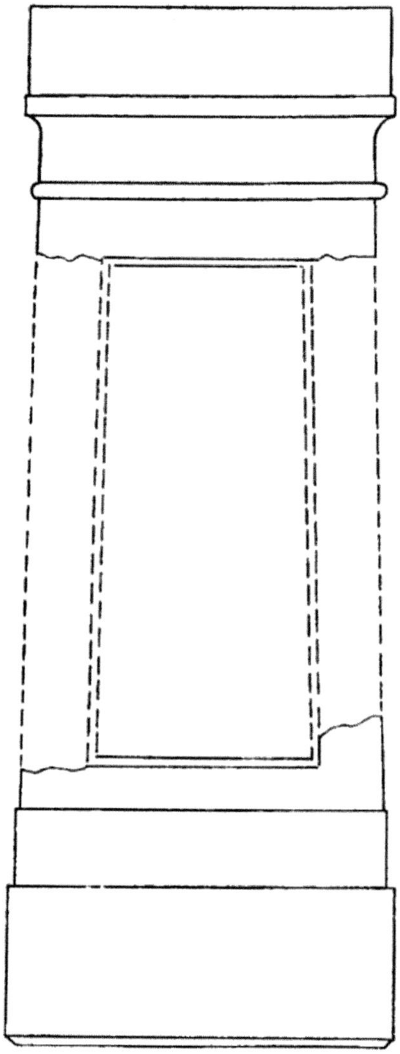
Fig. III.2. Naos Cairo CG 70011 including base. Reproduced from Habachi 1982, fig. 5.

King's titulary (preserved): nṯr nfr nb tꜣwy iꜥḥ-ms-sꜣ-nt.

Damnatio memoriae: no.

Roof type: pyramidal.

Architecture: plain sides.

Decoration: inscriptions on the surviving right doorjambs, decorated lintel. Left doorjamb very badly damaged.

Bibliography: Leclère 2003, 33; Wilson 2006, 212-213, pl. 30a; Leclère 2008, 176; Jansen-Winkeln 2014, 417.

10) Naos of the Cairo mosque of the emir Cheikho (fragment)

Provenance: unknown, possibly originally from Memphis.

Material: greywacke (?).

Size: uncertain; the naos is said to be 4.50 x 4 x 3.50 m by medieval Arab writers.

Beneficiary: the king is said to be 'beloved of' Ptah and of 'the gods who are in the temple of Ptah' (*nṯrw imyw ḥwt-ptḥ*) on the lintel.

King's titulary (preserved): nbty sꜣ-nt-spd-tꜣwy; ḥr nbw stp-nṯrw; ẖnm-ib-rꜥ; iꜥḥ-ms-sꜣ-nt.

Damnatio memoriae: yes.

Roof type: unknown.

Architecture: unknown.

Decoration: inscription on the lintel, registers with rows of gods (?).[324]

Bibliography: Stricker 1939, 215-220, pls. XXX-XXXII; Arnold 1992, 218; Spencer 2006, 22; Leclère 2008, 62-63; Jansen-Winkeln 2014, 436.

11) Naos Cairo CG 70010 (Fig. III.1)

Provenance: possibly from Memphis.

Material: granite.

Size: height 1.62 m.

Beneficiary: Neith 'who resides in *hwt-ka-ptah*' (*nt ḥryt ḥwt-kꜣ-ptḥ*) (king is 'beloved' of the goddess in the texts of the doorjambs).

King's titulary: ḥr smn-mꜣꜥt; nsw-bity iꜥḥ-ms-sꜣ-nt.

Damnatio memoriae: no.

Roof type: curved roof.

Architecture: cavetto cornice and torus moulding on the front; plain sides.

Decoration: inscriptions on doorjambs, decorated lintel.

Bibliography: Roeder 1914, 37-38, pl. 8; PM II, 874; Jansen-Winkeln 2014, 435-436.

12) Naos in two fragments: top (Cairo CG 70011) and base (Fig. III.2)

Provenance: Athribis (the base was found in the foundations of a house near the mosque of Sayeda Zenab in Cairo).[325]

Material: granite (?).

Size: restored height about 3 m.

Beneficiary: Kem-wer 'the great god, foremost of *sekhet-hotep*' (*km-wr nṯr ꜥꜣ ḫnty sḫt-ḥtp*) (dedicatory text).

King's titulary (preserved): ḥr smn-mꜣꜥt; nsw-bity ẖnm-ib-rꜥ (var. *nṯr nfr nb tꜣwy ẖnm-ib-rꜥ*).

Damnatio memoriae: yes.

Roof type: flat.

Architecture: cavetto cornice, torus moulding, frieze of uraei.

Decoration: dedicatory text, registers with rows of gods.

Bibliography: Roeder 1914, 38-42, 185-198, pl. 12; PM IV, 66 (CG 70011), 72 (base); Vernus 1978, 84-86 (top); Habachi 1982, 224-233, pls. XLII-XLVI (base); Mysliwiec 1988, 49; Spencer 2006, 22; Leclère 2008, 246; Jansen-Winkeln 2014, 429-431.

---

324 The naos is almost completely destroyed and is known above all thanks to medieval descriptions.

325 Habachi 1982, 224.

Fig. III.3. Naos at Tell Nabasha, as found by Petrie. Photograph by Petrie (© Egypt Exploration Society).

Fig. III.4. Naos at Tell Nabasha, as found by Petrie. Photograph by Petrie (© Egypt Exploration Society).

13) Naos of Imet (fragmentary) (Figs. III.3-6)

Provenance: Tell Nabasha (still *in situ*).

Material: granite.

Size: fragment, height: more than 4.50 m.

Beneficiary: unknown, perhaps Wadjet.[326]

King's titulary (preserved): ḥr smn-mꜣʿt; nsw-bity [...].

Damnatio memoriae: ?

Roof type: curved.

Architecture: plain sides (?).

Decoration: inscriptions on doorjamb, decorated lintel.

Bibliography: Petrie 1888, 13, 34, pls. IV, IX; Petrie 1892, 64-66; PM IV, 8; Spencer 2007, 57; Leclère 2008, 494; Jansen-Winkeln 2014, 432; Nielsen/Gasperini/Mamedow 2016, 65.

14) Naos (doorjamb)[327]

Provenance: Thebes (?).

Material: granodiorite.

Size: height: 1.73 m (jamb). Suggested height of the whole monument: 2.50-2.80 m; suggested width: 1.30-1.70 m.[328]

Beneficiary: 'Ptah south of his wall, Tatenen, the eternal one, lord of years, great of strength, who is on the great seat' (*ptḥ rsy inb=f tꜣ-ṯnn nḥy nb rnpwt ʿꜣ pḥty ḥry st wrt*), (king is 'beloved' of the god in the text of the doorjamb).

King's titulary (preserved): nṯr nfr nb tꜣwy iʿḥ-ms-sꜣ-nt.

Damnatio memoriae: no.

Roof type: low-pitched pyramidal (?).

326 It has been suggested that the naos might host the statue of the goddess Wadjet, dedicated by Ramses II and whose base has been discovered at the site: Leclère 2008, 494.

327 The jamb was seized by the police from an antique dealer in 1987 and then placed in a storehouse of the enclosure of Karnak. Now it is kept in the magazine Cheikh Labib: Thiers 2012, 981.

328 Thiers 2012, 986.

Fig. III.5. Naos at Tell Nabasha, present-day situation, looking south. Photograph by the Tell-Nabasha Project.

Fig. III.6. Naos at Tell Nabasha, present-day situation, looking west. Photograph by the Tell-Nabasha Project.

Fig. III.7. Naos fragments from Abydos. Reproduced from Petrie 1902, pl LXVIII.

Architecture: unknown.

Decoration: inscriptions on the surviving doorjamb.

Bibliography: Thiers 2012, 981-989; Jansen-Winkeln 2014, 447.

15) Naos (?) (fragment)

Provenance: found near an old fish market in Cairo (Wilkinson MSS, VI.203).

Material: unknown.

Size: unknown.

Beneficiary: unknown.

King's titulary: unknown.

Damnatio memoriae: ?

Roof type: unknown.

Architecture: unknown.

Decoration: unknown.

Bibliography: unpublished; see PM IV, 72; Jansen-Winkeln 2014, 436.

16) Naos (fragments) with the names of Apries and Amasis (?)[329] (Fig. III.7)

Provenance: Abydos.

329 Of this monument, Petrie discovered nearly half of two sides of the pyramidal roof, bearing the cartouches of Apries, and two fragments with the cartouches of Amasis that might belong to the sides of the naos. The naos would have been ordered by the first king and subsequently usurped by the second one. However, the possibility cannot be ruled out that the fragments with Amasis' names belong to another granite monument.

Material: red granite.

Size: unknown.

Beneficiary: unknown.

King's titulary: *ẖnm-ib-rˁ; iˁḥ-ms-sꜣ-wsir.*

Damnatio memoriae: no.

Roof type: pyramidal.

Architecture: unknown.

Decoration: decorated roof.

Bibliography: Petrie 1902, 31-32, pl. LXVIII; Gauthier 1915, 122; Effland/Effland 2013, 83, fig. 11; Jansen-Winkeln 2014, 375.

To this list should probably be added at least one other naos from Kom el-Ahmar. In 2005, besides the fragment which can perhaps be identified as a corner of a naos (no. 3 of the preceding list), the Minufiyeh Archaeological Survey led by Joanne Rowland saw another red granite block at the site, with a text in six columns of hieroglyphs with the cartouches of Amasis.[330]

In 2006, two other granite blocks were found. One is an undecorated fragment from the bottom left corner of a naos;[331] the other one,[332] also very likely part of a naos, shows the bottom register with the last three figures of a row of deities: one standing baboon followed by two baboons on a sledge; behind them there is a fragmentary column of hieroglyph: [...] *prt-ḫrw n rˁ nb ir=f di ˁnḫ ḏd wꜣs ꜣwt-ib ḏt*. The following year, the mission brought to light the upper corner of a naos in red granite (no. 4). The interior presents a *kheker*-frieze, while the exterior back side is undecorated, but polished. More interestingly, the left side of the fragment has part of a row of deities, all facing the same direction, the front of the monument. Traces of a throne of a god are still visible; this is followed by Geb, Nut, Wadjet and Shesmetet,[333] all standing and holding a *was*-staff. A dedicatory text, running above the gods and then down the side of the naos, informs us that the monument was made 'to his mother (*mnw=f n mwt=f*) Hathor who resides in the *set-weret* (*ḥt-ḥr ḥry-ib st-wrt*)[334] and the gods who are in the Upper Mansion (*nṯrw imyw ḥwt-ḥry-tp*), being a great house in granite (*pr wr m mꜣṯ*) [...]'.[335] Even though the name of the king on these last blocks is missing, they should probably be attributed to Amasis, who had dedicated at least two other naoi at the site. This seems to be corroborated by the fact that the dedicatory text with Hathor's name and those of the two other naoi from the same site – Louvre D 29 and Leiden AM 107 – present the same atypical writing for the word *mnw*, 'monument', consisting only of the bilateral sign *mn* and the phonetic complement *n*. Moreover,

330 Rowland/Wilson 2006, 11-13, fig. 5; Rowland/Billing 2006, 4-5; Rowland/Billing 2009, 7; Jansen-Winkeln 2014, 426; Billing/Rowland 2015, 104-105, fig. 3.

331 Rowland 2007, 70-71, figs. 2-3; Rowland/Billing 2009, 7; Billing/Rowland 2015, 105-106, fig. 4.

332 Rowland 2007, 70-71, fig. 4; Rowland/Billing 2009, 7-8; Jansen-Winkeln 2014, 761.

333 On this goddess, see Leitz 2002, VII, 123-125. For other examples, all dated to the Graeco-Roman Period, of the presence of Shesmetet in rows of gods just behind Wadjet, see *Edfu* I 201, 13; IX, pl. 24a; *Dendera* II 59, 13, pl. 98; VII 62, 51; IX 32, 13.

334 The only other goddess to be bestowed with this epithet is Isis in the Graeco-Roman Period: *Edfu* I 490, 9-10; IV 247, 3.

335 Rowland 2007, 70; Rowland/Billing 2009, 7-8; Jansen-Winkeln 2014, 761; Billing/Rowland 2015, 107.

Fig. III.8. Leiden naos, left wall, damaged cartouche in dedication text. Author's photograph.

the naos shows both a dedicatory text and rows of deities, a characteristic which seems to be an innovation introduced during the reign of Amasis, as we shall see.

It should be added that fragments of at least two smaller wooden shrines survive from the reign of Amasis. The first one (Louvre N 504), of unknown provenance, is a gilded wood back panel with glass-paste inlays.[336] The preserved scene shows a kneeling Amasis, with the cartouche containing his throne name, offering Maat to an enthroned falcon-headed Sopdu, the 'great god' (*spd nṯr ꜥꜣ*). Among the finds of a cache in the north-west corner, sector one, of the animal necropolis at North Saqqara, there was a fragment – now in Toronto (969.137.2) – of the painted and gilded cavetto cornice of a naos with a red and blue silica paste inlay and with the king's throne name inlaid in gold leaf: [...] *nṯr nfr nb tꜣwy ẖnm-ib-rꜥ ꜥnḫ ḏt*.[337] In a cache in the south-east corner, sector one, of the animal necropolis, there was also a wooden panel fragment (British Museum EA 68169) with a tenon for attachment and with the inscription *sꜣ rꜥ iḥꜥ-ms-sꜣ-nt*, possibly from a naos or other item of temple furniture.[338]

The monolithic shrines of the reign of Amasis display substantial differences with each other. They vary in shape, size, form of the cavity, and material. The latter is mainly granite, but quartzite (naos of Sais) and granodiorite (naos dedicated to Ptah) are also used. Some of them present a cavetto cornice and torus moulding, with (Louvre D 29 and naos from Athribis) or without (Cairo CG 70010) a frieze of uraei.

Not only the number, but also the striking dimensions of many of the surviving naoi of Amasis exceed those created by the other kings of the 26th Dynasty. With its height of 1.90 m, the naos of Leiden is one of the lowest shrines in stone ever produced during his reign. Only the naos Cairo CG 70010 for Neith, perhaps from Memphis, and the naos for Osiris from Sais are definitely smaller. Both the naos Louvre D 29 and the one dedicated to Ptah are approximately 2.50 m in height, while the naos set up at Athribis was about 3 m in height. But much larger monolithic shrines were also created. The restored height of the naos of Tell Nabasha is more than 4.50 m. The block reused in the mosque of Cheikho in

336 Yoyotte 1972, 220, pl. 9; Teeter 1997, 39 n. 21; Arveiller-Dulong/Nenna 2011, 368-369; Jansen-Winkeln 2014, 466-467.

337 Emery 1967, 143; Needler 1969, 30; Bianchi 1983, 31, fig. 2; Martin 1979, 50 no. 160; Green 1987, 10; Jansen-Winkeln 2014, 442.

338 Martin 1979, 50 n. 61 ('shrine-door of Amasis'); Green 1987, 12; Jansen-Winkeln 2014, 442.

Cairo Citadel was part of a large monolithic naos which medieval Arab accounts describe as 4.50 m height, 4 m width and 3.50 m depth.[339] The most impressive surviving naos is surely the one, still *in situ*, at Mendes; with its height of around 7.80 m, it surpasses any other shrine of the period. And the other three naoi at the site must also have had the same height. Moreover, according to the account offered by Herodotus (II, 175), from Elephantine Amasis brought a monumental monolithic shrine which is said to have been 21 x 14 x 8 cubits, to stand in the temple precinct of Sais.[340]

With the exception of the naos dedicated to Hathor from Kom el-Ahmar, the cavities of all the naoi of Amasis do not present any decoration and, as far as I know, the naos still *in situ* at Mendes is the only one presenting an internal arrangement, consisting of a sort of 'shelf' on its internal back wall. As for the roofs, at least four types were chosen: low-pitched pyramidal roof (naoi of Shu, Ra, and Geb of Mendes), pyramidal (Leiden AM 107; naoi from Sais and Abydos), curved (Louvre D 29; Cairo CG 70010; naos of Tell Nabasha), and flat (Cairo CG 70011 and naos of Osiris of Mendes). It should be noted, on the basis of the surviving monuments, that the pyramidal roof was prevalently, if not exclusively, adopted in association with a peculiar form of the cavity, i.e. wider than deep or high, and in monuments dedicated to Osirian forms (Leiden AM 107 and naos from Sais). The naos of Abydos with pyramidal roof and with Apries' cartouches, and perhaps usurped by Amasis, might also have been dedicated to the local Osirian form.

The different sizes, proportions, and architectural forms of the naoi of Amasis' reign indicate that there was not a preferred or specific model which had to be followed, although we cannot figure out why, in planning one of these monuments, a particular shape, material, or type of roof were adopted. It also seems evident that adapting the dimensions to a round number of cubits was not considered important.

This great variety might of course be due to many factors. To obtain the desired result, many aspects, as well as more general aesthetic reasons, were very likely taken into consideration, such as the availability of material, the impact of the monument on the temple context, and – as in the case of the Leiden naos – the nature of the beneficiary deity.

The majority of the naoi are rather slender shrines, higher than wide, and monumentality was often sought. In the case of the Leiden naos, more unusual geometries were explored and used. The compactness and squat appearance of the shrine is slightly attenuated by the soaring pyramidal roof. However, the peculiar form of the cavity and the proportions of the naos, with the height of its central body that seems too low in comparison with its width and depth, create a unique visual effect.

2. The *damnatio memoriae*

On the Leiden naos, the Horus name of Amasis, written inside a *serekh* on the four faces of the roof, and the cartouches in the two mirrored dedicatory texts were intentionally erased. The rest of the king's titles – *nṯr nfr nb tꜣwy* – were left untouched, as well as, rather interestingly, the Horus name *smn-mꜣꜥt*, without *serekh*, at the very beginning of the two identical dedicatory inscriptions. On the roof, all the signs of the Horus name *smn mꜥꜣt*

339 Leclère 2008, 62-63.

340 Arnold 1999, 85; Leclère 2008, 172.

were so grossly erased that they are still recognizable. On the contrary, on both the side walls of the naos, the cartouches of the dedicatory text with the throne name, Khnemibra, were selectively effaced, so that only the first sign, *rꜥ*, is clearly visible (Fig. III.8).

Other naoi also present traces of *damnatio memoriae*.[341] It is worth noticing that there is no consistency in the way the king's names were damaged. On the other naos from Kom el-Ahmar (Louvre D 29) all the names of Amasis, both inside the *serekh* and in the cartouches, have been completely chiselled out. In the dedicatory inscriptions, the Horus name written without *serekh* is intact (just like on the Leiden naos), but also the *nebty* name *sꜣ-nt-spd-tꜣwy* and the Horus of Gold name *stp-nṯrw*.[342] On the lintel of a naos preserved in the mosque of the emir Cheikho in Cairo,[343] the cartouche with the king's name *iꜥḥ-ms-sꜣ-nt* seems completely damaged, while the two cartouches with the throne name only preserve the first sign, *rꜥ*, as on the Leiden naos. On the naos of Athribis, the cartouches surmounted by the sun disk between two feathers and standing on the *nbw*-sign, which decorated the top of the monument, have been treated in various different ways.[344] Some of them were completely effaced, those with the throne name may present either only the sign *rꜥ* or the signs *rꜥ* and *ib*, while in some cartouches with the king's name the sign *nt*, Neith, has not been erased. In the dedicatory text, the hieroglyphs of the Horus name, written without the *serekh*, were erased in a way that leaves them still partially readable, while the cartouches with the throne name still present the signs *rꜥ* and *ib*. But not all the naoi suffered a similar fate: on the monumental shrines of Mendes, on the naos of Sais dedicated to Osiris, on the naos Cairo CG 70010 possibly from Memphis, on the naos perhaps from Thebes dedicated to Ptah, and on the fragments discovered in Abydos, the king's names remained intact.

There is no certain proof of the identity of who was responsible for the *damnatio memoriae* of Amasis, and it is also unclear why in some places the monuments of Amasis were attacked and in others – such as Mendes, Bubastis, Tell Defenneh, Tell el-Maskhuta, Elephantine, or Abydos – they seem to have been left undisturbed. Even more problematic is the fact that in some localities they were not treated in a consistent manner.

At Sais the majority of the king's objects do not present traces of *damnatio memoriae*, with the exception of the sphinx discovered in the surroundings of Santa Maria Sopra Minerva in Rome,[345] and probably originating from Sais. The inscription is on the front of the sphinx, in three columns; the first two had the titulary with the cartouches of the king, the third column the name and epithets of Osiris. The inscription has been effaced so that only the hieroglyphs for the divine names survive; in the first column only the sign of *rꜥ* of *sꜣ rꜥ*, and of *nt* in 'Iah-mes-sa-neith', survive. In the second column only the sign of *rꜥ* of the throne name Khenem-ib-Ra is intact, while in the third column only the signs for *mry* have been erased.

341 On the *damnatio memoriae* of Amasis, see also Müller 1955, 57 n. 5; Bresciani 1967, 279; De Meulenaere 1968, 184; De Meulenaere 1975, 182; Gozzoli 2000, 79 and n. 73; Bolshakov 2010, 45-53; Klotz 2010, 135.

342 Piankoff 1933, 162-171.

343 Stricker 1939.

344 Vernus 1978, 84-86; Habachi 1982, 228-229, 232-233.

345 In Rome, Musei Capitolini, Palazzo dei Conservatori (inv. MC 0035): Ensoli Vittozzi 1990, 28-31; Lollio *et al.* 1995, 162-163; Arslan 1997, 391; Perdu 2012, 182-183.

In the territory of Memphis many inscriptions do not present *damnatio memoriae*, but others – among which also the sarcophagi of Amasis' wife Nekhtbastetru and son Iahmes discovered at Giza[346] – have been purposely damaged.

The prevailing view among Egyptologists today is that the defamation of Amasis' memory took place, very likely, during the early phase of the Persian rule in Egypt. According to Herodotus (III, 16), Cambyses, among other crimes, would have ordered the exhumation, desecration, and burning of the corpse of Amasis.[347] Perhaps, the 'usurper' Amasis underwent a *damnatio memoriae* so that the conqueror Cambyses could present himself as the lawful descendant of the legitimate pharaoh Apries.[348] The people who were actually involved in cancelling the names of Amasis on the naoi and other royal monuments in different Egyptian sites could indeed have hardly acted on their own initiative; probably, they were just following orders. And, if it was Cambyses who gave the order to mutilate the king's monuments, this complicated task might only be carried out by educated Egyptians.

However, the men who erased the hieroglyphs of Amasis' names did not act following the same rules. In many cases the names of the gods were left untouched, though in other cases they were expunged like the other signs. The fact that in several cartouches (as on the Leiden naos) the names of the gods Ra and Neith were left undisturbed suggests that the attackers were able to read hieroglyphs.

It also remains intriguing why at Kom el-Ahmar the Horus names written without the *serekh* were not obliterated, as the rest of the king's titulary. Evidently, the men in charge of this operation attacked the cartouches – and in many cases only fixed parts of them – and the *serekhs*. Being not immediately visually identifiable, perhaps the rest of the titulary escaped the attention of the attackers, or was simply regarded as unimportant for the same reason. It is also peculiar, however, that the signs of the Horus names within the *serekh* were erased in a way that left them still clearly readable. If this was purposely made, it is possible that the men were trying to follow the orders of the Persians, but at the same time were reluctant not only to disturb the Egyptian gods, but also to destroy the eternal memory of the king.

3. The decorations

It seems that during the reign of Amasis there was no production of naoi with just one ritual scene occupying the whole surface of the outer walls, or with standard offering scenes. Images of the king presenting offerings or performing a ritual in front of one god – or a limited number of deities – appeared on monolithic shrines as early as the Middle Kingdom[349] and throughout the New Kingdom[350] and the 25th Dynasty,[351] until

346 Bolshakov 2010.

347 For a discussion of the impious behaviour attributed to Cambyses by Herodotus, see Kahn 2007, 103-112.

348 Herodotus I, 1-3 reports a legend according to which Cambyses was a son by Cyrus of a daughter of Apries. A similar story is found also in two other Greek authors, Ctesias fragment 13a and Atheneus XIII, 10. On the transition of power from Apries to Amasis, see Ladynin 2006, 31-56.

349 See the naos in granite of Senusret I from Karnak (Cairo JE 47276): Pillet 1923.

350 See the naoi of Ramses II Cairo CG 70003 and CG 70004 from Tanis and CG 70005 from Abu Simbel (Roeder 1914, 11-24, pl. 6), and the naos from Tell el-Maskhuta (Mysliwiec 1978).

351 Cairo CG 70007 of Shabaka from Esna (Roeder 1914, 25-28, pl. 7).

the Late[352] and Graeco-Roman Period,[353] but they are not so far attested in the whole 26th Dynasty.

On the basis of the available surviving monuments, the arrangement of texts and decorations of Amasis' monolithic shrines can be divided into two main types. The majority of them have inscriptions and images confined to the front. In this case, their side walls are usually plain, without architectural elements such as a cavetto cornices, torus mouldings, or uraeus friezes. During the 26th Dynasty, before Amasis' reign, this simple decoration is seen on a naos of Nekau II from Athribis (Cairo CG 88205),[354] with texts on the lintel and all around the door-thickness. A variant is found on the naos of Apries Cairo JE 43281,[355] with inscriptions on the lintel and jambs, but also with a decoration on the front of the pyramidal roof. The four monumental naoi of Mendes presented inscriptions both on the doorjambs and lintel, and the Osiris naos also has a winged sun-disk at the centre of the lintel. Usually, however, the inscriptions are only on the doorjambs. These consist of names and titles of the king, followed by the epithet 'beloved of' a deity, very likely the one housed inside the niche; the lintel can show just a winged sun-disk (naos of Tell Nabasha), which can be flanked by the text 'Behdety, great god, with dappled plumage' (*bḥdty nṯr ꜥꜣ sꜣb šwt*; naos from Sais), or, more simply, 'Behdety' (Cairo CG 70010). Unfortunately, nothing can be said about the lintel of the naos for Ptah from the Theban area, since only a doorjamb of this monument survives.

The second type of decoration consists of superimposed registers with rows of gods on the outer walls, as in the naoi from Kom el-Ahmar, in the naos from Athribis, and probably in the naos originally from Memphis and of which only a block conserved in the Cairo mosque of Cheikho survives. The descriptions given by Arab medieval authors indicate that the latter was decorated with hieroglyphs and images of gods portrayed in different attitudes. According to Abd el-Latif (13th century), the naos presented 'un grand nombre de figures d'astres, de sphères, d'hommes et d'animaux. Les hommes y sont représentés dans des attitudes et des postures variés; les uns sont en place, les autres marchent, ceux-ci étendent les pieds, ceux-là les ont en repos; les uns ont leurs habits retroussés pour travailler, d'autres portent des matériaux; on en voit d'autres enfin qui donnent des ordres par rapport à leur emploi',[356] while el-Maqrizi (1364-1442) wrote: 'on voyait dessus des figures sculptées et de l'écriture. Sur la face de la porte étaient des images de serpents qui présentaient leur poitrail'.[357]

---

352 Cairo CG 70018 from Abydos, with the names of Nekhtnebef and Nekhthorheb (Roeder 1914, 53-55). The fragment British Museum EA 1106 from Bubastis has images of Nekhthorheb uplifting the sky and offering to Bastet (Rosenow 2008, 247-266).

353 The drawings and description published in the *Description de l'Égypte* (DE IV, pl. 38; DE T IV, 95-98) show a monolithic naos, with pyramidal roof and probably of Ptolemaic date, recorded at Qaw el-Kebir in the 19th century and with images of a king offering to deities. It is not clear whether, in this case, they are part of rows of gods or just of standard offering scenes (Spencer 2006, 28). On the naos of Domitian, on the side and internal walls, there are registers with scenes with the king offering to one, two, or more deities (Rondot 1990, 308-320).

354 Habachi 1982, fig. 2, pl. XL; Gozzoli 2017, 160.

355 Perdu 1990, pl.2b.

356 Stricker 1939, 216.

357 Stricker 1939, 217-218.

Fig. III.9. Naos Brussels E 5818, corner (© KMKG – MRAH).

Fig. III.10. Naos Brussels E 5818, rear. (© KMKG – MRAH).

Even though naoi with registers of divine images might have existed before the late 26th Dynasty,[358] the first known examples are the naos Cairo CG 70008 in sandstone from el-Baqlieh (Hermopolis Parva),[359] and the naos Brussels, Musées royaux d'Art et d'Histoire E 5818 (Figs. III.9-10), made of a dark black stone and discovered at Sais.[360] Since both these monuments date to the reign of Apries, it is highly possible that the presence of superimposed registers with rows of divine images on naoi was an innovation of this king. This new way for monolithic shrines to convey religious ideas and themes was abandoned in the immediately following dynasties, but was used again both by Nekhtnebef in the naos from Saft el-Henna (CG 70021),[361] with at least six registers of deities, and by Nekhthorheb in a fragmentary naos from Bubastis, with at least four registers,[362] while it remains uncertain whether registers with sequences of gods were adopted in naoi after the 30th Dynasty. Three grey fragments from a naos reused in the mosque at Mit Gharitah, in the north-east Delta, with at least six registers of gods, have been dated by Ahmed Kamal to the Ptolemaic Period,[363] even though an earlier date, as suggested by Neal Spencer,[364] remains possible.

Another peculiarity of the reign of Amasis is the presence – on the naoi of the Louvre and Leiden – of superimposed registers with divine figures also on the doorjambs, a kind of decoration that is not attested with certainty on any other naos of the Late Period, when the jambs usually show only the royal titulary and the name of the deity housed within. One exception might be the basalt fragment of the front of a naos now in Verona, showing registers of rows of gods and part of a cartouche containing the elements *rꜥ* and *kꜣ* and which therefore might have belonged to Nekhtnebef.[365]

The number of the registers may also vary. In the reign of Apries, the naos Cairo CG 70008 has four registers on the side walls and on the rear, while the fragmentary naos Brussels E 5818 has eight registers. The Leiden naos of Amasis has only three registers on the front and two registers on the side walls and the rear. This is perhaps partly due to the limited height of the monument. However, the small number of registers allowed the divine figures to be represented at a larger scale than those found on any other naos of the period. The naos Louvre D 29 has one register more on each side than the Leiden one, while, owing to their fragmentary state, the number of registers on the other naoi of Amasis with rows of gods (naos from Athribis, fragments from Kom el-Ahmar, and the one in the mosque of the emir Cheiko) remains unknown. Apart from the uncertain case of the fragment of naos in the mosque of the emir Cheiko, in all the other three naoi with rows of gods Amasis also added a dedicatory text, which is absent in the shrines of Apries.

358 See Spencer 2006, 19-20.

359 Roeder 1914, 29-36, pls. 9-11a; Zivie 1975, 104-112; Jansen-Winkeln 2014, 361-363.

360 Speleers 1923, 87-88; Capart 1924; Kaper 2003, 264; Jansen-Winkeln 2014, 354-355. See also two fragments in Cairo (22/11/55/1 and 30/5/24/5), which might be part of a naos: Spencer 2006, 20 and n. 6. For a discussion on naoi depicting rows of deities, see Spencer 2006, 19-30.

361 Roeder 1914, pls. 17-33. A basalt fragment of a naos now in Verona (inv. 30297) with registers of rows of gods may also have belonged to Nekhtnebef: Clère 1973; Bolla 2007, 6, 25, fig. 4.

362 Spencer 2006.

363 Kamal 1904, 193-199.

364 Spencer 2006, 27.

365 Clère 1973; Spencer 2006, 27.

The Leiden naos is the only one from Amasis' reign to present an elaborate identical decoration on all the four sides of the roof. Despite the fact that a pyramidal roof could provide a suitable surface to be filled with images and hieroglyphs, naoi with decorated roofs are very rare and, in the Late Period, they are limited to the end of the 26th Dynasty. The first examples date to the reign of Apries. On the front of its pyramidal top, a naos from Busiris (Cairo JE 43281) dedicated to 'Osiris-Andjety who resides in Djedu/Busiris' (*wsỉr-ʿnḏty ḥry-ib ḏdw*), has a winged solar disk with pendant uraei with *ankh* around their neck and with the inscription 'Behdet the great god'.[366] A similar motif also embellished another naos (Cairo CG 70009) of Apries, perhaps from Mendes and of which only the front of the pyramidal roof survives.[367] The halves of two sides of the pyramidal roof of a red granite naos, brought to light by Petrie at Abydos, were adorned with the cartouches of Apries flanked by images of the vulture Nekhbet and the cobra Wadjet and hieroglyphs. In all probability, a similar decoration was also present on the other two missing sides. Petrie also found two fragments with the name and *nsw-bity*-name of Amasis. It is uncertain whether these items were part of the side walls of the naos, of which nothing else would have survived, or parts of another granite monument.

It is evident that, even though in the creation of monolithic shrines Amasis took up motifs, ideas, and shapes originating in the reign of his predecessor, he did not renounce using original elements and innovations, such as the decoration on the four sides of the pyramidal roof, the presence of divine images also on the front, and the addition of a dedicatory text on the shrines with rows of deities.

4. The recipients: Osiris and the others

The majority of Amasis' surviving naoi were dedicated in the Delta – Memphis, Sais, Athribis, Tell Nabasha, Mendes, and, perhaps, in the ancient Kom el-Ahmar – where a great part of his building program was concentrated. Thebes remains, at present, the only probable witness to the presence of a naos in hard stone made by Amasis for an Upper Egyptian site (above, section III.1, no. 14), while at Abydos, where he is nevertheless attested thanks to other monuments, the king perhaps limited himself to adding his cartouches on a naos of his predecessor (*ibid.*, no. 16).

The exact number of the surviving monolithic naoi from the 26th Dynasty is uncertain, since it is difficult to ascertain whether some fragments originally belonged to shrines in hard stone or other types of monuments. However, on the basis of the available documents, it seems that the production of naoi increased consistently towards the end of the dynasty. For Psamtek I, Nekau II, and Psamtek II, there are no more than two naoi each, while the surviving naoi of Apries are not more than seven. A fragment of the upper part of a naos (Cairo JE 47580)[368] from Nub-Taha, in the southern Delta, but perhaps originally from Heliopolis, contains a dedicatory text which starts on the lintel and continues on the roof and the rear, stating that Psamtek I made a naos (*sḥ-nṯr*) for 'his father Atum lord of Iunu, lord of the *hut-aat*' (*tm nb ỉwnw nb ḥwt-ʿꜣt*). In addition, the fragment in

366 Perdu 1990, pl. 2b; Jansen-Winkeln 2014, 359-360.

367 Roeder 1914, 36-37; Perdu 1990, pl. 2a; Jansen-Winkeln 2014, 361.

368 PM IV, 58; Perdu 2002, 103-104; Jansen-Winkeln 2014, 9.

basalt of a naos of the same king now in the museum of Florence (inv. 8691) might also have been set up originally in Heliopolis.[369] A quartzite naos (CG 88205)[370] from the reign of Nekau II was originally installed for 'his mother Nebet-hetepet' (*mwt=f nbt-ḥtpt*) at Athribis; two inscriptions, running all around the cavity in opposite directions, bear the king's names followed by the epithets 'beloved of' Hor-Khenty-khety and Osiris-Khenty-khety. The naos was then usurped by his successor Psamtek II. Of this king, the museum of Brussels has a naos in granite (E 5283),[371] of unknown origin and bearing part of the king's titulary. Besides the naos of Abydos, perhaps later usurped by Amasis, king Apries dedicated a naos (Cairo CG 70008), discovered at el-Baqlieh, to Thoth 'who separates the two contenders' (*wp-rḥwy*),[372] a naos to Osiris-Andjety at Busiris (Cairo JE 43281),[373] and the naos Brussels E 5818[374] at Sais, while the naos in quartzite Cairo CG 70009[375] might have been installed at Mendes. The lion door-bolt in bronze discovered at Horbeit (Cairo JE 48887) with the king's cartouches – and the mention of Hormerty 'lord of Shedenu' (*ḥr-mrty nb šdnw*), 'the gods and the living *bau* who are in Shedenu' (*nṯrw bꜣw ꜥnḫw imyw šdnw*), and the 'gods in the *hut-aat* in Shedenu' (*nṯrw m ḥwt-ꜥꜣt m šdnw*) – might have been used for a door of a local naos.[376]

The number of Apries' naoi was doubled by his successor, and indeed, only with the kings of the 30th Dynasty the naoi in hard stone would outnumber those produced during the reign of Amasis.

The reasons why this king, of non-royal descent, ordered so many naoi may have been various. One might assume, following Erhart Graefe,[377] that these monuments had to replace more ancient shrines in wood. But it is also possible that Amasis promoted a specific programme for the creation of completely new naoi, ideated and carved to pay homage to a wider number of deities. Perhaps, after obtaining the throne from Apries, he wanted to mark the beginning of a new reign, emphasising his role of king on a religious and ritual level in order to obtain legitimacy for his rule from the traditional Egyptian gods.[378]

At the base of the choice of which deities were to be singled out as beneficiaries of monolithic naoi there were, of course, religious aspects linked to the place where these monuments were dedicated, as in the case of the naoi at Mendes for four great Egyptian deities regarded as *bas* of the local ram god. But not rarely Amasis opted for local aspects of important national gods, showing once again a certain degree of originality, as in the case of the naos of Sais for Osiris 'in the house of Sekhmet', or the naos Cairo CG 70010 for

369 Botti 1949, 124-125, pl. 2; Perdu 2002, 143-144; Jansen-Winkeln 2014, 25-26.

370 Habachi 1982, 216-219, fig. 2, pl. XL; Jansen-Winkeln 2014, 272; Gozzoli 2017, 160.

371 Speleers 1923, 87; Jansen-Winkeln 2014, 321; Gozzoli 2017, 142.

372 Roeder 1914, 29-36, pls. 9-11a; Zivie 1975, 104-112; Jansen-Winkeln 2014, 361-363.

373 Perdu 1990, 43-44, pl. 2b; Jansen-Winkeln 2014, 359-360.

374 Speleers 1923, 88-89; Capart 1924; Jansen-Winkeln 2014, 354-355.

375 Roeder 1914, 36-37; Perdu 1990, 42-43, pl. 2a; Jansen-Winkeln 2014, 361.

376 PM IV, 26-27; Gourlay 1979, 364-365. Gauthier 1915, 109 n. 2 mentions another naos of Apries, the fragment Cairo JE 43285 from Mendes, which, however, might be part of a statue base (Leahy 1984a, 65). See also two fragments in Cairo (22/11/55/1 and 30/5/24/5) with a row of deities and which might be part of a naos: Spencer 2006, 20 and n. 6.

377 Graefe 2011, 164.

378 See also Gozzoli 2009, 181.

Neith 'who resides in *hut-ka-ptah*',[379] both created in honour of two otherwise unattested forms of these gods.

However, among the preeminent aspects of Amasis' religious policy, there was the maintenance and support of the worship of Osiris. In this, he was acting in line with a general trend which, starting from the Third Intermediate Period, greatly favoured Osiris among the Egyptian gods.[380] Some of his predecessors had already dedicated monolithic naoi to local Osirian forms. Shabaka of the 25th Dynasty ordered a naos[381] in granite for Osiris *ḫnty sḥ-nṯr*[382] at Esna, while at Busiris Apries built a naos for Osiris-Andjety 'who resides at Busiris' (*wsỉr-ʿnḏty ḥry-ỉb ḏdw*).[383] However, with his two naoi at Kom el-Ahmar, and one each at Mendes, Sais, Athribis, and perhaps Abydos, Amasis seems to have been interested in the creation of monolithic shrines specifically made for Osiris, more than any other king of the Late Period. The high number of Amasis' naoi for Osiris has a parallel in other typologies of monuments – chapels, offering-tables, sphinxes – dedicated to the god by the king.

The increased popularity of Osiris in the Late Period is testified by numerous chapels erected for the god at Karnak, which were built starting from the Third Intermediate Period and where his cult was intimately connected with that of Amun. At least three chapels date to the period of the divine adoratress of Amun Ankhesneferibra,[384] daughter of Psamtek II. In particular, two of them, located inside the enclosure of Amun, in the area between the great hypostyle hall and the temple of Ptah, were erected during the time of Amasis. The chapel of Osiris Wennefer Neb-djefau (*nb ḏfꜣw*) was dedicated by Ankhesneferibra and Amasis,[385] while the chapel of Osiris lord of eternity-*neheh* (*nb nḥḥ*) was consecrated by Ankhesneferibra and the kings Amasis and Psamtek III.[386]

It has been suggested that both these chapels hosted a copy of the Abydene fetish.[387] If in the chapel of Osiris Wennefer Neb-djefau the wall facing the entrance of the sanctuary presents an image of the Abydene fetish, protected by four lion-headed uraei, represented on the jambs of the door, the wall facing the entrance of the sanctuary of the other Osirian chapel is occupied by two hymns to the god, both ending with the wish that his beautiful face might be benevolent towards the king (*ḥtp ḥr=k nfr n nsw-bỉty ḫnm-ỉb-rʿ sꜣ rʿ ỉʿḥ-ms-sꜣ-nt ʿnḫ ḏt*). While the religious ideas of the first chapel are strongly connected with the theology of the House of Life of Abydos,[388] in the second one they are focused on the

379 Leitz 2002, V, 428.

380 On Osiris in the first millennium BC, see Coulon 2010. See also: Topozada 2003, 527-533 for some observation on the cults of Osiris and Isis at Memphis at the time of Amasis.

381 Cairo CG 70007: Roeder 1914, 25-28, pl. 7; PM VI, 117; Jansen-Winkeln 2009, 20-21.

382 For other examples of this epithet bestowed to Osiris, see Leitz 2002, V, 860.

383 Cairo JE 43281: Perdu 1990, pl. 2b; Jansen-Winkeln 2014, 359-360.

384 On Ankhesneferibra, see Leahy 1996, 145-165; Gozzoli 2017, 27-32.

385 Coulon 2003, 47-60; Defernez 2004, 35-47; Coulon/Defernez 2004, 135-190.

386 Traunecker 2010, 155-194. In the same area, there is another anepigraphic chapel, stylistically similar to the other chapels of Ankhesneferibra (Coulon/Defernez 2004, 137). Another chapel, dedicated to Osiris *pꜣ-mry=s* by the divine adoratress and Psamtek III, is located west of the enclosure of Montu. It is worth mentioning that two doorjambs with Amasis' name were recovered in the south-eastern area of the sacred lake: Masson *et al.* 2009, 17. See also Thiers 2012, 286.

387 Traunecker 2010; Coulon 2011.

388 Coulon 2011.

Fig. III.11. Fragment of Osiris chapel from Coptos, now London UC 14468 (courtesy of the Petrie Museum of Egyptian Archaeology, UCL).

themes of water and inundation and aim at presenting Osiris as a 'beloved one' (*mrty*), a living force, granting nourishment to gods, men, and the dead.[389]

According to Petrie, Amasis also built a small Osiris chapel at Coptos, south of the third pylon.[390] The Petrie Museum houses a sandstone fragment (UC 14468) (Fig. III.11) from this locality, which might be dated to the reign of Amasis; it features the head with *atef*-crown and shoulder of Osiris 'Wennefer, the great god, who resides at Coptos' (*wsỉr wn-nfr nṯr ꜥꜣ ḥry-ib gbtyw*), with beard and holding the *heqa*-sceptre and flail.[391] He was followed by an image of Isis, of whom only name and parts of her epithets survive: 'Isis the great, the god's mother, lady of the sky, lady of the gods' (*ꜣst wrt mwt nṯr nb pt ḥnwt nṯrw*).

However, both private and royal sources indicate that, in Upper Egypt, it was at Abydos that Amasis best showed his interest in the Osiris cult. In the inscriptions of one of his statues,[392] the high-ranking official Peftjawyneith, active during the reigns of Apries and Amasis, offers information on renovation works carried out in the area of the temple of Khentyamentiu during the reign of Amasis. He states that the king himself ordered him to do works in Abydos, in order 'to restore (*mr*) Abydos': 'I did much in making excellent

389 Traunecker 2010.

390 Petrie 1896, 17: 'A small chapel of Osiris, built by Aahmes Sineit, stood by the temenos to the south of the Third pylon in line with the south wall. Only the lower course, with ribbing of papyrus stems on it, remains *in situ*; but a slab with a figure of Osiris was found in it'.

391 Stewart 1983, pl. 22 n. 49; Gabolde/Galliano 2000, 112 cat. 82. See also PM V, 123.

392 Naophorous statue Louvre A 93: Jelinkova-Reymond 1956, 275-287; Lichtheim 1980, 33-36; Leahy 1984; Heise 2006, 229-233; Klotz 2010, 128-129; Spencer 2010a, 454-456.

(*smnḫ*) Abydos, until I put everything belonging to Abydos in its place... I built the temple of Khentyamentiu as a perfect work for eternity (*m k3t mnḫ nt ḥḥ*) as His Majesty had ordered, that he might see that Ta-wer prospered. I surrounded it with walls (*sbty*) of bricks, the shrine *ʿrḳ-ḥḥ* was of one block of granite (*m m3t wʿ*). An august chapel (*ḥḏ-šps*) was of electrum. The sacred equipment, amulets and cult objects were of gold, silver and all precious stones. I built the *wpg*-sanctuary, surrounded by its altars, and I dug (*šd*) pits and provided (him) with trees'. Peftjawyneith goes on, declaring to have 'endowed (*sfḏ*) the temple of Khentyamentiu' with every necessary thing and to have established the 'village of Osiris' (*grgt wsỉr*), an agricultural estate, to have 'restored (*sm3w*) the House of Life' after it was in ruins, to have established the provisions of Osiris, and to have made a new sacred god's bark (*wỉ3*) in cedar. Once again, as in the hymns in the chapel of Osiris lord of eternity-*neheh*, the inscription ends with a petition for Amasis, stressing his personal connections with the divine beneficiary of the works: '... May he (Osiris) give life to his son Amasis' (*dỉ=f ʿnḫ n s3=f ỉʿḥ-ms-s3-nt*).

Peftjawyneith's account tallies with the scanty archaeological evidence.[393] The works undertaken in the *wpg*-sanctuary, very likely the Osirian tomb at Umm el-Qaab, can be related with a later cult at the site.[394] Here, Émile Amélineau found a fragmentary stela of Amasis, with the king 'beloved of Hor-sa-aset of Ra-setjau' and possibly connected to the Osiris burial in the tomb of king Djer of the 1st Dynasty.[395] In the Osiris temple precinct in Kom el-Sultan, Petrie discovered foundation deposits of Apries and Amasis,[396] a red granite offering-table with an inscription in which Amasis is said to be 'beloved of Osiris foremost of the West, the great god, lord of Abydos' (*mry wsỉr ḫnty ỉmntt nṯr ʿ3 nb 3bḏw*),[397] and quarry marks on foundation blocks mentioning the king as 'beloved of Osiris lord of Abydos',[398] besides the fragmentary granite roof of a naos with the cartouches of Apries and the fragments with those of Amasis. It is unclear whether Amasis usurped the naos of his predecessor, simply adding his own names, or whether his fragments belong to another granite naos. However, it is interesting that in one of these fragments, the name of Amasis is not followed by the usual epithet *s3 nt*, 'son of Neith', but by *s3 wsỉr*, 'son of Osiris'.

The inclusion of the name of Osiris inside a royal cartouche is unusual. A significant precedent is represented by Sety I, who, at Abydos, modified the cartouche with his name by replacing the sign of the seated god with the head of the Seth-animal by the sign of Osiris followed by the *tỉt*-knot. Amasis might have been inspired by his ancient predecessor's cartouches; and indeed, in Amasis' case, the epithet *s3 wsỉr* is not attested outside the territory of Abydos. It is also striking that in the surviving texts on the lower part of a red granite obelisk[399] found at Mensha (Ptolemais), not far away from Abydos, the name of Amasis is followed, as usual, by the epithet *s3 nt* when he is said to be 'beloved of Ptah-Sokar' or 'Ra-Harakhty, the great god, lord of the sky', but, in the

393 Petrie 1902, 31-33; Petrie 1903, 19-20.
394 Effland 2006; Effland/Effland 2013, 78-89.
395 O'Connor 2009, 133-134; Klotz 2010, 129.
396 Petrie 1902, 32, pl. LXX.
397 British Museum EA 610: Petrie 1902, 32, pls. LXIX, LXX, fig. 10; PM V, 43; Jansen-Winkeln 2014, 446-447.
398 Petrie 1902, 19, pl. XLVIII; Kemp 1968, 147, pl. XLI, b.
399 Cairo CG 17029: Kuentz 1932, 59-60, pl. XV; PM V, 36; Selim 1991, II, 299-300; Jansen-Winkeln 2014, 445-446.

one column where the king calls himself 'beloved of Osiris, foremost of the West, the great god, lord of Abydos', his name is followed by the epithet *sꜣ wsir*. The same filial relationship was also expressed, as we have seen, on the final petition on the statue of Peftjawyneith and must have been one of the local religious characteristics, which stressed and defined the bond between king and god.

Osiris plays a major role also on some blocks of Amasis now in the White Monastery Church at Sohag. One block preserves the lower part of an enthroned Osiris,[400] while another[401] has an image of a mummiform Osiris with white crown, called '[lord of Aby]dos', [*nb ꜣb*]*ḏw*. On another block,[402] stylistically similar to the quarry marks found at Abydos, the king was very likely labelled as '[beloved of] Osiris lord [of Abydos]', [*mry*] *wsir nb* [*ꜣbḏw*]; in a cartouche visible on one of the interior jambs of the north portal, the name of Amasis appears to be followed, once again, by the epithet 'son of Osiris', instead of 'son of Neith'.[403] Other fragments depict episodes from a *sed*-festival for Amasis.[404] Since Osiris is the only deity to appear in this context with any frequency and Abydos is the only toponym mentioned, David Klotz has pointed out that it seems tenable that the blocks from Sohag came from an Amasis-period sanctuary in which the god was a key figure, and that the best candidate seems to be Abydos itself; moreover, since all of Amasis' objects related to Osiris at Abydos were found at Kom el-Sultan, he has convincingly hinted that the blocks from Sohag should also derive from the same building. Even though the actual function of this building remains uncertain, it might have been, as has been suggested, a *ka*-chapel for the celebration of the divine kingship of Amasis, appropriately decorated with scenes of his *sed*-festival.[405]

Another site comprising a construction with scenes relative to a *sed*-festival for Amasis was Sais. Two quartzite blocks, one from Rosetta and one from el-Nahhariya but both originally from Sa el-Hagar, show the king involved in his jubilee. The first block features Amasis turned towards the right, wearing the so-called *heb-sed* robe and the white crown and holding the *heqa*-sceptre and flail; behind him there is a group of protective emblems. The king is preceded by the *iunmutef* priest, of whom only the caption survives, and by two Wepwawet standards, represented as facing each other and of different sizes.[406] On the block from el-Nahhariya, a scene shows a Lower Egyptian king in a *heb-sed* robe under a baldachin, identified as the god Geb, seated with both his hands on the head of Amasis who is portrayed with the uraeus and kneeling in front of him; *iunmutef* and canine-headed figures in the *henu*-pose, representing the souls of Nekhen, take part in the event.[407]

Unlike Abydos, where all the attention seems to have been paid to Osiris 'lord of Abydos', at Sais Amasis dedicated objects to more than one local Osirian form, perhaps because these objects were originally placed in different religious contexts, involving different aspects of

400 Another block shows a row of mummiform deities: Klotz 2010, 159, fig. 5b-c.

401 Klotz 2010, 133, 159, fig. 5a.

402 Vernus 1975, 67, pl. VI; Klotz 2010, 133-134.

403 Klotz 2010, 133, 160, fig. 6a.

404 Klotz 2010, 132.

405 Klotz 2010, 134-135. See also Marlar 2007, 1251-1252; O'Connor 2008, 80-81, 111-113, who has proposed that the smaller structures at Kom el-Sultan were royal *ka*-chapels, going back to the Old Kingdom.

406 Habachi 1943, 385, fig. 105; Wilson 2006, 312; Jurman 2010, 97-98, pl. 24; Rummel 2010, 161. On the *iunmutef* priest and the *sed*-festival, see Rummel 2010, 157-165.

407 Habachi 1943, pl. XXVII, b; Wilson 2006, 314; Rummel 2010, 167-168. See also Habachi 1982, 231; Leclère 2008, 175.

Fig. III.12. Sfinx of Amasis, now in Rome, Musei Capitolini, MC 0035 (Photo: Archivio Fotografico dei Musei Capitolini).

Fig. III.13. Offering table of Amasis, now in Baltimore, Walters Art Gallery, 22.122 (Photo: The Walters Art Museum, Baltimore).

Osiris. One block, now completely eroded, which seems to have been lying with the blocks at the bottom of the 'Great Pit' of Sa el-Hagar, preserves a heaven sign surmounting an inscription for 'the king of Upper and Lower Egypt Khenem-ib-Ra, given life; beloved of Osiris who is in Sais'.[408] On a basanite sphinx of Amasis, discovered in 1883 in the vicinity of Santa Maria Sopra Minerva in Rome, the king is '[beloved of] Osiris, the great god, foremost of the *hut-bit*' (*wsỉr nṯr ꜥꜣ ḫnty ḥwt-bỉt*; Fig. III.12);[409] also the inscriptions of two similar black granite offering-tables – one in the British Museum (EA 94)[410] and the other in the Walters Art Gallery of Baltimore (22.122, Fig. III.13)[411] – state that they were expressly made by the king for 'his father Osiris, the great god, foremost of the *hut-bit*' (*ỉr n ỉt=f wsỉr nṯr ꜥꜣ ḫnty ḥwt-bỉt*). On the basis of their inscriptions, it is plausible to assume that Amasis dedicated these three monuments in the *hut-bit* itself, the major local Osirian cult-place.[412]

In the inscription on the surviving doorjamb of the fragmentary naos in quartzite from Sa el-Hagar, Amasis presents himself as 'beloved of Osiris in the House of Sekhmet' (*wsỉr m ḥwt-sḫmt*), an otherwise unattested form of the god. The presence of Sekhmet at Sais is attested by other sources.[413] Penelope Wilson has suggested that, given the important

408 Habachi 1943, 374; Wilson 2006, 311.

409 In Rome, Musei Capitolini, Palazzo dei Conservatori (MC 0035): Ensoli Vittozzi 1990, 28-31; Lollio/Barberi/Parola/Toti 1995, 162-163; Arslan 1997, 391; Perdu 2012, 182-183.

410 Taylor/Strudwick 2005, 126-127; Jansen-Winkeln 2014, 418.

411 Steindorff 1946, 88-89 no. 292, pl. 55; Jansen-Winkeln 2014, 418.

412 El-Sayed 1975, 199-208; Wilson 2006, 31-33, 259-262.

413 El-Sayed 1982, 136.

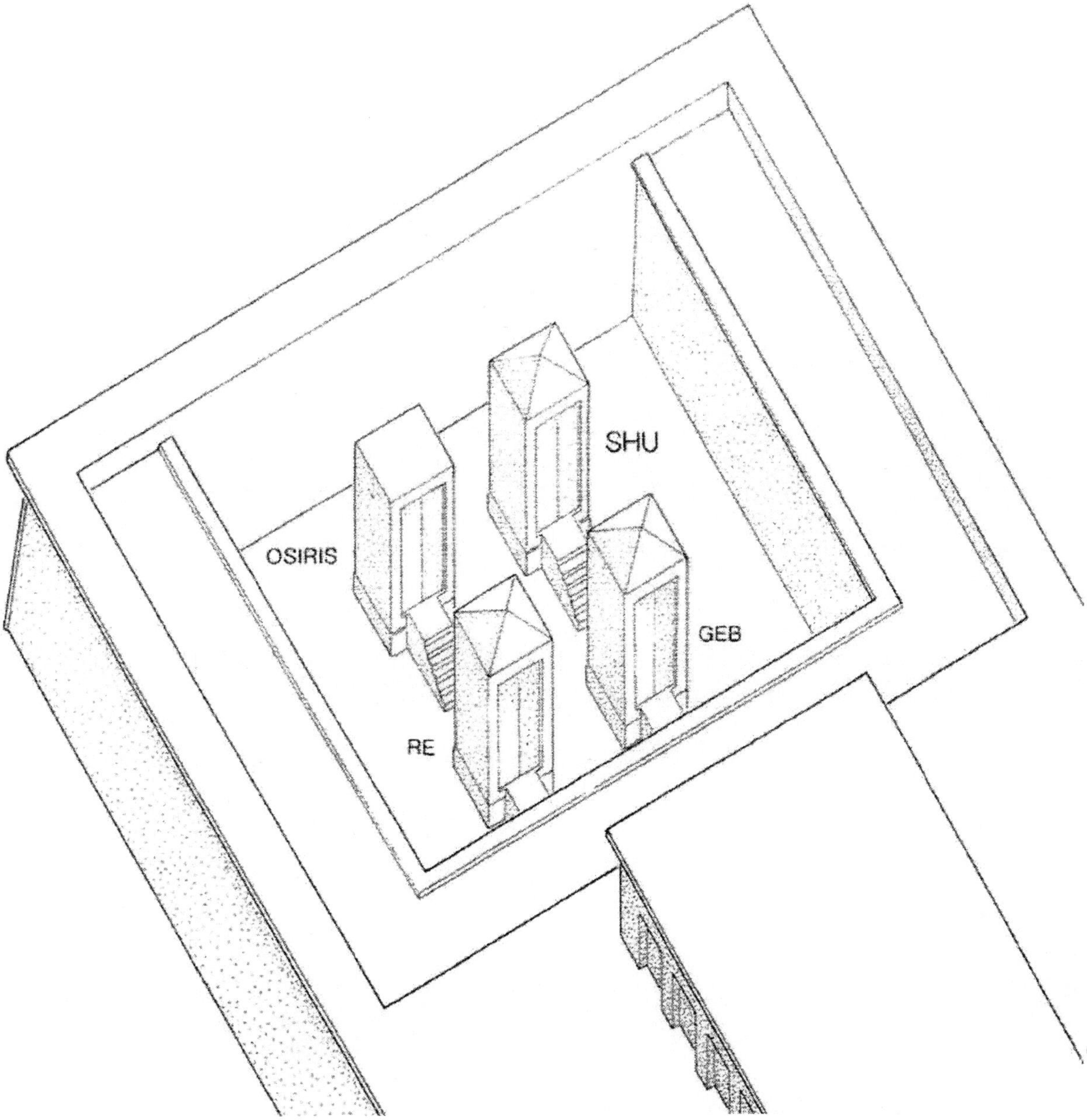

Fig. III.14. Reconstruction of court with shrines in the Banebdjed temple at Mendes. Reproduced from Arnold 1999, fig. 42.

medical tradition at Sais, the 'House of Sekhmet' was perhaps linked to the local medical institution, where Osiris might also have been worshipped.[414]

Amasis also appears in another Osirian context, that is in the chapels in Ayn el-Muftella, in the Bahariya Oasis. In particular, the decoration of room 121 of the complex B,[415] built by the local governor Djedkhonsuiuefankh in the king's name, includes numerous forms of Osiris and was focused on the god's connections with vegetation and, as in the Leiden naos, his resurrection.[416]

Osiris was also present at Mendes, where his naos is part of an architectural complex built by Amasis that included four monolithic shrines, dedicated to four deities – Ra, Shu, Geb, and Osiris himself – regarded as the four *bas* of the main local god, Banebdjed.

414 Wilson 2006, 213 and n. 16.

415 The so-called second chapel in Fakhry 1942.

416 Labrique 2005; Labrique 2007; Labrique 2013, 259, 263-264.

The four naoi were erected in an open-air court and created a quadrant based on the four cardinal points. The naos of Shu still stands in situ in the south-west corner of the court and faces north, but the original arrangement of the other three naoi is uncertain. According to Bothmer[417] the naos of Geb was in the north-west corner, while the naoi of Ra and Osiris were in the south-east and north-east corners, respectively. Leclère[418] has instead suggested that the position of these two last shrines should be reversed. Moreover, according to Leclère and Arnold (Fig. III.14),[419] all the four naoi faced north, while Redford[420] proposed that one pair was 'facing the other in a square pattern'.

The naos of Athribis is also an expression of the specific Osirian theology of the site. The monument was dedicated to 'Kem-wer, the great god, foremost of *sekhet-hotep*'[421] and might have been donated by the king in the temple he built in the north area of the town, north-east of kom A. Labib Habachi[422] has assumed that the naos was made for a jubilee of the king's, as the decoration of the front, just beneath the opening in the middle, presents two structures usually linked with the *sed*-festival ceremony, viz. the *ỉtrt* of Upper and the *ỉtrt* of Lower Egypt. The first one is flanked by three canine-headed gods representing the souls of Nekhen of Upper Egypt and by Isden in the guise of a baboon; the second *ỉtrt* is followed by three hawk-headed deities representing the souls of Pe of Lower Egypt, and by another baboon labelled as *ḥḏ wr*,[423] the 'Great White one'; each of these two groups ends with the images of two superimposed recumbent lions called *ꜣkr*.[424]

It is worth mentioning that the Athribis naos is the only monolithic shrine with images of Amasis in front of gods. Rather unusually, ritual scenes are here located also on the area just above the cavetto cornice, which itself is decorated with a row of royal cartouches and under which there is the dedicatory text. On the left side, the king stands with his arms down in front of an image of Osiris 'in the *sekhet-hotep*' (*wsỉr m sḫt-ḥtp*), kneeling on a lion-bed under a baldachin (Fig. III.15). The legend accompanying the figure of Amasis is damaged, but can be restored as [*dwꜣ*] *nṯr* [*sp*] *4*, '[worshipping] god four [times]'. Behind Osiris there is the goddess *Mnḫt-štꜣt*, the 'Secret cloth', followed by four groups of deities, each composed of three seated male gods holding a *was*-staff; the first divine group represents 'the gods who preside over *sekhet-hotep*' (*nṯrw ḫntyw sḫt-ḥtp*), then there are 'the gods who are in the secret mansion' (*nṯrw ỉmyw ḥwt-štꜣt*),[425] 'the gods who are in the palace' (*nṯrw ỉmyw stp-sꜣ*),[426] and *mḏḥ m* [...]. On the right side of the top, the king once again performs the *dwꜣ nṯr sp 4* and stands with his arms down in front of a god, very

---

417 Bothmer 1988, 206.

418 Leclère 2008, 325.

419 Arnold 1999, 82.

420 Redford 2010, 157-158.

421 For other examples of Osiris as 'foremost of the *sekhet-hotep*', see a private statue of the time of Psamtek I (Vernus 1978, 91) and the statue BM EA 957 of the Ptolemaic Period (Vernus 1978, 209).

422 Habachi 1982, 231. See also the discussion of this decoration by Jurman 2010, 99-100.

423 In the Saite period this deity is also attested, always as a baboon, on the naos Cairo CG 70008 of Apries, on the block Vienna 213 (Arnold 1999, 77), and on the sarcophagus of Aspelta (Dunham 1955, 90). See also Leitz 2002, V, 601.

424 Leitz 2002, I, 82-83.

425 No other example of this group of deities: Leitz 2002, IV, 463.

426 No other example of this group of deities: Leitz 2002, IV, 466.

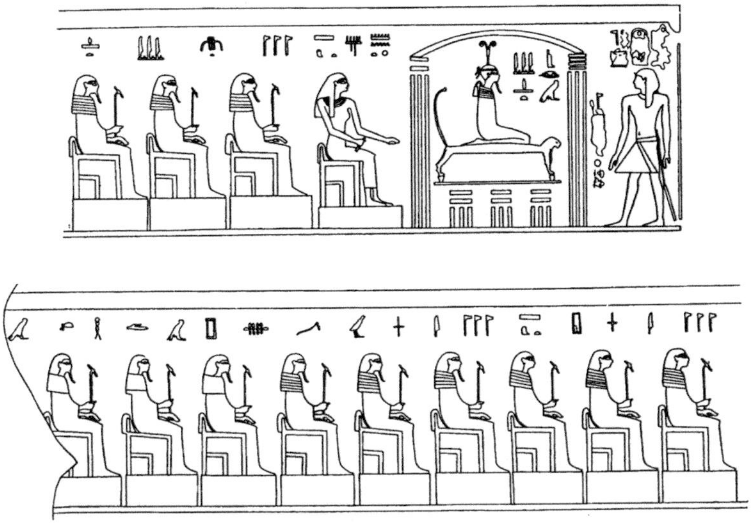

Fig. III.15. Naos of Athribis, left side, upper register. Reproduced from Habachi 1982, 228, fig. 7.

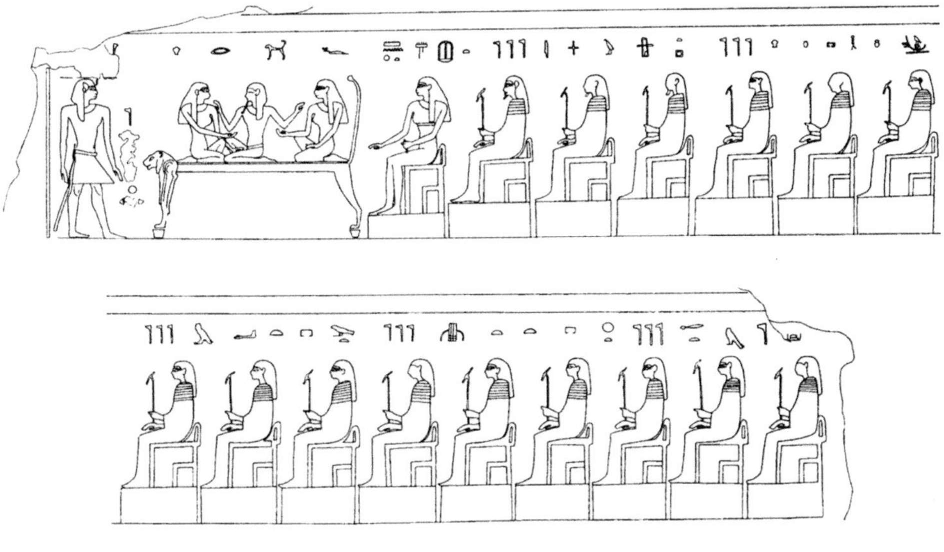

Fig. III.16. Naos of Athribis, right side, upper register. Reproduced from Habachi 1982, 232, fig. 10.

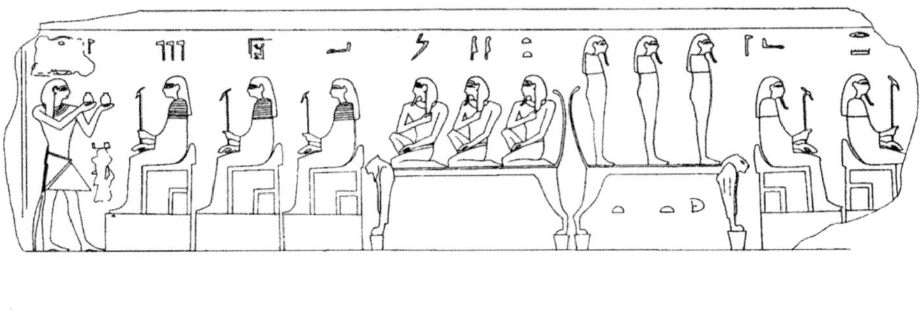

Fig. III.17. Naos of Athribis, rear, upper register. Reproduced from Habachi 1982, 233, fig. 12.

likely Osiris himself, called 'the one on his bed' (*ḥry nmỉt=f*),[427] kneeling on a lion-bed and extending his arms to a goddess to either side, who may perhaps be identified as Isis and Nephthys (Fig. III.16). The scene is followed by another personification of cloth, *Mnḫt-ḥbt*,[428] the 'Festive cloth', and by four other groups of deities, the 'gods who are in the great mansion' (*nṯrw ỉmyw ḥwt-ʿȝt*),[429] 'the gods who reside in the house of the *henu*-barque' (*nṯrw ḥryw-ib pr-ḥnw*),[430] 'the gods in the great chamber' (*nṯrw m ʿt-wrt*),[431] and 'the gods who preside over the house of the Great Ennead in the mound of the god' (*nṯrw ḫntyw pr-psḏt ʿȝt m ỉȝt-nṯr*).[432] The top register of the rear wall instead presents two rows of gods, arranged symmetrically and both looking towards the front of the naos (Fig. III.17). On the left, the king is shown standing and offering two *nw*-vases to three seated gods, called *nṯrw ỉmn-ʿ*, and three deities kneeling upon a lion-bier, labelled as *mȝʿtyw*.[433] On the right, the scene is only partially preserved: the image of the king is lost, as well as the figure of the first god in front of him, but two seated gods, named [...] *rmn nṯr*, and three standing mummies upon a lion-bier are still visible.

The surfaces of the naos below the dedicatory text are now lost. It is therefore not possible to know whether similar figures seated on thrones or placed on lion-biers were present also in the other registers, or if their location in the top register, above the cavetto cornice, meant to highlight their importance in relation to the image of the god preserved inside the niche of the naos. However, parts of the bottom of the monument fortunately survive. The left side is very badly damaged: the king is represented kneeling and offering two *nw*-vases to a row of seated gods, whose names have disappeared. On the right side, the king, in the same attitude as on the left side, faces anthropomorphic seated deities holding *was*-staves, with cobras on pedestals in between: *ȝst m trỉ*, 'Isis in the reeds' (?),[434] the cobra *snfy*, 'Bloody one',[435] *nb ḥḥ*, 'Lord of million',[436] the cobra *tm-ḥʿw*, 'Complete of limbs',[437] the god *nb-rḥn*,[438] two cobras back to back with their tails intertwined labelled as *mm-tȝ*,[439] the goddess Nebet-hetepet, the cobra *rȝ-wȝḥ*, 'the one with an enduring mouth',[440] the god *nḫt*, 'Strong one', three cobras named as *nʿw wr*,

427 This epithet, rather common in the Graeco-Roman period, started being used in the Saite period (Leitz 2002, V, 365). Besides the naos of Athribis, it occurs on the stela Brussels E 7429 (Limme 1979, n. 17).

428 Both Mekhet-shetat and Mekhet-hebet are attested for the first time on the naos of Athribis (Leitz 2002, III, 316). Subsequently, they are mentioned on the altar Turin 22055 of Nekhthorheb from Athribis (Habachi 1977, 95). Menkhet-hebet is represented on a block of Darius I from Abusir (Naville 1890, pl. 7A), while Menkhet-shetat is mentioned in the 'Book of traversing eternity' (Herbin 1994, VI, 8).

429 No other example of this group of deities: Leitz 2002, IV, 463.

430 No other example of this group of deities: Leitz 2002, IV, 534.

431 No other example of this group of deities: Leitz 2002, IV, 472.

432 Cf. Leitz 2002, III, 143 and IV, 537.

433 The naos of Athribis is the only example of this group of deities for the Saite period: Leitz 2002, III, 230-231.

434 No other example of this form of Isis is known. Leitz 2002, I, 78 suggests the reading 'im Röhricht'.

435 This deity is known from only two other examples dated to the New Kingdom: Leitz 2002, VI, 382.

436 Leitz 2002, III, 703. This deity is attested from the Middle Kingdom to the Graeco-Roman period. In the Saite period he appears also on the naos Brussels E 5818 (Capart 1924, 23, pl. II). His name might be read also *nb ḥḥw*, 'Lord of millions' (Leitz 2002, III, 703-704) or *nbw ḥḥw*, 'Gold of millions' (Leitz 2002, IV, 180).

437 This is the only attestation of this deity: Leitz 2002, VII, 426. On the connection between the verb *tm* and the term *ḥʿw* or *ỉwf*, see Wilson 1997, 1143.

438 The reading of the name of this otherwise unattested deity is uncertain: Leitz 2002, III, 685.

439 Of this deity there is only one mention dated to the New Kingdom: Leitz 2002, III, 278.

440 No other example of this deity: Leitz 2002, IV, 607.

the 'Great serpent',[441] *ḳmꜣ-ỉrw*, 'He who creates the form',[442] followed by a cobra whose name is lost. Above this divine row, the lower part of another register, showing the feet of various figures, survives: the king is in front of male and female deities and a group of three figures on the same low base.

Even though some of the place-names associated with the groups of gods – such as *ḥwt-ꜥꜣt*, *ꜥt-wrt*, *ḥwt-šṯꜣ*, and *ỉꜣt-nṯr* – can be found in many temple complexes, it seems likely that in this context some of them, if not all, might refer to local cult places. On an altar of Nekhthorheb from Athribis, Osiris and Isis 'in *ỉꜣt-nṯr*' and the goddesses Menkhet-hebet and Menkhet-shetat are quoted.[443] The material brought to light in the area of the temple built by Amasis in Athribis is very scanty and consists of fragments of a sphinx and of a baboon statue and a stela with the images of Osiris and Isis 'in the necropolis' (*ẖꜣst*).[444] However, according to Barbara Ruszczyc,[445] the temple might be identified with the local Osirian *ḥwt-ꜥꜣt*, a sanctuary for the celebration of the solar rebirth.[446] The presence of the naos in this context would have been particularly appropriate. Kem-wer is an Athribian Osirian manifestation, which seems to represent the god during the critical phase of his mummification and interment.[447] The theme of the awakening of Osiris, with the god on lion-biers and assisted by all the groups of deities represented, is certainly preeminent in the decoration of the naos. If Kem-wer, through his association with the *sekhet-hotep*, a land rich in water and vegetation, can connect his resurrection with the vegetal world,[448] the *ḥwt-ꜥꜣt* stresses above all his connections with solar theology. Through the two symmetric scenes on the top of the naos, the Athribian Osiris was able to link himself and his rebirth with two fundamental themes, the inundation and the rising sun.

The meaning of the naoi Amasis made for Osiris at Kom el-Ahmar is particularly uncertain. The issue is made even more complicated by the fact that, unlike the other places where he decided to locate monolithic shrines, no other building activity on behalf of this king has so far been registered at the site, and by the fact that the connections between the town and Osiris Hemag and Osiris Merty, who do not seem to be specific local forms of the god, are apparently obscure.

---

441 This is the most ancient known example of this deity: Leitz 2002, III, 531.
442 Leitz 2002, VII, 188.
443 Turin 22055: Habachi 1977, 94-95.
444 Vernus 1978, 450-451.
445 Ruszczyc 1976.
446 Vernus 1978, 420.
447 Vernus 1978, 429.
448 Vernus 1978, 431.

Chapter IV

The role of the naos

1. The recipient of the naos: Osiris Hemag

Osiris Hemag, to whom the naos of Leiden AM 107 was dedicated, did not fail to draw the attention of scholars.[449] In 1996, I made an attempt to present an account of this important and interesting Osirian form in the volume *A study on the Egyptian god Osiris Hemag*.[450] Before returning here to the issue of the meaning of the epithet *ḥmȝg*, which is central to the understanding of the significance and function of the naos, it is perhaps useful to present a list of the documents mentioning the term *ḥmȝg* which are not included in my volume; some of them escaped my attention, while others have been published more recently.

For *hemag* as a divine epithet, see:

1. block-statue Cairo JE 36997bis[451] (22nd-25th Dynasty, from the Karnak Cachette), belonging to the *hem-netjer* priest of Amun and Osiris (*ḥm-nṯr n ỉmn ḥm-nṯr n wsỉr*) Amenmes (*ỉmn-ms*), with an image on the front of 'Osiris Hemag, the great god, lord of the sky' (*wsỉr ḥȝmꜥgȝ nṯr ꜥȝ nb pt*); see Fig. IV.1 below;
2. statue Museo Archeologico Nazionale, Naples 237[452] (25th-26th Dynasty, unknown provenance), belonging to the vizier (*ṯȝty*), great mayor in Memphis (*ḥȝty-ꜥ wr mn-nfr*), god's father and master of secrets in Heliopolis (*ỉt nṯr ḥry-sštȝ ỉwnw*), *sȝ mr=f*, dignitary (*sȝb*), *hem-netjer* priest of Atum 'who resides in his city' and Osiris Hemag (*ḥm-nṯr ỉtm ḥry-ỉb nỉwt=f wsỉr ḥmȝg*), *hem-netjer* priest of Ipet[453] (*ḥm-nṯr n ỉpt*), Harkhebi (*ḥr-(m-)ȝḫ-bỉt*);
3. Theban tomb TT 33 of Pediamenopet (25th-26th Dynasty), room XV, with images of Osiris Hemag (unpublished);[454]
4. Chapter 142 of the Book of the Dead: a) p. Colon. Aeg. 1027 (68e,14)[455] (26th Dynasty), *wsỉr m ḥmȝgȝ*; b) *pṯȝ-šrt-n-ȝst*[456] (26th Dynasty, reign of Amasis), *wsỉr m ḥmȝgȝ*; c) p. Vatican 38603[457] (Ptolemaic Period): *wsỉr m ḥmȝgȝ*;

---

449 See, for example, Yoyotte 1961, 94; Chassinat 1966-1968, II, 479-489; El-Sayed 1975, 208-213; Derchain 1990, 221, 225; Favard-Meeks 1991, 367-368.

450 Zecchi 1996.

451 Brandl 2008, 178-179, pls. 112-113, 161d; Jansen-Winkeln 2009, 511.

452 The statue is dated to the 18th Dynasty, but was re-inscibed for Harkhebi: Lillesø 1987, 230-234; Cantilena/Rubino 1989, 47, fig. 3.2, pl. II; Jansen-Winkeln 2009, 374; PM VIII, 547.

453 On the existence of *ipt* in Heliopolis, see Yoyotte 1954a, 91; Postel/Régen 2005, 236-237, 267-168 n. ll; Iwaszczuk 2013, 309-311.

454 Von Bissing 1938, 22-23; PM I, 55; Traunecker 2008, 34; Traunecker/Régen 2013, 33; Traunecker 2014, 218.

455 Verhoeven 1993, I, 270; II, 103*.

456 Munro 2011, pl. 28.

457 Albert 2013, pls. 16c-d.

5. fragment of a basalt statuette of a man with text on back-pillar,[458] in Musei Capitolini, Palazzo dei Conservatori, Rome, inventory number 2156 (Late or Ptolemaic Period, found in the Castro Pretorio): 'Osiris Hemag, who resides in Bubastis' (*wsỉr ḥmk ḥry-ỉb bꜣstt*);
6. stela Louvre C 318[459] of the reign of Nekhtnebef, discovered in the vicinity of the Serapeum at Saqqara, but dedicated by Naes, son of Hetepimen, from Tanis: among nine deities of this city there is also an image of Osiris Hemag, with the epithets 'lord of the great city, the great god' (*wsỉr ḥmꜣg nb nỉwt wrt nṯr ꜥꜣ*) and pronouncing the words: 'I have given you all life, stability and dominion, all the health (coming) from me' (*dỉ.n(=ỉ) n=k ꜥnḫ ḏd wꜣs nb snb nb ḫr=ỉ*);
7. papyrus Hohenzollern-Sigmaringen II, 1, 24,[460] containing a litany to different Osirian forms (late 4th century BC): 'Osiris Hemag in the house of *hemag*' (*wsỉr ḥmꜥgꜣ m ḥwt-ḥmꜥgꜣ*);
8. statue Yale Peabody Museum ANT 264191, of Horpakhepesh (Ptolemaic Period),[461] who held the title, among several others, of '*hem-netjer* priest of Osiris Hemag' (*ḥm-nṯr wsỉr ḥmꜣg*);
9. second western Osirian chapel (*Dendera* X 324, 9), in a geographical list of the Coptite nome: 'Osiris Min in *hemag*, the bull high-raised of arm in the Coptite province' (*wsỉr mnw m ḥmꜣg kꜣ fꜣỉ-ꜥ m nṯrwy*).[462]

Another possible occurrence of this Osirian form – written *ḥmkꜣ* and translated as 'the bandaged one' – is in an ostracon in demotic of the Ptolemaic Period,[463] containing an invocation to various gods to appear in a dream.

For other mentions of the 'house of *hemag*', see:

1. first western Osirian chapel (*Dendera* X 271, 2-4), in an invocation to Sokar-Osiris: 'the great god who resides in Iunet (*nṯr ꜥꜣ ḥry-ỉb ỉwnt*)... the statue of gold, who comes out from the house of gold, your relics are created in the house of *hemag*' (*sḫm n nbw bs m ḥwt-nbw wtṯ ỉḫt=k m ḥwt-ḥmꜣg*);
2. third western Osirian chapel (*Dendera* X 401, 12), words spoken by the king: 'I have protected the right leg in the *imentet*-province and *iq*-province, (I) place it in the house of *hemag*' (*ỉr.n=ỉ nht nt wꜥrt wnmyt m ỉmntt ỉḳ rdỉ(=ỉ) st r ḥwt-ḥmꜣg*);
3. third western Osirian chapel (*Dendera* X 402, 4), words spoken by the king: 'I carried Qebehsenuef in Nedjefet-pehet, I place him in the *hemaket* in Iunet' (*ỉšš=ỉ ḳbḥ-snw=f m ndft pḥt rdỉ.n=ỉ sw r ḥmꜣgt m ỉwnt*);

458 Bosticco 1952, 39 doc. 547; Malaise 1972, 182; Roullet 1972, 111; Lollio Barbieri/Parola/Toti 1995, 170-171. According to PM VIII, 113 the statue is 'probably a Roman imitation'.

459 Yoyotte 1987, 196-197; PM III, 780; Guermeur 2005, 286.

460 Quack 2000, 78, pl. X; Smith 2009, 204.

461 Klotz/LeBlanc 2012, 645-698.

462 See also Leitz 2012, 75-76.

463 Reading uncertain: Ray 1976, 67. See also the block from Sais quoted by Habachi 1943, 373 and Zecchi 1996, 12 doc. 7 (26th Dynasty?), with an image of *wsir ḥmꜣg nṯr ꜥꜣ ḫnty ḥwt-bỉt*, and now published in Wilson 1998, 4, pl. I.4; Leclère 2003, 34; Wilson 2006, 219-220, pl. 31e; Jansen-Winkeln 2014, 759. For the blocks from Behbeit el-Hagar, see now Favard-Meeks 2003, 97-108, pls. 25-29.

4. third western Osirian chapel (*Dendera* X 414, 3-4), in a list of epithets of the god Iremawa (*ỉr-m-ʿwꜣy*): 'the great god in the house of gold (*nṯr ʿꜣ m ḥwt-nbw*)... efficient of hand carrying the vase in the *hemaket* on the day of wrapping Osiris' (*ꜣḫ ḏrt ẖr ʿ m-ḫnt ḥmꜣgt m hrw nw n wsỉr*).

For *ḥmꜣg* as verb, see:

1. third western Osirian chapel (*Dendera* X 413, 13-14), words spoken by Shesmu: 'receive for yourself the divine stone with all its effluxes, you are enveloped with it' (*mn n=k ʿꜣt-nṯr m rḏw=s nbw ḥmꜣg.tw ỉm=s*).

It should also be noted that in the inscriptions of a small statuette in faience of the Late Period, belonging to the *ḥmꜣg* priest Harkhebi, it is the god Ptah-Sokar who is called *ḥry-ib ḥmꜣg*.[464]

Even though a deity called *ḥmꜣgt(y)* appears in the list of Memphite gods engraved on the south wall of the chapel of Ptah-Sokar in the temple of Sety I at Abydos,[465] Osiris seems to have begun adopting the epithet Hemag during the Third Intermediate Period. According to the available data, the most ancient attestations of the use of the term *hemag* as an Osirian epithet are found on the statue of the priest Amenmes from Karnak,[466] dating from the 22nd to the 25th Dynasty, on a coffin of the same period belonging to a certain Yewerhen son of Ankhwennefer, found at el-Lahun,[467] where the god bears the epithets 'who presides over the *per-henu* (*ḫnty pr-ḥnw*),[468] great god, lord of the sky (*nṯr ʿꜣ nb pt*), ruler of eternity (*ḥḳꜣ ḏt*)', and on the statue of the priest Basa, very likely from Dendera and dated to the late 25th Dynasty or early 26th Dynasty.[469] However, it was only starting from the 26th Dynasty that Osiris Hemag became a key figure among the myriad of Osirian forms that populated the Egyptian pantheon. His origins are uncertain and, owing to the scarcity of documents before the Saite period, it is not possible to know where his cult might have begun. Contrary to what is often stated, there is no evidence that Osiris Hemag had a Saite origin;[470] rather than his first cult-centre, Sais should be regarded as just one locality where his worship was particularly important. In this respect, it should be noted that in the hymns or litanies to Osiris, Osiris Hemag is never referred to as a Saite god; moreover, outside the territory of Sais, he is usually not directly

---

464 Gubel 1991, 225-226.

465 Kees 1915, 57-59; Baines 1988, 124-133; Kitchen 1993, 87-104; Zecchi 1996, 85-86; Gaber 2015, 245-255.

466 Cairo JE 36997bis: Brandl 2008, 178-179; Jansen-Winkeln 2009, 511.

467 Petrie 1890, 40, pl. XXV.23; Zecchi 1996, 8-9 doc. 3. In Leitz 2002, II, 555 the coffin is dated to the Graeco-Roman Period.

468 This is the only example of this epithet. Acording to Yoyotte 1961, 92 in this context *per-henu* is the Osirian sanctuary in the XXIst Upper Egyptian province. In Leitz 2002, V, 809 it is regarded as that of Athribis. However, it is equally plausible that the epithet is a reference to the connections of Osiris Hemag with Memphis.

469 Chicago OIM 10729: Ritner 1988, 124-133, who dated the statue to the 22nd-23rd Dynasty. Guermeur 2005, 353-355 and Brandl 2008, 107-108 have suggested a date in the late 25th Dynasty or at the beginning of the 26th Dynasty on stylistic grounds.

470 See, for example, Gauthier 1922, 201; Posener 1936, 4, 13; Montet 1938, 138; Goyon 1967, 130; El-Sayed 1975, 208-213; Vernus 1978, 425 n. 3; Lloyd 1982, 168; El-Banna 1989, 125; and more recently Zivie-Coche 2004, 179, where the god is regarded as 'sans doute née a Saïs'.

connected by means of epithets to that site, nor associated with its deities;[471] rather he is associated above all with Memphis, or more rarely Kher-Aha, Behbeit el-Hagar, or Coptos. The most plausible candidates are indeed Memphis itself or the territory between this town and Heliopolis.[472]

Whatever his origin may have been, in the Late and Graeco-Roman periods his cult was well established in several localities of the Delta. Besides Memphis,[473] Heliopolis, and Kher-Aha,[474] it was present at Sais,[475] Behbeit el-Hagar,[476] Tanis,[477] Mendes,[478] Avaris,[479] Bubastis,[480] and possibly Kom el-Ahmar. On the contrary, the cult in honour of this Osirian form was not so widespread in the south of Egypt. The presence of Osiris Hemag seems to have been restricted to the area of the fourth, fifth, and sixth Upper Egyptian provinces. One of the most ancient *hem-netjer* priests of Osiris Hemag is known thanks to a statue from the Karnak Cachette and, interestingly, the god is represented in the tomb of Pediamenopet (TT 33) in el-Assasif in the Theban necropolis. Inside this impressive burial place there are three chapels (rooms XIV, XV, and XVI) where Pediamenopet, in his capacity as ritualist, prepares the ideal mummy of Osiris. One of these chapels is the 'house of natron' (room XIV) for the embalming of the divine body and where Ptah and Sokar reside; another chapel is the 'house of gold' (*ḥwt-nbw*) (room XVI), which is under the tutelage of Ptah and Sokar 'who presides over the house of gold' and where the body embalmed in the previous room is animated by the Opening of the Mouth. The central room (XV) is the 'house of *hemag*' presided by Osiris Hemag himself, who represents, as pointed out by Claude Traunecker,[481] the perfect result of the operations carried out in the two other chapels.

But the main forms of veneration in the Nile Valley were undoubtedly in Dendera and Coptos. In the former locality, the god was worshipped at least from the Third Intermediate Period until the Graeco-Roman Period. The earliest evidence of a priesthood for Osiris Hemag is offered by the above-mentioned statue from Dendera of the 25th-26th Dynasty belonging to a certain Basa,[482] who held several titles, among which those of '*hem-netjer* priest of Osiris-Sokar, *hem-netjer* priest of Ptah and Sekhmet who reside in Dendera, and *hem-netjer* priest of Osiris Hemag (*wsir ḥmꜣḳ*)'. Inside the third western Osirian chapel on the roof of the temple of Hathor, Osiris Hemag seems to be regarded as a local Osirian form,[483] while within the chapel of Sokar he is expressly called 'the great god who resides in Iunet' (*nṯr ꜥꜣ ḥry-ib iwnt*);[484] moreover, the temple also hosted a small room called

---

471 Zecchi 1996, 77-78.
472 Zecchi 1996, 85-90.
473 Zecchi 1996, 85-87.
474 Zecchi 1996, 87-90.
475 Zecchi 1996, 90-94.
476 Zecchi 1996, 94-96.
477 Zecchi 1996, 96-97. See also Zivie-Coche 2004, 111, 112, 179.
478 Zecchi 1997, 97.
479 Zecchi 1996, 97.
480 In the inscription of the statuette inv. 2156 in the Musei Capitolini, Palazzo dei Conservatori, Rome (Late or Ptolemaic Period), Osiris Hemag has the epithet *ḥry-ib bꜣstt*: Lollio Barbieri/Parola/Toti 1995, 170-171.
481 Traunecker 2008, 34. See also Traunecker 2014, 218.
482 Chicago OIM 10729: Ritner 1994, 205-205 (= Zecchi 1996, 8 doc. 2).
483 *Dendera* X 412, 9 = Zecchi 1996, 55 doc. 47.
484 *Dendera* II 160, 17 = Zecchi 1996, 47-51 doc. 40.

ḥmȝkt.[485] A similar room or chapel must also have existed at Coptos. In a hymn to Osiris and his resurrection in the first western Osirian chapel at Dendera, one reads: 'You are in Coptos, in the house of rejoicing (*in iw=k m gbtyw m ḥwt-ȝw-ib*), the *senut* is joining with your mummy (*snwt ḥr snsn sʿḥ=k*). Your son is after you as a king, Horus the mighty (*sȝ=k ḥr sȝ=k m nsw ḥr-nḫt*), and your secret form is in the house of *hemag* (*irw=k štȝ m ḥwt-ḥmȝg*)'.[486] Moreover, Osiris Hemag or the 'house of *hemag*' are mentioned in the geographical lists relative to the fifth Upper Egyptian province inscribed on the temples of Edfu,[487] Opet,[488] Dendera,[489] and Medamud.[490]

Unfortunately, the available data of the dynastic period do not provide any information on the nature and meaning of the word *hemag*. The Graeco-Roman sources, consisting above all of hieroglyphic inscriptions engraved on a few temples, are a little more generous. A substantive *ḥmȝgȝ* appears in two passages of the 'mysteries of Khoiak'[491] in association with the last envelopment of the mummy, but its exact meaning remains uncertain.[492] In the Graeco-Roman sources, however, Osiris Hemag, the house of *hemag*, and the word *hemag* are not specifically connected with cloth and fabrics; rather, they usually, and more frequently, appear in texts involving precious material, such as metals and costly stones (i.e. the final decoration of the mummy).

At Edfu Osiris Hemag is not present, whereas the 'house of *hemag*' is mentioned three times in the inscriptions of the local temple. In a scene where king Ptolemy IV Philopator lays bricks (*sḫt ḏbt*) in front of Horus, the god declares to give him 'your *pr-ḥmȝg* with [your] images (*irw*)'.[493] More interesting is a scene for the offering of the necklace (*rdi iry-ḫḫ*) to Hathor, where Ptolemy VIII Euergetes II is the one 'who is cautious coming out of the *hemag*' (*ip-ib pr m ḥmȝg*), when he brings electrum (*ḏʿm*) and turquoise (*mfkȝt*) to adorn the neck of the goddess;[494] moreover, he is the one with 'skilfull hands (*ȝḫ ʿwy*), Tatenen who makes excellent the fingers in the work of the craftsmen (*sȝḫ ḏbʿ m kȝt ḥmww*)... the venerable pillar, when fashioning with gold (*ḏd šps ḥr nbi m nbw*), who came into existence in the beginning to create minerals (*ḫpr m-ḥȝt ḥr ms ʿȝt*)'. One of the most descriptive texts on the nature of the *hemag* is perhaps in a scene for the offering of lettuce (*ḥnk ʿbw*) to Min, where both donor and recipient are connected with the *hemag*. Ptolemy VIII is mentioned as the one 'who makes great the dignity of the one who presides over the house of *hemag*' (*swr kfȝw n ḫnty ḥwt-ḥmȝgȝt*),[495] while the god is called 'Min in Behdet, who presides over Ombos, great beneficent god in the nome of Edfu (*mnw m bḥdt ḫnty nḇb nṯr mnḫ m wṯst-ḥr*)' and 'Atum in his *hemag*, divine image with costly stones and

485 *Dendera* VIII 128, 15-131, 6 and 133, 14-134, 7; Daumas 1980, 109-118; Derchain 1990, 219-242; Zecchi 1996, 51-53 doc. 42. See also *Dendera* X 401, 12 and 402, 4 with a mention of the '*ḥmȝgt* in Dendera (*m iwnt*)'.

486 *Dendera* X 282, 10-12 = Zecchi 1996, 53-54 doc. 44.

487 *Edfu* V, 110, XX = Zecchi 1996, 47 doc. 39.

488 *Opet* I, 278 = Zecchi 1996, 56-57 doc. 49.

489 *Dendera* X 324, 8-11 (Leitz 2012, 75-76).

490 *Médamoud* 69-70 (157) = Zecchi 1996, 58-59 doc. 51.

491 *Dendera* X 34, 9 (*ir tȝ rwḏ ʿrf m ḥmȝg irtw=s m ʿȝt nt ḥrw wʿ mi tmt nt ḥbs n rḥty*) and 46, 1-12 (*wḏʿ rȝ ḥr=f ir(t) sbn 4 ḥr ʿrf n tmt nt ḥmȝg*).

492 Chassinat 1966-1968, 479-489, where the 'house of *hemag*' is translated as 'salle de l'emmaillotement'; Zecchi 1996, 67-68. See also Koemoth 1998, 756.

493 *Edfu* II 61, 5 = Zecchi 1996, 41-42 doc. 36.

494 *Edfu* III 175, 8-176, 2 = Zecchi 1996, 42-44 doc. 37.

495 *Edfu* IV 270, 16.

gold' (or 'Atum in his divine *hemag*, prepared with costly stones and gold', *tm m ḥmꜣgꜣ=f nṯr šsp m ꜥꜣt nbw*).[496]

At Dendera, the inscriptions of the *ḥmꜣkt* strongly indicate a connection between the activities carried out within this chamber and the house of gold, and precious metals and stones.[497] Moreover, on the west wall of the first western Osiris chapel, Osiris is addressed as follows: 'You are in Memphis, in the house of gold, (in) the *ḥwt-ḥmꜣkt*, the *per-henu* is for your mummy' (*ỉn ỉw=k m ỉnb-ḥḏ m-ḫnt ḥwt-nbw ḥwt-ḥmꜣg pr-ḥnw n sꜥḥ=k*).[498] In a scene in the same temple dedicated to the offering of a garland for Hathor (*mꜣḥ r ḥꜣt=t*), the king is the 'eldest son of the venerable pillar (*sꜣ smsw n ḏd šps*), created by the one who is south of his wall within the house of gold (*ḳmꜣ n rsy ỉnb=f m-ḫnt ḥwt-nbw*), who casts a beautiful wreath of gold, adorned with costly stones within the house of *hemag* (*nbỉ wꜣḥ nfr m nbw sẖkr m ꜥꜣt m-ḫnt ḥwt-ḥmkꜣt*), lord of activities (*nb rꜣ-ꜥwy*)',[499] while the goddess gives the king 'the mountains giving you the products, the venerable minerals of the mining regions' (*dỉ=ỉ n=k ḏwy ḥr dt n=k ỉḫt ꜥꜣwt špswt nt ḫꜣwt*). In a ritual scene in the chapel of Sokar, Osiris Hemag bears the epithets 'beautiful of face, long of beard' (*nfr ḥr ḳꜣ ḫbswt*), which may be a reference to his pleasant aspect due to his association with metals and minerals.[500] In the first western Osirian chapel, Sokar-Osiris is addressed as 'the great god who resides in Dendera (*nṯr ꜥꜣ ḥry-ỉb ỉwnt*), the *djed*-pillar, sovereign and lord of Djedu (*ḏd ỉty nb ḏdw*), the eldest son created by Geb (*sꜣ smsw wtṯ gb*), who illumines his brothers [...] (*wpš snw=f m* [...]), statue of gold (*sḫm n nbw*), introduced in the house of gold (*bs m ḥwt-nbw*), your relics are created in the house of *hemag* (*wtṯ ỉḫt=k m ḥwt-ḥmꜣg*)'.[501]

An enlightening example of the meaning of *hemag* is offered by its use as a verb in an inscription on the propylon of Ptolemy III Euergetes at Karnak. In a scene, the king is represented offering a *wḏꜣ*-pectoral and a necklace, to which heart-shaped amulets are attached, to Montu-Ra, followed by Rayt-tawy.[502] In the title, one reads that the *wḏꜣ*-pectoral is offered 'to establish the heart' of the god (*r smn ỉb=f*) and that the 'the *nḏ-rꜣ*-amulet is for your *ỉb*-heart, the *ḥry-st*-amulet is for your *ḥꜣty*-heart, the *wḏꜣ*-pectoral is to adorn your throat (*r sẖkr ꜥm=f*), the electrum in its form (*ḏꜥm m sštꜣ=f*), the copper in its sacredness (*bḫt m ḏsr=f*), the precious minerals as a whole (*ꜥꜣt mỉ ḳd=sn*)...' And if Montu-Ra destroys the king's foes, the goddess Rayt-tawy 'envelops (or protects?) her Horus with the good things of her dignity' (*ḥmꜣg ḥr=s m ꜣḫw ḳfꜣt=s*).

The city of Coptos seems to have expressed, at least at first glance, a different idea of the meaning of the *hemag*. In the geographical list relative to the fifth Upper Egyptian

496 *Edfu* IV 271, 1-2 = Zecchi 1996, 45-47 doc. 38. The sentence ends with the expression *ḥꜣ m ỉwn* (or *ỉmn*) *n ḳꜣꜣ* (?), which could be translated as 'around by the colour of...' or 'around the skin of...'. See also Leitz 2012, 77.

497 Daumas 1980, 109-118; Derchain 1990, 219-242.

498 *Dendera* X 287, 3-4.

499 *Dendera* V 83, 2 = Zecchi 1996, 51 doc. 41. See also *Dendera* X 401, 12.

500 The epithets *nfr ḥr ḳꜣ ḫbswt* are bestowed on Osiris above all at Dendera (*LD* IV, 53b; *Dendera* I 134, 6; 135, 17; II 158, 4 and 14; IX 86,4; 117, 3-4; X 250, 9; 275, 11). In a few examples, they are connected with electrum and lapis-lazuli: *nfr ḥr ḳꜣ ḫbswt ḏꜥm ḫsbḏ tp*, 'beautiful of face, long of beard in electrum, and the head in lapis-lazuli' (*Dendera* IV 92, 12; 120, 10; 148, 7; 172, 10-11) or *nfr ḥr ḳꜣ ḫbswt ḏꜥm ḫsbḏ ỉnm*, 'beautiful of face, long of beard in electrum, and the skin in lapis-lazuli' (*Dendera* I 166, 16). See also *Edfu* I 149, 8-9, where Osiris is *nfr ḥr ḳꜣ ḫbswt ḫsbḏ tp km sšd ḫsbḏ tp*. On the epithet *ḳꜣ ḫbswt*, see also Leitz 2002, VII, 167.

501 *Dendera* X 271, 2-4.

502 *Urk.* VIII, 16; Aufrère 2000, 396-398.

province of the temple of Edfu, the main local god is addressed as: 'You are black of limbs, anointed of skin, your secret form is in the house of *hemag*' (*ntk km ꜥwt mrḥ inm irw=f štꜣ m ḥwt-ḥmꜣg*).[503] Even more interesting is the version in the temple of Opet at Karnak, where instead of the house of *hemag*, the god himself is quoted: 'I bring to you Coptos (*gbtyw*) with costly stones (*ꜥꜣt*)... You are black of limbs, anointed of flesh in your name of Osiris Hemag' (*ntk km ꜥwt mrḥ ḥꜥw m rn=k n wsir ḥmꜣg*).[504] In the temple of Dendera, the geographical text of Coptos connects Osiris Hemag with the local god Min: 'The son of Ra... comes to you, Osiris, Min in the *hemag*, the bull high raised of arm in the Coptite province (*wsir mnw m ḥmꜣg kꜣ fꜣi ꜥ m nṯrwy*)... He brings you Coptos with venerable costly stones and the Coptite province with its marvellous things (*in=f n=k gbtyw ẖr ꜥꜣwt špswt nṯrwy ẖr biꜣw=f*)...'.[505]

The reason for this tradition concerning the *hemag* in the fifth Upper Egyptian province is probably due to the fact that the local Osiris is occasionally placed in relation to a black resin named *mnn*, used in mummification.[506] In a significant passage of the embalming ritual, Osiris, 'foremost of the house of gold' (*ḫnty ḥwt-nbw*), is said to come from Coptos in order to bring 'the efflux (*rḏw*) coming out of his body, the *mnn* coming out of his limbs' and the 'divine stone (*ꜥꜣt-nṯr*) from the province of Bat, as he does for Min himself'.[507] According to the recipe engraved on the temple of Edfu for making the *ꜥꜣt-nṯr*, this was a substance purposely prepared by the priest of Min for the limbs of Min-Amun,[508] or, according to a variant,[509] to be given to Min, Osiris and Isis: 'the recipe of making the divine stone by the *sematy*-priest for the divine limbs of Min-Amun (*tp-rd n smꜣ tꜣ ꜥꜣt-nṯr in smꜣty r ḥꜥw nṯr mnw imn*) and all the images of wood and stone (*sšpw nb m ḫt inr*)'.[510] Many products are involved in the preparation of the *ꜥꜣt-nṯr*: first of all, an ointment made from ten *deben* of *mnn* and one *hin* of *ti-shepes* oil from the Bread of John tree is needed.[511] Then, all the necessary ingredients, which must be finely crushed (*nḏ snꜥꜥ*) and ground up through an Upper Egyptian sieve (*nkr m ḏꜥr šmꜥ*),[512] are added day after day, alternating days of cooking with days when they are left to rest, until on the nineteenth day 'two *kites* of all the real stones (*ḳdt 2 m ꜥꜣt nbt m mꜣꜥt*)', 'gold (*nbw*), silver (*ḥḏ*), real lapis-lazuli (*ḫsbḏ m mꜣꜥt*), real red jasper (*ḫnmt n mꜣꜥt*), real feldspar (*nšmt n mꜣꜥt*), real turquoise (*mfkꜣt n mꜣꜥt*), real faience (*ṯḥnt n mꜣꜥt*), and real carnelian (*ḥrst n mꜣꜥt*)'[513] are eventually included. On the twenty-first day, when the final product reached the right consistence, it was applied to the 'limbs of the god with a spatula' (*ḥꜥw-nṯr m isp*).[514] The 'divine stone' (*ꜥꜣt-nṯr*) was presumably laid upon the bandages of the mummy or upon a statue[515] and,

503 *Edfu* V 110, 8-9. The temple of Medamud (*Médamoud* 157) has the variant 'you are black of limbs, anointed of skin, your secret relic is in the temple of *hemag*' (*ntk km ꜥwt mrḥ inm spy=k štꜣ m ḥwt-ḥmꜣg*).

504 *Opet*, 278.

505 *Dendera* X 324, 8-10; Leitz 2012, 75.

506 Harris 1961, 173; Aufrère 1984, 1-4; Wilson 1997, 430-431.

507 Sauneron 1952, VII 6, 8. See also the passages IV 3, 6 and IX 7, 22.

508 *Edfu* II 214, 7-215, 2. See also Montet 1950, 20-23; Kurth 1994, 115-116; Leitz 2012, 78.

509 *Edfu* VI 165, 8-166, 4, in a scene *ḥnk ꜥꜣt-nṯr*, 'presenting the divine stone'(*Edfu* VI 165, 2-166, 10).

510 *Edfu* II 214, 7-8.

511 *Edfu* II 214, 9 (*sgnn n tišps n nḏm hn wꜥ mnnn dbn 10*); VI 165, 8 (*tišps nḏm hn wꜥ mnnn dbn 10*).

512 *Edfu* II 214, 9-10; VI 165, 8-9.

513 *Edfu* II 215, 4-5; VI 165, 15-16.

514 *Edfu* II 215, 9; VI 165, 18. For the word *isp*, see Wilson 1997, 111.

515 On the 'divine stone', see also: Sauneron 1962, 38-39; Aufrère 1982-1983, 16-17; Aufrère 1991, 329-342; Wilson 1997, 139.

when hardened, might appropriately be called 'stone' (*ꜥ3t*), even though its name might very well derive from the numerous minerals amongst its components.

The connections between the gold house, the *ꜥ3t-nṯr,* and the term *hemag* are strongly corroborated by another text from the temple of Dendera. In the third western Osirian chapel a scene[516] shows Osiris, as a mummy with an erect phallus and wearing the white crown on a lion-bier, and Anubis, standing in the act of touching the breast of the god and with the epithet '*ỉmy-wt*, who presides over the god's hall (*ḫnty sḥ-nṯr*), who wraps his father Osiris in the *wabet* (*nw ỉt=f wsỉr m wꜥbt*), who clothes his body with his wrappings (*ḥts ḏt=f m mnḫt=f*)'. Osiris is said to be 'foremost of the West (*ḫnty ỉmntt*), great god foremost of the house of the interment of Osiris (*nṯr ꜥ3 ḫnty pr-ḳrs-wsỉr*)' – that is Dendera – 'the venerable mummy who is on his bed (*sꜥḥ šps ḥry-nmit=f*), the burial of whose image started (*š3ꜥ.tw sm3-t3 n snn=f*), the secret form of the one who is on his bed in the house of gold (*sšt3 št3 ḥry-nmit=f ḫnty ḥwt-nbw*), whose corpse is embalmed with the work of the embalmers (*sdwḥ ḫ3t=f m k3t wt*)'. At the head and the foot of the couch are two kneeling images of the goddess Shentyt, one with the epithet 'foremost of the *hemaket* (*ḥm3kt*)'.[517] These are followed by a row of five deities: Iunmutef, a bull-headed Shesmu, Heka, Iremawa and Maaitef. Iremawa (*ỉr-m-ꜥw3*)[518] is 'the great god in the house of gold (*nṯr ꜥ3 m ḥwt-nbw*), great of fear (*wr nrw*), provided with forms (*ꜥpr ỉrw*), efficient of hand carrying the vase in the *hemaket* on the day of the wrapping of Osiris (*3ḫ ḏrt ḥr ꜥ m-ḫnt ḥm3gt m hrw nw n wsỉr*)'.[519] The last epithet of the god suggests a manual creative skill in the preparation, within the house of *hemag*, of a product to be used during the mummification of Osiris. And indeed Iremawa says: 'Take for yourself the oils of the fir trees, which make beautiful your front, your body rejoices thanks to them (*mn n=k ḥ3tt nt ꜥšw ntt snfr ḥ3t=k ḥꜥ ḥꜥ=k ỉm=sn*)'. But it is the inscription that accompanies the figure of Shesmu, a deity in charge of the preparation of wine, oils and unguents, which is even more interesting. He is 'the great god in the workshop, the venerable power in the house of gold (*nṯr ꜥ3 m ỉs sḫm šps ḫnt ḥwt-nbw*), pure of arms and efficient of hand in his work (*wꜥb ꜥwy 3ḫ ḏrt m k3t=f*), the venerable distiller of the prince of the white crown (= Osiris) (*šps nwd n sr-ḥḏt*), excellent of fingers in making beautiful the divine stone on that beautiful day when (Osiris) receives his burial (*ỉḳr dbꜥw ḥr snfr ꜥ3t-nṯr m hrw pn nfr n šsp ḳrst=f*)' and, as such, Shesmu turns to Osiris, saying: 'Receive for yourself the divine stone with all its effluxes (*mn n=k ꜥ3t-nṯr m rḏww nbw*), you are enveloped with it (*ḥm3g.tw=k ỉm=s*), you are bright (*b3ḳ=k*), you have received the divine stone to cover your limbs (*šsp.n=k ꜥ3t-nṯr r swnḫ ꜥwt=k*)...'.[520]

The origin of the epithet *hemag* remains unknown. In this respect, however, the presence of a deity called *ḥm3gt(y)* in the list of Memphite gods on the south wall of the chapel of Ptah-Sokar in the temple of Sety I at Abydos might be significant. The list has been recently studied by Hanane Gaber, who has drawn a parallel between it and Chapters 141-142 of the Book of the Dead.[521] Gaber has pointed out that the recipient of

516 *Dendera* X 412, 5-414,11, pl. 247.
517 *Dendera* X 412, 9.
518 Leitz 2002, I, 444-445.
519 *Dendera* X 414, 3-4.
520 *Dendera* X 413, 11-14.
521 Gaber 2015, 245-255.

the list was surely Osiris and that it aimed at enhancing his rebirth, also expressed by the image of the god lying upon a bed with erect phallus as represented on the north wall of the chapel. Nothing can be said about the deity *ḥmꜣgt(y)*, except that he is associated with the expression *ḥꜣ ỉnb rsy*, 'behind the south wall'[522] and that his name, like those of many other deities of the list, ends with the determinative of the seated god wearing a tight-fitting skullcap, straight beard and necklace counterpoise, suggesting that he was an aspect of Ptah. The name *ḥmꜣgt(y)* might be regarded just as the most ancient attestation of the Osirian epithet. Nevertheless, considering the role of Ptah as divine craftsman and his own connection with the house of *hemag*,[523] the possibility cannot be ruled out that the name *ḥmꜣgt(y)* was a manifestation of Ptah or an independent deity linked to the mineral world, and that only later it was identified with Osiris.

However, on the basis of the documents, it is possible to maintain that the house of *hemag* was a complementary chamber of the house of gold, and that the term *hemag* denotes an adornment or envelopment, or the act of adorning or enveloping the statue or mummy of a god with amulets, pectorals, or with the 'divine stone' – which all have in common that they are created from precious and semi-precious materials. The intrinsic character of the *hemag*'s components – precious metals such as gold and silver, semi-precious metals such as copper, and gemstones – determines the proprieties of the *hemag* itself. Reliability, corrosion resistance, longevity, and also brightness and intensity of colour result in durability, incorruptibility, and splendour of the body of Osiris with his *hemag*, while the blackness of the 'divine stone' may be related to the ideas of renewal and regeneration. Osiris Hemag's body can potentially be surrounded by almost the entire variety of minerals and metals known at the time. Minerals and metals had a divine origin and nature,[524] and the bodies of the gods might be envisaged as – or embodied in – images of gold, silver, and precious stones. As divine emanations, they participated in the cycle of renewal and transformation of the cosmos, had a protective and invigorating power, and contributed to the return of life to Osiris and the Osirianized dead.[525]

Another crucial issue, connected with Osiris Hemag's identity, concerns his iconographic variants. The most ancient known image of an Osiris explicitly named Hemag goes back to the Third Intermediate Period. On the front side of a block-statue dated to a period from the 22nd to the 25th Dynasty and found in the Karnak Cachette (Cairo JE 36997bis),[526] the owner *ꜣImn-ms*, who was *hem-netjer* priest of Amun and Osiris, is represented standing and performing the censing (*ỉr snṯr*) in front of Osiris. The god is portrayed as seated on a throne placed on a *mꜣꜥ*-base, wearing *atef* crown and collar, his body wrapped in a garment, with prominent elbows and hands crossed on the chest holding flail and *heqa*-sceptre. Between the two figures, there is an offering-table with a

522 According to Kitchen 1993, 98, fig. 6, who has suggested a theoretical reconstruction of the sanctuaries of Ptah and Sokar at Memphis on the basis of the Abydos list, the expression might be a reference to the location of the deity and his chapel in the precinct of Sokar at Memphis.

523 For example, the above-mentioned statuette in faience (Gubel 1991, 225-226). The 'overseer of the craftsmen' Basa had, among others, the titles of '*hem-netjer*-priest of Ptah and Sekhmet dwelling at Dendera and *hem-netjer*-priest of Osiris Hemag'. See also *Dendera* V 83.

524 For minerals and metals, see: Aufrère 1982-1983, 3-21; Aufrère 1991, 311-314, 413-431; Aufrère 1993, 7-24; Aufrère 1997, 113-144; Aufrère 1999, 357-371.

525 Daumas 1956, 1-17; Aufrère 1982-1983, 20-21; Beaud 1990, 59-61; Aufrère 1991, 341-345, 389-392, 801-804.

526 Brandl 2008, 178-179, pls. 112-113, 161d (22nd-25th Dynasty); Jansen-Winkeln 2009, 511 (25th Dynasty).

Fig. IV.1. Cairo JE 36997bis, block-statue of Amunmes with depiction of Osiris Hemag (Karnak Cachette Database – Fonds B.V. Bothmer, CLES, © Brooklyn Museum, CLES – IFAO).

lotus flower and two *hes*-vases. Above the god, his name and epithets are given: 'Osiris Hemag, the great god, lord of the sky' (*wsỉr ḥ3mꜥg3 nṯr ꜥ3 nb pt*). The whole scene is surmounted by an elongated hieroglyph of the sky (Fig. IV.1). It is perhaps worth noticing that the only other example of Osiris Hemag as 'lord of the sky' is on a contemporary coffin (22nd-25th Dynasty) from the necropolis of el-Lahun.[527]

Another image of Osiris Hemag survives, from the breast upwards, in a block from the lustration room of the main mosque of Sa el-Hagar, which might be dated to the Saite period. He is non-mummiform, wears a tripartite wig, and holds a *was*-staff, while the inscription connects him with Sais: 'Osiris Hemag, the great god, foremost of the *hut-bit*' (*wsỉr ḥm3g nṯr ꜥ3 ḫnty ḥwt-bỉt*) (Fig. IV.2).[528] A similar iconography was adopted in the 30th Dynasty in the temple at Behbeit el-Hagar, where the god is usually depicted

527 Zecchi 1996, 9.

528 Zecchi 1996, 12 doc. 7; Wilson 1998, 4, pl. I.4; Leclère 2003, 34: Wilson 2006, 219-220, pl. 31e; Jansen-Winkeln 2014, 759. Unfortunately, the cartouche of the king is illegible. The block was transferred to the SCA Office in 1998 (register no. 985).

Fig. IV.2. Sa el-Hagar, SCA reg. no. 985, block with depiction of Osiris Hemag. Photograph by Penelope Wilson.

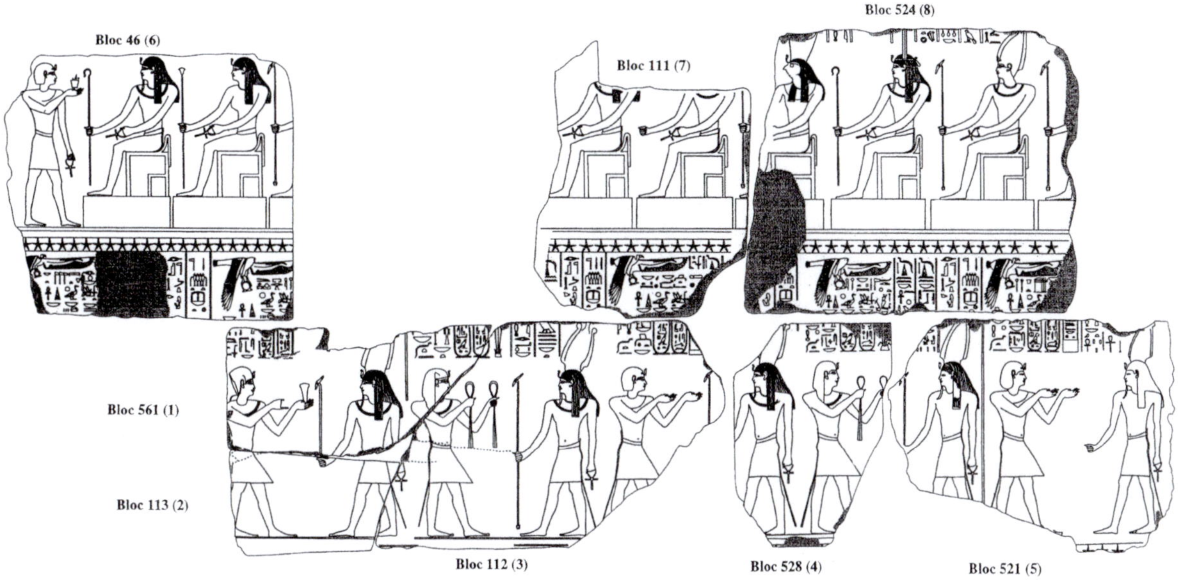

Fig. IV.3. Behbeit el-Hagar, temple walls depicting Osiris Hemag. Reproduced from Favard-Meeks 2003, 103, fig. 5.

striding, wearing a *shendyt* and a tripartite wig surmounted by the *atef*-crown, and holding a *was*-staff and an *ankh*-sign (Fig. IV.3).[529] In the same dynasty, on the stela of the priest Naes son of Hetepimen found at Saqqara,[530] we find a Tanite version of this Osirian form among a group of nine gods of Tanis: Amun-Ra, Mut, Khonsu-Neferhotep, Horus of Mesen, Henut-wat, Montu-Ra, Min-Ra, Osiris Hemag, and Khonsu the child.

529 Favard-Meeks 2003, 103. See also Favard-Meeks 2009, 137-138.
530 Louvre C 318: Yoyotte 1987, 196-197; Guermeur 2005, 285-287.

Fig. IV.4. Hibis temple, double representation of Osiris Hemag. Reproduced from Davies 1953, pl. 3.

Osiris Hemag, named the 'lord of the great city' (*nb nỉwt wrt*),[531] is represented standing and mummiform, wearing the *atef*-crown, and holding a composite *ankh-was-djed*-staff.

However, it is in the 27th Dynasty that we encounter a new kind of iconography for Osiris Hemag. In the third register of the north wall of the sanctuary in the temple of Hibis in el-Kharga Oasis, the god is depicted twice among deities which seem to be representative of the first Lower Egyptian province.[532] In both examples, he is lying within a sarcophagus surmounted by two eyes and a row of stars, and on a bier embellished with the feet and the head of a lion, with a downward tail; the bier is kept off the register line by small supports beneath the lion's legs. The first Osiris Hemag is said to be 'in Tjepehet-djat' (*wsỉr ḥmꜣḳ r tpḥt-ḏꜣt*), 'the cavern of djat'; he is nude, wears a beard and a tripartite wig, and his legs look as if he is walking. His right arm is bent towards the forehead, the other hand towards his erect phallus, while Isis, in the guise of a hawk, hovers above the god's member. The second one is named 'Osiris Hemag in *hut-ka*' (*wsỉr ḥmꜣḳ m ḥwt-kꜣ*) and differs from the first one because of his shorter beard and because the left hand is at his side (Fig. IV.4).

The two Osiris figures are followed by 'Amun-Ptah of Tjepehet-djat' (*ỉmn-ptḥ n tpḥt-ḏꜣt*) as a mummified ram on an oval containing a mummiform figure, and by 'Tatenen lord of Tjepehet-djat' (*tꜣ-tnn nb tpḥt-ḏꜣt*), represented as a standing dwarf.[533] Neither Tjepehet-djat nor the *hut-ka* is associated with Osiris Hemag anywhere else.[534] The fact that the god appears under nearly identical iconographies suggests that

531 On *niwt wrt*, see Zivie-Coche 2004, 111-112.

532 Davies 1953, pl. 3, III; Cruz-Uribe 1988, 12; Sternberg-el Hotabi 1994, 254; Zecchi 1996, 21-22 (doc. 12), 74-75, fig. 1.

533 In the magical papyrus Leiden I 383, col. 11, 7 (3rd century AD), one reads: 'I am the noble dwarf who is in Tepehet[-djat]', *ink pw nm šps nt m tpḥt*[*-ḏꜣt*]': Griffith/Thompson 1904, 82-83. Yet to my knowledge there is no other example of Amun-Ptah associated with the Tjepehet-djat. However, the epithet 'he whose name is hidden in the Tjepehet-djat' (*imn rn=f m tpḥt-ḏꜣt*) is shared both by Amun-Ra (*Dendera* II 125, 18-126, 1) and Ptah-Tatenen (*Urkunden* VIII, 196). For Tatenen and the Tjepehet-djat, see also *Edfu* I 329, 13-330, 1; *Dendera* XIII 60, 4-5; Leitz 2014, 179-180.

534 For other associations between Tjepehet-djat and Osiris or Osiris-Sokar, see the 'Ritual of Embalming': Sauneron 1952, 3, 20-3, 21; 5, 15.

the two toponyms shared similar ideas on the nature of this Osirian form. A place-name Tjepehet-djat, translated by Borghouts as the 'Blocked Cavern', is attested in Hermopolis[535] and Armant,[536] but the most famous one was in Memphis. Its exact nature is uncertain. Although it could be associated with many gods, Borghouts has shown that the toponym was likely connected with the *shetyt* and that it could be regarded as a place for Ptah and his craftsmen, and above all as a tomb or cenotaph for this god or Osiris.[537] Since the term rarely occurs before the Graeco-Roman Period, the examples in the Hibis temple are particularly interesting, above all for their association with Osiris Hemag and the *hut-ka*. Considering that Ptah might be represented as a dwarf,[538] and that dwarfs were involved in the craft of goldworking,[539] the presence of Tatenen as a dwarf together with Osiris Hemag in the Tjepehet-djat might be a reference to the connections of this Osirian form with precious metals and costly stones. Moreover, it cannot be ruled out that in this context *hut-ka* might just be an abbreviation for Hut-ka-ptah, that is Memphis;[540] in this respect, it is worth mentioning that, in a geographical list of the temple of Edfu, Tjepehet-djat is said to be 'in Hut-ka-ptah' (*tpḥt-ḏꜣt ḫnt ḥwt-kꜣ-ptḥ*),[541] and that at Dendera the goddess Hathor may be called 'the very great in Tjepehet-djat, noble and powerful, mistress of Hut-ka-ptah' (*wrt ꜥꜣt m tpḥt-ḏꜣt špst wrt ḫnwt ḥwt-kꜣ-ptḥ*).[542] However, *hut-ka* usually denotes a cenotaph for a king, or more generally a funerary chapel, but it may also be a place for the celebration of funerary rituals associated with the tomb of a god.[543] In this context, the two toponyms, therefore, might be not only theologically, but also physically linked, since they might refer to two different sections of Osiris Hemag's grave at Memphis – that is the funerary chapel for the rituals on behalf of the god (*ḥwt-kꜣ*), and the tomb itself (*tpḥt-ḏꜣt*) where the god's body was supposed to rest and revive.

The lying position of the god on a lion bier, the nakedness, the striding legs, and the erect phallus are characteristic attributes of Osiris Hemag also at Dendera. In the upper register of the south wall of the chapel of Sokar, Osiris Hemag, 'the great god who resides at Dendera' (*wsỉr ḥmꜣk nṯr ꜥꜣ ḥry-ib ỉwnt*), is represented in a scene for the offering of cloth (*mnḫt*) with Neper, Sokar-Osiris, Tefnet, Isis, and Nephthys. The text underlines the high status of this Osirian form, a deity who governs everything – the sky, the earth, the world of the dead, kings, men, and gods – and whose word cannot remain unheeded; he is 'the eldest son of Geb (*sꜣ wr tpy n gb*), king in the sky (*nswt m ryt*),[544] ruler of the stars (*ḥkꜣ*

535 Borghouts 1971, 20.

536 The god Montu could be called 'he whose name is hidden in the Tjepehet-djat in Armant' (*imn rn=f m tpḥt-ḏꜣt m iwnw šmꜥ*): Mond/Myers 1940, pl. 90, 3.

537 Borghouts 1971, 194-198. See also Smith 1985, 107-108; Smith 1993, 77; Wilson 1996, 1162-1163; Stadler 2003, 76; Smith 2005, 126; Leitz 2014, 179-180, 182-183.

538 Sandman-Holmberg 1946, 182-185; Dasen 1993, 91-92.

539 Montet 1952, 1-11.

540 See Cruz-Uribe 1988, 12.

541 *Edfu* I 329, 13-14.

542 *Dendera* III 134, 5.

543 On *ḥwt-kꜣ* see Régen 2006, 266; Pasquali 2008, 364-366 (with bibliography). In the territory of Memphis, at Ra-setjau, there was a *ḥwt-kꜣ* of Sokar (Pasquali 2008, 365 n. 47).

544 This is the only example of this epitet: Leitz 2002, IV, 338.

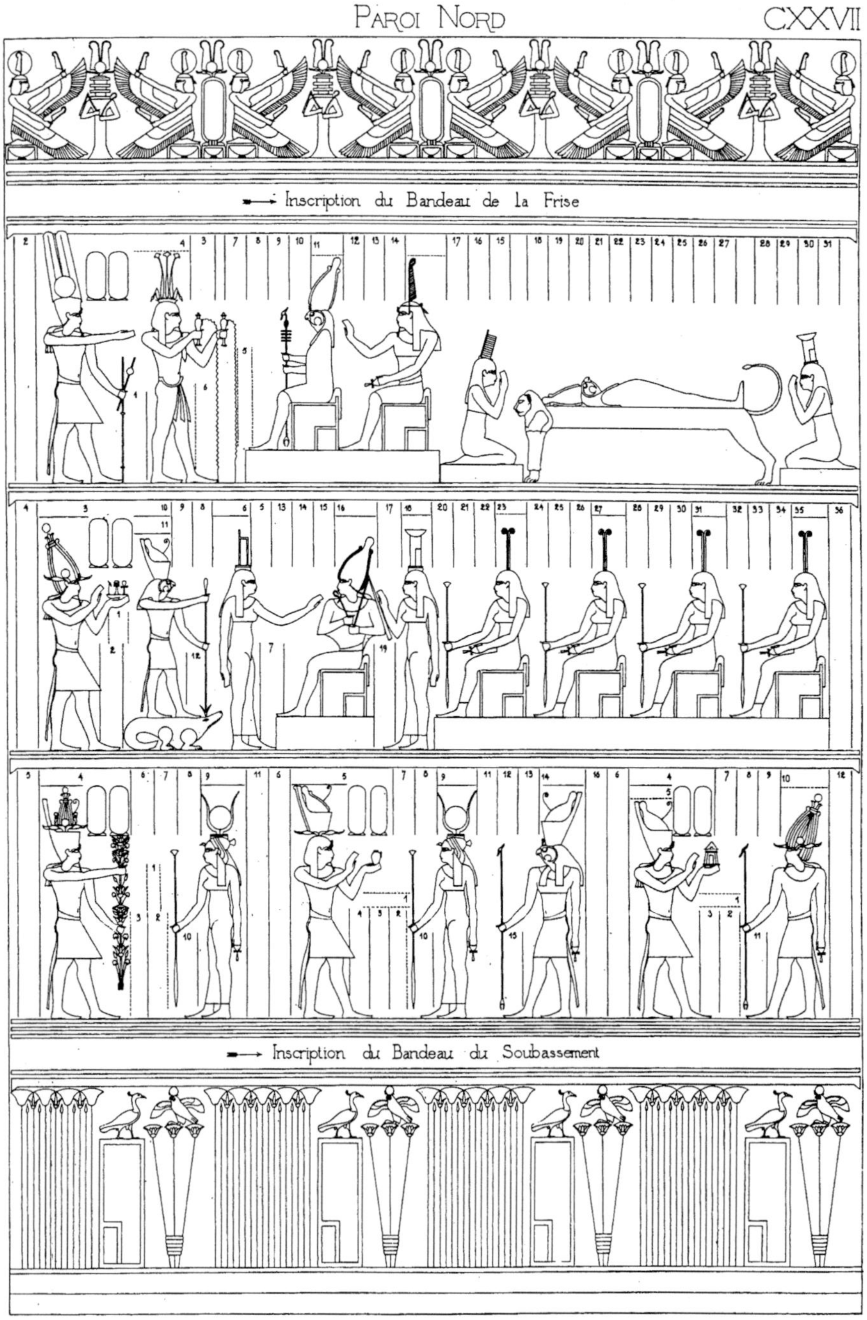

Fig. IV.5. Dendera, Hathor temple, chapel of Sokar, north wall. Reproduced after *Dendera* II, pl. CXXVII.

ḫꜣbꜣsw),[545] great sovereign in the realm of the dead (*ỉty ꜥꜣ m ỉgrt*)[546]... king of the kings of Upper Egypt (*nsw n nsww*),[547] king of the kings of Lower Egypt (*bỉty n bỉtyw*)[548] – they come

545 Osiris bears this epithet only in the Graeco-Roman Period: *Edfu* I 317, 3; 383, 8; 490, 1; *Dendera Mammisis* 126, 10.

546 This epithet and its variants (*ỉty ỉgrt, ỉty m ỉgrt, ỉty ꜥꜣ m ꜥt ỉgrt, ỉty ꜥꜣ m spꜣt ỉgrt*) are typical of Osiris: Leitz 2002, I, 591-593.

547 With the exception of this example, this epithet is ascribed to Osiris only in the New Kingdom: Chapter 185 of the Book of the Dead (Budge 1913, 36); tomb of Amunemhotep (TT 41: Assmann 1991, 22, 137, 196); Cairo JE 32020 (Rammant-Peeters 1983, 151, pl. 12.34).

548 No other example of this epithet is known for Osiris.

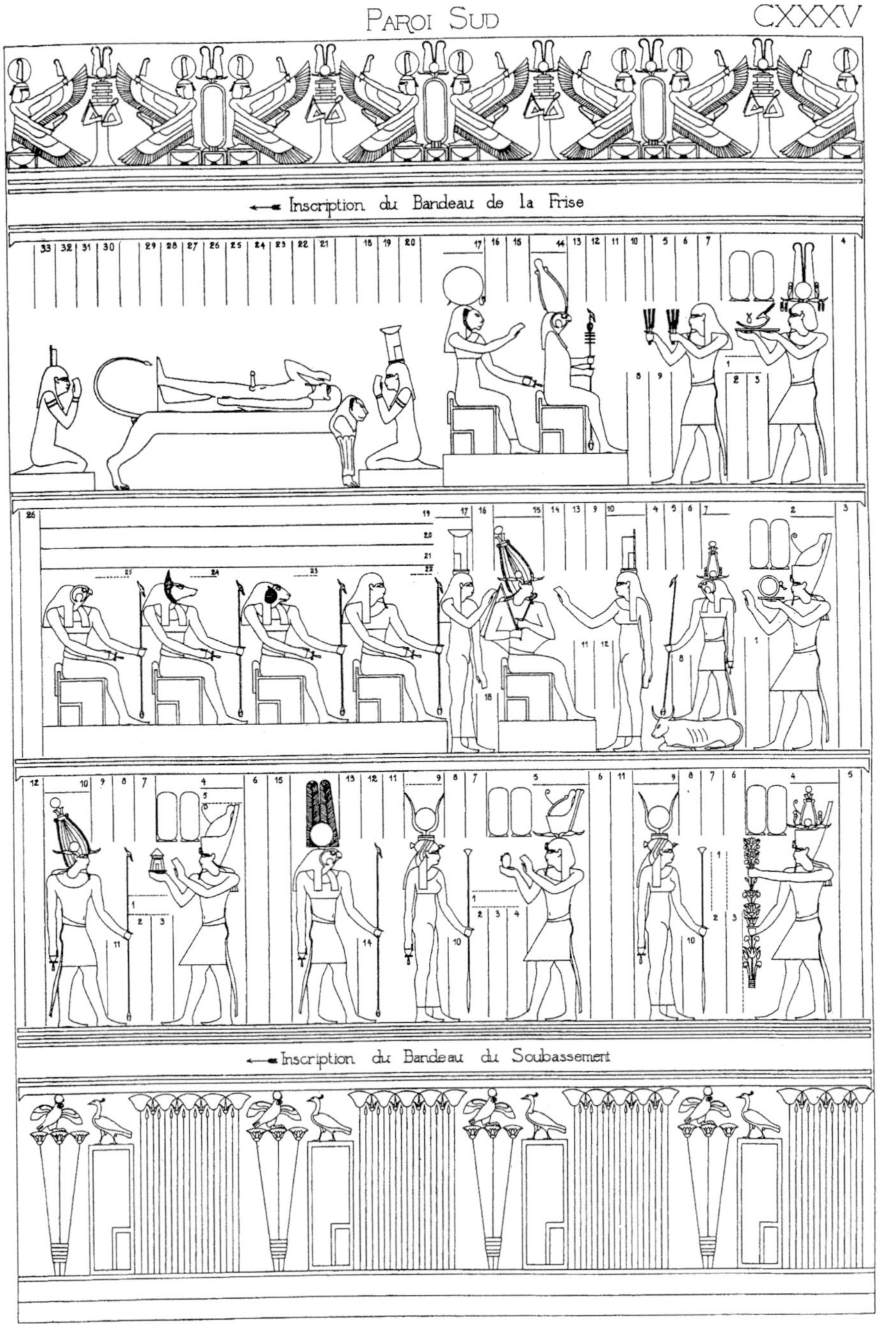

Fig. IV.6. Dendera, Hathor temple, chapel of Sokar, south wall. Reproduced after *Dendera* II, pl. CXXXV.

to him bowing (*ii=sn n=f m ksw*) – chief of the necropolis with what is in it (*ḥry-tp imnt ẖr imyt=s*),[549] who gives orders to gods and men (*wḏ mdw n nṯrw rmṯ*)'.[550] The scene has a parallel in the upper register of the north wall, where the king performs the Opening of the Mouth (*ir wp-r3*) for Sokar-Osiris, who is represented twice. The king, who is preceded

549 Besides this example, the epithet *ḥry-tp imnt*, attested only in the Graeco-Roman Period, is ascribed to Sokar-Osiris (*Edfu* V 67, 7) and Anubis (*Edfu* IV 276, 9; *Dendera* XI 177, 8).

550 No other example of this epithet is known. For similar epithets referring to Osiris' authority to command, see for example: *wḏ mdw n nṯrw sp3wt* (*Dendera* X 71, 13); *wḏ mdw n imyw t3 pn* (*Deir Chelouit* III, 150); *wḏ mdw m itrty* (*Dendera* II 82, 8). Also Sokar-Osiris can give orders to gods, *wḏ mdw n nṯrw* (Petrie 1908, pl. 28).

by the god Hapi, is in front of a falcon-headed Sokar-Osiris – seated on a throne, with the *atef*-crown and holding a *was-ankh-djed*-staff with both his hands – , Shu, and Sokar-Osiris, portrayed as a falcon-headed mummy with the *atef*-crown and lying on a lion bier between Isis and Nephthys (Fig. IV.5).[551] Unlike Sokar-Osiris, Osiris Hemag is represented naked and ithyphallic, with striding legs and with his right arm towards his face, while his left arm is down at his side; the god is flanked by Isis and Nephthys,[552] kneeling and weeping (Fig. IV.6).

A very similar image appears on the west wall of the third eastern Osirian chapel; the difference is in the standing position of Isis and Nephthys, in the presence of four canopic jars under the lion bier, and in the fact that in this case Osiris Hemag is a northern deity, being 'Osiris Hemag in Behbeit el-Hagar' (*wsỉr ḥmꜣg m ḥbỉt*) (Fig. IV.7).[553] A more elaborate scene, with the king kneeling and offering incense, is depicted on the west wall of the third western Osirian chapel (Fig. IV.8).[554] The title of the scene makes reference to purifications for the god during his 'beautiful feast' when he receives his 'burial'.[555] Osiris Hemag's lion couch is flanked by Shentyt and Merkhetes, kneeling and making lamentation; once again, the god is nude, ithyphallic, with striding legs, wearing a tripartite wig, and with his right arm towards his face and the left arm at his side. When compared with the previous examples, other deities are in attendance. Anubis is at the foot of the bier; it is interesting that, when this god attends this kind of scenes, he holds a small vase or a piece of cloth, or touches Osiris' chest. In this case, instead, he raises both his arms, as if he is adoring him, but perhaps also to indicate that the process of embalming is actually concluded and that he has just to assist in the awakening of the deceased god. Behind him is Hor-sa-aset, the heir, with one arm raised and the other down at his side. As in the temple of Hibis, Isis flies above in the guise of a hawk called 'the falcon of gold' (*bik n nbw*), extending the *ankh*-sign toward the erect member of the god. This is the only example in a temple showing Anubis in a scene with the striding Osiris. As suggested by Lanny Bell,[556] the protruding legs of the resurrecting Osiris seem to interfere with the presence of Anubis, who is generally depicted with a mummified Osiris.[557] The legend accompanying Osiris Hemag, 'the great god in the *shetyt*' (*wsỉr ḥmꜣk nṯr ꜥꜣ m štyt*), is particularly interesting since it gives information on the kind of materials from which the image of the god, and his bier too, were created: 'wood, gold and divine stone, length 1 cubit, bier in gold' (*ẖt nbw ꜥꜣt-nṯr ḳꜣ mḥ 1 nmỉt m nbw*).

There seems to be a sort of contradiction between the meaning of the epithet *hemag* and the iconography adopted for Osiris Hemag. According to the available sources, this Osirian form never shows itself dressed up in his *hemag*. With the exceptions of the statue from the Karnak Cachette, the stela Louvre C 318, and one very late example in the temple of Philae, where the god is represented as a lion-headed mummy with an

---

551 *Dendera* II 151, 5-152, 10, pl. CXXVII.

552 *Dendera* II 160, 17-161, 2, pls. CXXXV, CXLII.

553 *Dendera* X 233, 13, pls. 107, 136.

554 *Dendera* X 423, 9-10, pls. 257, 280.

555 The title of the scene is: *mn n=k snṯr swꜥb=f snn=k mnwr twr=f ḏt=k snṯr sꜣḳ-ḏt=f ḥr wꜥb ꜥt=k m ḥb=k nfr n šsp ḳrst=k*.

556 Bell 2008, 27.

557 *Dendera* X, pls. 243, 247, 255. In another example, with a Sokar-Osiris with moving legs, Anubis is represented at the head of the bier (*Dendera* X, pl. 108).

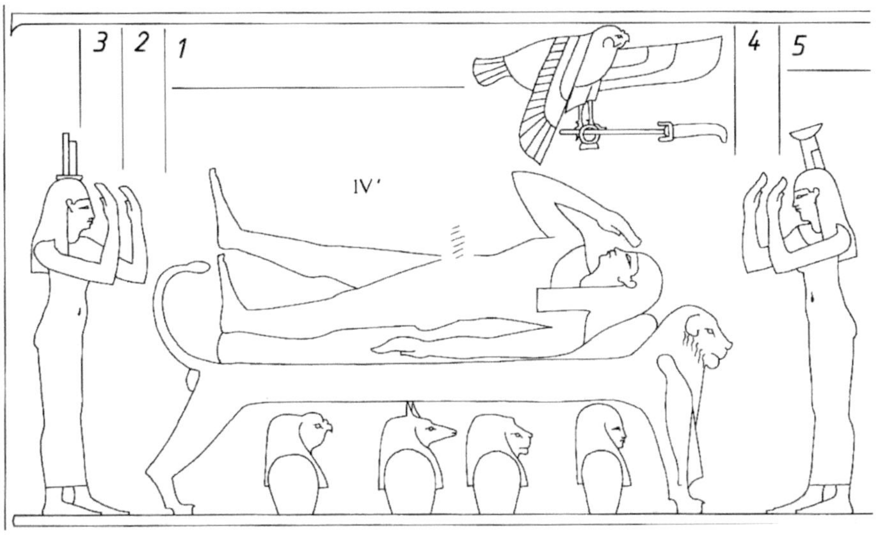

Fig. IV.7. Dendera, Hathor temple, third eastern Osiris chapel, detail of west wall. Reproduced after *Dendera* X, pl. 107.

Fig. IV.8. Dendera, Hathor temple, third western Osiris chapel, west wall. Reproduced after *Dendera* X, pl. 239.

uraeus on the forehead,[558] he is not even depicted mummiform. Rather, he is preferably represented as a living deity, standing and wearing a *shendyt* kilt and a tripartite wig or crowns (like in Sais and in the temple of Behbeit el-Hagar), or, more characteristically (like in the temples of Hibis and Dendera), lying on a lion bier, naked and ithyphallic and with striding legs. But this discrepancy is only apparent. The *hemag* is a medium through which Osiris can reach a new phase. Thanks to the mineral nature of his envelopment,

558 Bénédite 1893, 126, pl. XLI; Zecchi 1996, 55-56 (doc. 48), 76, fig. 3. The lion-headed Osiris Hemag appears inside the room of Osiris of the local temple in a row of gods associated with Khnum 'who shapes on the potter's wheel, who fashions the divine flesh of Osiris, foremost of the house of gold, in life' (*ḳd ḥr nḥp ḳd ḥʿw nṯr n wsir ḫnty ḥwt-nbw m ʿnḫ*). For the lion-headed Osiris, see also Fakhry 1942, 144; Cauville 1983, 116 n. 261.

Osiris turns into an awakening and living god. After his embalming has been completed and his body has been wrapped with precious or semi-precious materials, the god becomes Hemag, but, when represented as such, he prefers to abandon his special clothing in order to appear as an active deity. The iconography does not describe the *hemag* itself, but the effects that it produces.

Indeed, the fact that Osiris Hemag is represented nude, ithyphallic, with striding legs and with the right arm bent towards his face, as if he were stretching and wiping the sleep from his eyes, suggests that he is waking up.[559] His figure is not constrained by bandages or wrappings. There is no trace of the mummification process in these images: his nude body is whole and intact. And there is nothing in Osiris Hemag of the immobility of many other Osiris figures represented on lion biers.[560] The reawakening of the god manifests itself to the viewer in the most dynamic way. The movement of the legs seems to indicate that he is experiencing the last phase of the resurrection process, as if he were ready to leave his bier and inaugurate a new life. Moreover, his physique is sexually imposing. Thanks to the regenerating power of the minerals and metals that compose the *hemag*, he is not only a reawakening god but also an engenderer, ready to generate his heir. The strong sexual connotations of the *hemag* are also expressed in the texts. In a scene of the temple of Edfu, the king, who is called 'the ruler as child, who makes great the dignity of the foremost of the house of *hemag*' (*ḥḳꜣ m nḫn swr ḳfꜣw n ḫnty ḥwt-ḥmꜣgt*), offers lettuce (*ḥnk ꜥbw*),[561] a symbol of sexual power, to Min 'Atum in his *hemag*'. The god, 'male of the gods' (*ṯꜣy nṯrw*)[562] and 'fierce one, who repels with his member' (*ḥsꜣ-šnꜥ ỉrf m nfrw=f*),[563] gives the donor, whose 'heart is warm for pleasure', his 'phallus to copulate with women' (*dỉ=ỉ n=k npḥ ḥr smꜣ nfrwt srf ỉb=k ḥr nḏmnḏm*).[564] Moreover, in a scene for the offering of clothing (*ḥnk mnḫt*) at Dendera[565] to Sokar-Osiris, Tefnet, Nephthys, Isis, and Osiris Hemag, the latter bears the epithets of 'ejaculating ram' (*bꜣ sty*) and 'who presides over women' (*ḥry nfrwt*).[566] The fact that both these epithets are usually bestowed to male gods with a vivid sexual character – such as Ba-neb-djedet, Amun-Ra, Min, Sobek, Khnum, and Heryshef – and that they are not otherwise ascribed to Osiris,[567] enhance their sexual meaning in this specific context, aiming at stressing the forceful and potentially procreative function of this Osirian form. And indeed, the goddess Isis, who is represented kneeling at the foot of the lion bier on which Osiris Hemag lies, is the 'god's mother and main royal wife

---

559 Zecchi 1996, 79; Bell 2008, 28.

560 For Osirian 'bed scenes' in temples, see: a) Abydos, temple of Sety I: Otto 1967, pls. 16-17 (north and south walls, chapel of Ptah-Sokar); Calverley 1938, pl. 62 (east and west walls of room 11, Osiris complex); b) Qurna, temple of Sety I: Otto 1968, 100-105; c) Hibis temple: Davies 1953, pls. 3, 4, 20; d) Karnak, temple of Opet: Varille 1956, 110-111, pl. XIX; e) Dendera, chapel of Sokar: *Dendera* II, pls. CXXVII, CXXXIV-CXXXV, CXLII; Osiris chapels: *Dendera* X, pls. 87-90, 105-108, 116-119, 134-137, 236-239, 247, 252-256, 258-264, 268, 271, 275-282; f) Philae, roof temple: Bénédite 1893, pls. XXXV, XL.

561 *Edfu* IV 270, 6-271, 4 = Zecchi 1996, 45-47 doc. 38.

562 Leitz 2002, VII, 452-453.

563 There is no other example of this epithet: Leitz 2002, V, 480.

564 *Edfu* IV 271, 1-3.

565 *Dendera* II 159, 17-161, 4, pls. CXXXV, CXLII = Zecchi 1996, 47-51 doc. 40.

566 *Dendera* II 160, 17.

567 See Leitz 2002, II, 697 and V, 364-365. The only exception is in a scene for the offering of the lotus (*sḫm nḫb*) in the temple of Dendera, where *bꜣ sty* is one of the epithets of Osiris-Neferhotep: Ryhiner 1986, 98.

of Wennefer, true of voice' (*mwt nṯr ḥmt nsw tpyt n wnn-nfr mꜣʿ-ḫrw*)[568] and, after the offspring of the couple is assured, can be called the 'one who places his (= Osiris') son on his throne forever, rising as ruler of eternity' (*rdi sꜣ=f ḥr nst=f nḥḥ ʿḥʿ m ḥkꜣ n ḏt*).[569]

From the first attestations of Osiris Hemag in the 10th-11th centuries BC to his first depictions on a lion bier in the 27th Dynasty, a few centuries have passed. In this span of time, the sources are not helpful in catching a glimpse of this Osirian form. Though the first documents on Osiris Hemag can help us in reconstructing the diffusion of his cult and the associations with other deities, they offer almost nothing for the understanding of his identity. Still, the iconography involving the lion bier seems to mark his first true emergence.

A damaged image of Osiris with a tripartite wig, with a kestrel flying above his member, and with one arm raised towards his face and the other at his side, but with legs together, is already portrayed in the Osiris complex of the temple of Sety I at Abydos;[570] a variant, featuring Sokar-Osiris 'who is in his barque' with one hand grasping his phallus and with one arm towards his face, is present on the north wall of the Ptah-Sokar chapel of the same temple.[571] As far as I know, the variant with striding legs appears for the first time a little later, on the internal lid of a Theban wooden coffin of a private individual dating to the 21st Dynasty (Fig. IV.9).[572] Here, above Osiris, there is a large *rs*-hieroglyph ('awake'), a reference to the god's resurrection; the deity is depicted in a very similar way to the image of Osiris Hemag in the third western Osirian chapel of Dendera, with also the detail of Isis in the guise of a kestrel flying above the bier and extending the *ankh*-sign held in its claws towards the erect member of the god. It is interesting to note that, at Dendera, the only other Osiris to be depicted with striding legs, nude, ithyphallic, and with one arm raised towards his face, is the Osiris of Abydos.[573]

According to the available data, at the very beginning of his existence Osiris Hemag was perhaps portrayed only in a rather stereotyped way, as the statue of *ỉmn-ms* from the Karnak Cachette seems to suggest (Fig. IV.1). However, since he had to embody ideas connected with his divine rebirth after the experience of death, one rather chose for him, at least from the 27th Dynasty, an Osirian image whose attitude and details would perfectly describe that special moment of his life. Indeed, since a more appropriate iconography was available, one did not fail to adopt it for Osiris Hemag, but when and where this happened is hard to tell. In this respect, it is worth noticing that the iconography of the god as lying on a bier, nude, ithyphallic, with striding legs, one arm raised towards to his face with the other at his side, was certainly well known during the reign of Amasis, since it is used to depict Osiris 'the ram of Djedet, who presides over the house of gold' in one of the chapels at Ayn el-Muftella in Bahariya Oasis.[574]

Therefore, the question arises whether the reign of Amasis was decisive in the construction of a new definition and representation of Osiris Hemag and in a reformulation of the god's nature. This seems highly possible, considering that the Saite

568 Leitz 2002, V, 135.
569 *Dendera* II 161, 3-4.
570 Calverley 1938, pl. 62.
571 Otto 1967, pl. 16.
572 Sarcophagus of Imeneminet, Louvre E 5534: Ziegler 1990, 73; Luft 1998, 429.
573 *Dendera* X, pl. 187.
574 Room 121 (second chapel of Djedkhonsuiuefankh, reign of Amasis): Labrique 2007, 1062, 1065.

Fig. IV.9. Louvre E 5534 (© Musée du Louvre / Christian Décamps).

kings undoubtedly contributed in a dynamic and intense way to the diffusion of the god's worship, even before king Nekhthorheb of the 30th Dynasty included a cult in Osiris Hemag's honour in the temple of Behbeit el-Hagar.[575] The god is depicted in the above-mentioned block (which was part of a temple wall) from Sais (Fig. IV.2), where the god was probably venerated. And the first king to link his name to that of the god was, as far as we know, Nekau II, who chose for himself the epithet of 'beloved of Osiris Hemag', preserved on two quartzite blocks discovered by Labib Habachi in Rosetta and el-Nahhariya,[576] and believed to have been transferred from Sa el-Hagar to these localities in the Middle Ages to be reused in buildings of this period.[577] The decision that Osiris Hemag could be imagined as an ithyphallic god lying naked on a lion-bier might have a Memphite origin. As we have seen, this iconography was certainly used in the temple of Hibis to describe a Memphite Osiris Hemag and subsequently was adopted in the south of Egypt, at Dendera. It is interesting that this iconography was rejected or regarded as uninteresting for Osiris Hemag in the very north of the country, at Sais and Behbeit el-Hagar, where he is a living and striding god (Fig. IV.3), or at Tanis, with its mummiform version of the god – though this provisional conclusion may be mistaken due to a lack of documents. As we shall see, the Leiden naos, discovered at Kom el-Ahmar, not far away from Memphis, seems to present Osiris Hemag as a god associated with the territories of Memphis and Heliopolis; this peculiar monument might be an expression of the Memphite tradition concerning Osiris Hemag and evidence for a new approach to and interest in this peculiar Osirian form during the reign of Amasis.

Osiris Hemag is not represented on the outer walls of the naos, even though images of Osiris above a bier are not unusual on naoi of the Late Period. On a naos of Apries, a prone figure upon a bier is named '[...] Osiris-Mert(y)', with crowns represented beneath the bed;[578] on the naos of Amasis from Athribis, 'Osiris in Sekhet-hotep' is depicted seated upon a bier; in a similar pose is also a god, presumably another Osirian form, called 'the one on his bed' (*ḥry nmỉt=f*), flanked by two goddesses also on the bier.[579] On the naos of Saft el-Henna of Nekhtnebef, there is a prone figure, whose face is not preserved, with Nephthys and Isis, and crowns represented above the god's body,[580] while on a naos of Nekhthorheb from Bubastis, the god, not accompanied by an inscription, is depicted with a frontal view of the face, wearing a tripartite wig, arms crossed over his chest, hovering upon a lion bier, and flanked by two mourning goddesses kneeling on pedestals.[581] However, on the Leiden naos Osiris Hemag is not physically absent, since the monument hosted, with all probability, a statue of the god. That Osiris Hemag is not portrayed on the naos, which certainly is one of the most significant tributes he ever received by a reigning king, is even more striking in consideration of the presence of images of three other Osirian forms in the upper register of the left outer wall. Osiris Hemag does not appear on the outer walls because its decoration does not intend to

575 Favard-Meeks 1991; Zecchi 1996, 94-96; Favard-Meeks 2003, 97-108, pls. 25-29.
576 Habachi 1943, 378-380, 396 = Zecchi 1996, 10-11 docs. 5 and 6.
577 Habachi 1943, 403-406. See also Wilson 2006, 311-315.
578 Cairo CG 70008: Roeder 1914, pl. 9.
579 Habachi 1982, 230, pls. XLIIIA and XLIVA.
580 Cairo CG 70021: Roeder 1914, pl. 32.
581 Fragment British Museum EA 1079: Spencer 2006, pl. 13.

Fig. IV.10. Sais, naos of Amasis for Osiris. Photograph by Penelope Wilson.

describe its contents. Neither are the available surfaces of the outer walls used to display rituals carried out by the pious king on behalf of the recipient of the naos or of gods connected to him. Rather, they are functional to its divine owner; they narrate something on the functions of the monument itself and of the theology related to the deity inside. At the same time, the unusual architectural shape of the internal niche was very likely created on the basis of the shape of the statue it had to contain. The cavity is wider than it is deep or high and it seems to be ideal to receive a statue of a lying god.[582]

In the Saite period, during the reigns of Apries and Amasis, a small number of naoi was produced, all dedicated to Osirian forms, with pyramidal roofs and cavities similar to that of the Leiden naos; the first one is a naos for Osiris-Andjety of Busiris dedicated by Apries,[583] then Amasis also made a similar naos for Osiris of the 'Mansion of Sekhmet' at Sais (Fig. IV.10). On these two monuments, however, the inscriptions are limited to lintel and jambs. The Leiden naos may have hosted an image very similar to the gneiss statue from Horbeit in the Cairo Museum (CG 38424),[584] which has been dated to the 26th Dynasty and represents the god in the process of resurrection, wrapped as a mummy lying prone on a plinth with both his arms at his sides, with his face slightly

582 Yoyotte 2001, 75.

583 Cairo JE 43281: Perdu 1990, pl. 2b; Jansen-Winkeln 2014, 359-360.

584 Daressy 1906, 114, pl. XXIII; Hornung/Bryan 2002, 176-177; Goddio/Fabre 2015, 126, 134-137. See also Spencer 2006, 21. On the production of statues of Osiris in stone in the Late Period, see Coulon 2016.

upraised, and with a headdress made of gold and electrum consisting of two ostrich plumes and a solar disk on ram's horns. Its length of 55.5 cm is fairly close to the ancient Egyptian cubit of about 52.5 cm, which also corresponds to the length of the image in 'wood, gold, and divine stone' of Osiris Hemag as indicated in the temple of Dendera.[585] A statue of this kind, or more likely rather resembling the iconography of the god as shown on the walls of the temples of Hibis and Dendera, could easily have been laid down in the cavity of the naos, with its width of 99 cm. However, in this case, the Leiden naos would be the first monument to conceive Osiris Hemag as a lying deity, rather than standing or seated on a throne.[586]

The Leiden naos of Amasis is extraordinary not only for its design, but also because it perhaps heralded a new direction in the way of regarding this Osirian form. The naos was conceived and then created in a way that had to reflect the full nature of Osiris Hemag. Even without looking at the statue of the elusive Osiris Hemag inside it, both its shape and decoration evoke a resurrecting god.

2. The dedicatory text

In at least three or four naoi, Amasis adopted a kind of decoration that is known for the first time in the reign of Apries,[587] consisting of rows of gods depicted in two or more registers on the outer walls. This kind of decoration seems to disappear from the naoi of the 27th, 28th, and 29th Dynasties, to be reused during the 30th Dynasty. On some of his naoi – Leiden AM 107, Louvre D 29, and Cairo CG 70011 from Athribis – Amasis also added a dedicatory text running along the top of the outer walls. To these shrines one should also add the fragmentary block, found at Kom el-Ahmar and probably belonging to a naos of Amasis, with part of a dedicatory text to Hathor.[588] Dedicatory texts were already present on free-standing naoi at least as early as the 18th Dynasty,[589] as in the case of the ebony shrine for Amun from Deir el-Bahari (CG 70001a),[590] and continued to be used on monolithic naoi through the Third Intermediate Period – as in the naoi for Bastet of Osorkon II (CG 70006)[591] and for Osiris of Shabaka (CG 70007)[592] – and the Late Period – as in the little naos in red granite of Psamtek I (Cairo JE 47580)[593] – until the Roman age, as in the limestone naos of Domitian for the god Tutu (Cairo 2/2/21/14).[594] Nevertheless, the combination on the same monument of rows of deities with dedicatory texts seems to be an innovation of the reign of Amasis.

---

585 *Dendera* X 423, 9-10.

586 Nothing can at present be said of the images of Osiris Hemag in the tomb of Pediamenopet (TT 33), which remain unpublished.

587 Naos Cairo CG 70008 from el-Baqlieh (Roeder 1914, 29-36, pls. 9-11a; Zivie 1975, 104-112; Jansen-Winkeln 2014, 361-363); naos Brussels, Musées royaux d'Art et d'Histoire E 5818 (Speleers 1923, 88-89; Jansen-Winkeln 2014, 354-355). See also the two fragments in Cairo (22/11/55/1 and 30/5/24/5) with row of deities and which might be part of a naos: Spencer 2006, 20 and n. 6. For a discussion of naoi depicting rows of deities, see Spencer 2006, 19-30.

588 Rowland/Billing 2009, 7-8; Billing/Rowland 2015, 107.

589 See also a fragment with Senusret I's name, which might have been part of his naos and with the inscription *ir.n=f m mnw* [...]: Pillet 1923.

590 Roeder 1914, 3-5.

591 Roeder 1914, 25.

592 Roeder 1914, 25.

593 Gauthier 1923, 170-171. For the examples of the 30th Dynasty, see Spencer 2006, 64-65.

594 Rondot 1990, 306.

The dedicatory texts on the three naoi of Amasis follow a similar model. They are all to be read from the front towards the rear and start with the expression 'may live' (*ꜥnḫ*), followed by the complete titulary of the king, as in the naos Louvre D 29 dedicated to Osiris Merty, or by his Horus name (*ḥr smn mꜥꜣt*) and throne-name, as in the case of the Leiden naos for Osiris Hemag and in CG 70011 dedicated to Kem-wer. These are followed by the expression 'he has made as his monument for his father', *ỉr.n=f m mnw=f n ỉt=f*,[595] and name and titles of the beneficiary deity. The inscription on the fragment with Hathor's name fits with the gender of the beneficiary deity, featuring the variant [...] *mnw=f n mwt=f*. Then, some information on the typology of the monument and its material are given. In the latter fragment, the shrine is called a *pr-wr*, while the monument for Kem-wer is actually called *ḥḏ šps m bḫn*, 'an august shrine in *bekhen*-stone'.[596] Even though the term *ḥḏ šps*, written here with the sign of the mace inside a chapel,[597] may refer to the sanctuary, or a free-standing naos or portable chapel,[598] its use in a dedicatory text to denote a monolithic naos is unusual.[599]

On the other two naoi for Osiris, the term used to describe the monument is *kꜣr*, which, together with *sḥ-nṯr*, is the usual term to refer to free-standing naoi in their own inscriptions. While *sḥ-nṯr* might refer to different kinds of structures[600] – temporary booth made of light material, temple sanctuary, sacred barque shrine, individual rooms in the temple or the temple itself, portable shrine or naos – the term *kꜣr* has a more restricted range of meanings, denoting above all the portable shrine, the shrine of the sacred barque, or the temple's naos which kept the god's image.[601] Moreover, unlike *sḥ-nṯr*, which is already present in the dedicatory text of a naos of the 18th Dynasty,[602] the term *kꜣr* is not attested in this kind of inscriptions before the 26th Dynasty,[603] even though it already occurs in Egyptian texts of the Old Kingdom. It should be noted that in a few dedicatory texts – for example the naos CG 70021 of Nekhtnebef from Saft el-Henna,[604] the naos from Bubastis of Nekhthorheb dedicated to 'Khonsu-Horus, lord of joy, son of Bastet',[605] and the limestone naos in Cairo 2/2/21/14 of Domitian for the god Tutu[606]– the word for naos is simply written with the ideogram of the shrine's façade, and it remains therefore uncertain whether it should be read as *kꜣr*. However, when adopted for this specific purpose and in this specific context, it is not clear whether *sḥ-nṯr*, *kꜣr*, as well

595 On this formula, see Leahy 1987, 57-64; Castle 1993, 99-120.

596 For two other monolithic naoi said to be made in *bekhen*-stone, see Cairo CG 70019 in greywacke (?) dedicated by king Nekhtnebef to Min of Coptos (Roeder 1914, 25) and the naos from Kus by Ptolemy II Philadelphus for Horus son of Isis (*Urk.* II, 73-74). See also Varille 1934, 93-102.

597 Roeder 1914, pl. 88 (18).

598 *Wb.* III 209, 1-8; Wilson 1997, 696.

599 A mention of *ḥḏ šps* occurs also in the inscriptions of the statue of the high-ranking official Peftjawyneith, recording the works he did for Amasis at Abydos: Klotz 2010, 145-146 and n. 136.

600 Spencer 1984, 114-119; Wilson 1997, 890.

601 Spencer 1984, 125-130; Wilson 1997, 1082-1083.

602 See the naos CG 70001a: Roeder 1914, 3-5. For the following periods, see for example the naos Cairo CG 70007, dedicated by Shabaka to Osiris *ḫnty sḥ-nṯr* from Esna (Roeder 1914, 25), and the naos Cairo JE 47580 in red granite, dedicated by Psamtek I to Atum lord of Heliopolis (Gauthier 1923, 170-171).

603 See also the naos Cairo CG 70019 of Nekhtnebef to Min of Coptos (Roeder 1914, 25).

604 Roeder 1914, 79.

605 Rondot 1989, 251, pl. XXXIII.

606 Rondot 1990, 306-307.

as *ḥḏ šps*, can be regarded as synonyms, or whether they were distinguished to reveal something of the nature or physical appearance of the naoi.

In their dedicatory texts, both the Leiden naos and that in the Louvre offer a more detailed description of themselves. Not only do they specify their own typology (*k3r*), but what is also given is their dimension – though merely through a rather generic 'great' (*ꜥ3*) – and material (*m3ṯ*, 'granite'). *M3ṯ* is a rather common term for granite, both black and red.[607] According to the Egyptian texts, a *k3r*, although it could be made of wood, was usually made of stone, particularly of granite.[608] It is also worth noting that the two naoi of Amasis defined as *k3r* are both dedicated to an Osirian form. The use of the term *k3r* in these two shrines, rather than *sḥ-nṯr* or *ḥḏ šps*, as in CG 70011 for the god Kem-wer, might of course be casual or due to geographical reasons, both the monuments being from Kom el-Ahmar. Nonetheless, it should be noted that the shrines prepared for Osiris are usually designated as *k3r*. The connections between the god and this term are indeed not rare: they go back to the Middle Kingdom[609] and were carried on in the New Kingdom, when, for example in Ramses II's temple at Abydos, the king declares to have made 'as his monument for his father Osiris (*ir.n=f m mnw=f n it=f wsir*), who presides over the Westerners, lord of Abydos, the making for him of a shrine (*irt n=f k3r*) and a place of repose for the king of Upper and Lower Egypt, who follows Osiris in his temple of Millions of Years in Abydos'.[610] Moreover, starting from the Third Intermediate Period, the rare epithet *nb k3r*, 'lord of the shrine', can be bestowed on Osiris.[611] The connections between Osiris and the term *k3r* continued in the following period. The 'Book of Traversing Eternity' (I, 23-24)[612] mentions a 'secret shrine' (*k3r št3*) of Osiris, which, according to François-René Herbin, might denote the Osirian sanctuary in Busiris. It is therefore not surprising that Amasis chose this term in dedicatory texts on naoi purposely created for this deity.

A final sentence, which varies on each naos, concludes the dedicatory text. The naos CG 70011 for Kem-wer ends with the short phrase *ir=f* [*di ꜥnḫ*], just to emphasize the king's role as donor of the monument. On its side walls, the naos Louvre D 29 for Osiris-Merty presents a more interesting final phrase, which explains one of the purposes of the shrine, 'on which are placed the name of the gods who follow him. May he be given life!' (*wd rn n nṯrw imyw ḫt=f ḥr=f ir=f di ꜥnḫ*). The dedication on the rear wall specifies that Amasis 'made as his monument for the gods who are in the temple of Osiris Merty, so that their name is enduring forever. Hereby he acts, the one who has been given life and all the stability and dominion, all the health and joy of his heart on the seat of Horus, forever' (*ir.n=f m mnw=f n nṯrw imy ḥwt wsir mrty rwḏ rn=sn ḏt ir=f di ꜥnḫ ḏd w3s nb snb nb 3w ib=f ḥr st ḥr ḏt*). One of the main purposes of this naos was to record the names of those deities

---

607 Takàcs 2008, 114-115.

608 Spencer 1984, 127, 129. The naos (*k3r*) of Nekhthorheb at Edfu is made of 'black granite' (*m3t km*): *Edfu* I 10, 3. See also *Edfu* V 5, 3.

609 See the stela of Ikherneferet, who boasts to have fashioned, in Abydos, the gods who are in Osiris' following and 'to have made their *k3rw* anew': Sethe 1924, 71 (6).

610 KRI II, 544 (7).

611 Leitz 2002, III, 764. The first example of this epithet occurs in CT VI, 267t. For the god Osiris, see Budge 1912, pl. 50; Bénédite 1893, 126, 9.

612 Herbin 1994, 109. See also *Edfu* II 23 (112).

housed, as the text says, inside the temple of its beneficiary.[613] Moreover, the dedicatory text highlights the importance of the reward received by Amasis for his action, a reward consisting in all the means by which he is able to rule Egypt. But the naos of Leiden ends with a different and perhaps more effective sentence: *nn sp i͗rt mi͗tt ḏr-bꜣḥ*, 'never had the like been done before!' After having explained what and for whom he has acted, Amasis speaks with pride of having done something new for his father Osiris Hemag. The legitimacy of his rule derives not only from the fact that he has fulfilled his role as donor of a marvellous naos in granite, but also from the novelty of the monument itself.

3. Great gods, small gods: divine beings in action

3.1. Gods and demons

One of the distinguishing characteristics of the Leiden shrine is the presence, on all the outer walls, of different figures, which might be ascribed to distinctive categories of divine beings. Some of them – for example Horus, the three different Osiris figures, the goddesses Isis and Nephthys, Anubis and the couple Shu and Tefnet – are undoubtedly among the key divinities of the Egyptian pantheon. A few others might just simply be defined as 'minor deities', while others belong to a class of divine entities usually called 'genii' or 'demons', even though in the Egyptian language there is no word that can be literally translated as such.[614] Indeed, one of the main issues regarding their nature is if they can be regarded as ontologically differentiated from the other deities. In this respect it is interesting that, on the naos, the main Egyptian gods can occupy specific sections, such as the upper registers of the left and right walls, and can be physically distinguished, as for example being seated on a throne. On the other hand, Horus and Isis seem to be in harmony with all the other divine figures; on the front and in the lower register of the left wall, they mingle with other deities who carry out their ambivalent – both malevolent and benevolent – functions for Osiris Hemag. A difference in importance, diffusion of cult, iconography, and in the set of qualities that makes a god (*nṯr*) different from other gods (*nṯrw*) does not imply a difference on an ontological level. In this specific context, if a distinction exists, it lies in the function that these groups of gods are called to carry out, in their relation to Osiris Hemag, and in the ideas that they have to convey. Yet, it is precisely the class of the so-called 'demons' that makes the decoration of the naos unique.

3.2. Roof

Another interesting peculiarity of the naos is the identical decoration on the four faces of its pyramidal roof. On each side, the symmetrical scene shares a vertical column of hieroglyphs – *di͗ ꜥnḫ wꜣs nb ḏd nb ꜣwt-i͗b nb mi͗ rꜥ*, 'giving all the life and dominion, all the stability and all the joy, like Ra' – and is dominated by the *i͗my-wt* emblem, a headless animal skin hanging from a pole placed into a pot, and by Amasis' *serekh*, on

613 Spencer 2006, 21-22.

614 For a discussion of the nature and functions of the so-called Egyptian 'demons', see Te Velde 1975, 980-984; Meeks 2001, 375-378; Lucarelli 2006, 203-212; Szpakowska 2009, 799-805; Lucarelli 2010; Kousolis 2011; Lucarelli 2013, 99-105; and, above all, Lucarelli 2011.

which there is a hawk without crown. Behind the Horus name there is the inscription *nṯr nfr ḫnty pr ꜥꜣ ꜥnḫ ḏd mỉ rꜥ ḏt*, 'the beautiful god, who presides over the *per-aa*, living and stable like Ra, forever'. A similar decoration appears on the other naos from Kom el-Ahmar (Louvre D 29), likewise dedicated to an Osirian form. The first difference is the position of the scene, which in this case is not placed on the undecorated arched roof, but just on the lintel, above the niche. At the centre, the symmetrical scene has a vertical text, a shorter variant of the one on the Leiden shrine: *dỉ ꜥnḫ ḏd wꜣs mỉ rꜥ*; unlike the naos of Osiris Hemag, the *serekh* is surmounted by a hawk with the white crown on the right and with the red crown on the left, and is followed by the epithets *nṯr nfr nb tꜣwy*, 'the beautiful god, lord of the two lands', and the cartouche; then, there is the inscription *ḥr nfr ḫnty pr ꜥꜣ ꜥnḫ ḏd ꜣwt-ỉb=f ḥr st ḥr mỉ rꜥ ḏt*, 'the beautiful Horus, who presides over the *per-aa*, living and stable, may he be joyful on the throne of Horus, like Ra, forever'. But the most significant variation is that, instead of *ỉmy-wt*, in front of the royal *serekh* there are the goddesses Nephthys on the right and Isis on the left, represented standing with their hieroglyphic emblems on their heads and holding the *was*-staff in one hand and the *ankh* in the other.

The *ỉmy-wt* is a very ancient emblem, appearing for the first time on a vase from Hierakonpolis of Naqada II date and then on a few labels at the very beginning of the dynastic period from Abydos.[615] The emblem was involved in the coronation ceremonies, the *sed*-festival, the royal burial, and funerary practices.[616] It was also closely associated with Anubis and, particularly from the New Kingdom onwards, it occurs frequently in funerary contexts. Evidently, on the Leiden naos, the king preferred to show his close link with the *ỉmy-wt*, whose presence on a monument dedicated to Osiris is as appropriate as that of Isis and Nephthys. Not only the kind of decoration, but also its location on the roof are proof of a certain degree of originality on the part of the king. The pyramidal roof, which might also be evocative of a royal tomb, is not merely the apex of the monument under which Osiris Hemag reposes, but, thanks to the repetition of an identical decoration on its four sides, contributes to unravelling part of the function of the shrine and of its donor. Both Amasis and the *ỉmy-wt*, a funerary emblem but also a symbol of healing and rebirth,[617] cooperate in the safeguarding of Osiris Hemag. The link between the *ỉmy-wt* and the king is emphasised first of all by their proximity, but also by the presence of an *ankh*-sing looped around the head of a *was*-sceptre inserted in the pot and extending towards the beak of the hawk on the *serekh*. However, the striking juxtaposition of the king's name with the fetish *ỉmy-wt* on the naos might have more than just a funerary function. During the 1st Dynasty, and up to the 3rd Dynasty, the *ỉmy-wt* is prevalently represented next to the royal *serekh*,[618] and it should be noted that, according to the available sources, Amasis was the only king of the 26th Dynasty to have adopted such an ancient iconography.[619] By the Old Kingdom, if not earlier, the *ỉmy-wt* may indeed appear in scenes for the celebration of the *heb-sed*, as for instance in the blocks from the temple

---

615 DuQuesne 2005, 102, 106-108.
616 Köhler 1975; Köhler 1980; DuQuesne 2005, 102-105.
617 DuQuesne 2000, 53-60.
618 Logan 1990, 61-69; DuQuesne 2005, 106-108.
619 Köhler 1975.

of Niuserra, where the *ỉmy-wt* is paraded or placed before the king.[620] It is therefore possible that, also in this context, the old motif of the royal *serekh* in front of the *ỉmy-wt* emblem served to evoke the theme of the *sed*-festival. In this respect, it is also relevant that the *ỉmy-wt* is here a source of life and power for Amasis, who appropriately, to stress his legitimate rule, presents himself as the 'beautiful god, foremost of the great house' (*nṯr nfr ḫnty pr ꜥꜣ*).[621] Before being used by Amasis on the Louvre and Leiden naoi, the epithet *ḫnty pr ꜥꜣ* was adopted by Senusret I in a naos found south of the western obelisk of the seventh pylon at Karnak (Cairo JE 47276).[622] In the inscriptions on the left side of the front of the monument, the king is said to be 'beloved of Amun-Ra, lord of the thrones of the two lands, the beautiful Horus, foremost of the great house (*ḥr nfr ḫnty pr ꜥꜣ*)'. This royal epithet is another peculiar and original characteristic of the Leiden naos. It might refer to an actual royal building, perhaps at Memphis. But, at the same time, the use of the term *pr ꜥꜣ* to denote a royal residence, rather than the pharaoh himself,[623] seems a refined archaism, a sort of homage to more ancient traditions.

3.3. Front

Great attention was given to the decoration of the front of the naos, which, also in this case, presents strong original elements. This was the main view, very likely the first to be visible to those who approached the monument. The design on the lintel is not to be found on any other Egyptian monolithic naos. The centre is occupied by a structure surmounted by a frieze of uraei. Although nothing is represented inside, this should be taken as a representation of a shrine or burial place of Osiris. In this respect, it might be worth mentioning, for instance, the burial chamber of the tomb of Mutirdis (TT 410) of the beginning of the 26th Dynasty, which shares religious themes and ideas with the Leiden naos. Its decorations on the east, west and south walls, regarded by Jan Assmann as a unity,[624] show the regeneration of Osiris by Horus in the presence of thirty-six deities.[625] On the south wall, Osiris is represented lying prone – that is in a position similar to the one that he probably also had inside the naos – on a lion couch and inside a structure decorated by two lines of cobras rearing on top, which are said to exert an apotropaic function (*ỉꜥrwt stpwt sꜣ*).[626] On the Leiden naos, the image of the resting place of Osiris, whose statue was actually lying just below, has been featured as the focal point of the decoration of the front, attracting not only the two rows of gods represented on each of its sides, but presumably also those watching the monument.

Like many gods depicted on the other faces of the naos, the deities of the front have a strong funerary and apotropaic character. On each side of the structure with uraei, there is a group of two figures, consisting of Anubis lying on a shrine with a recumbent lion

620 Von Bissing/Kees 1923, pls. 4 no. 11a, 5 no. 12c, 10 no. 24, 12 no. 32, 13 no. 33a, 24 no. 72; Du Quesne 2005, 108. See also a block (Cairo CG 1747), perhaps a lintel of Pepy II from Saqqara, with two figures of the king inside a shrine seated back to back and wearing the red and white crowns. To the right, the *imy-wt* is placed between the king and the Wepwawet standard: DuQuesne 2005, 109.

621 Cf. Blöbaum 2006, 32.

622 Pillet 1923; Macadam 1946, 61, pl. 9.

623 Goelet 1982, 585; Jurman 2006, 19.

624 Assmann 1977, 14-15.

625 Assmann 1977, 91; Roberson 2013.

626 Roberson 2013, 62-63.

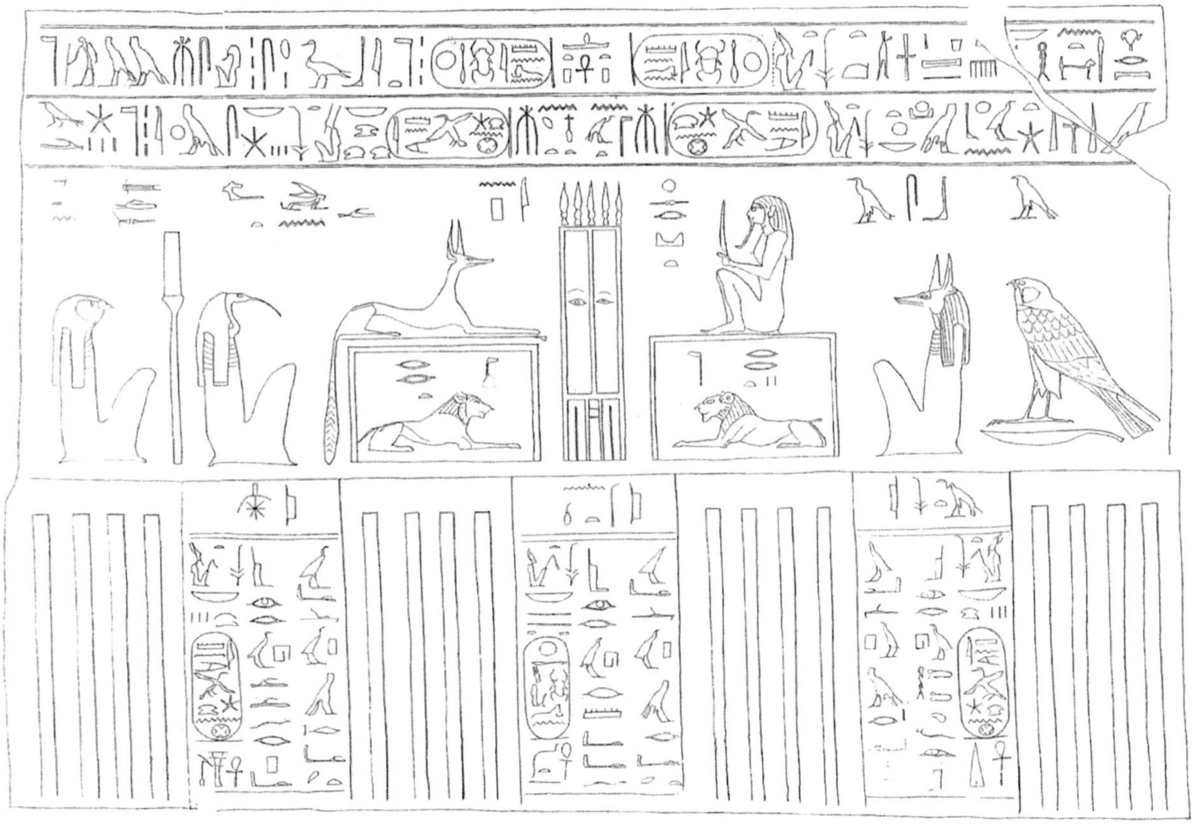

Fig. IV.11. Sarcophagus of Psusennes, detail. Reproduced after Montet 1951, pl. 88.

called *ỉwꜥ nṯr*, 'heir of the god', inside. A variant of this motif occurs on other monuments starting from the Third Intermediate Period. The most ancient example is to be found on the sarcophagus for Merenptah and later usurped by Psusennes I,[627] which shows, at the centre, a structure imitating a palace façade with two eyes inside and a frieze of *khekeru* at the top; on the left side there is Anubis on a shrine, but on the other side a deity called *ḫsr-ḏw*, 'He who repels evil', is represented squatting on the shrine and holding a knife (Fig. IV.11). In this case, the two lions inside the structure are called *rrt/rrty*, which might be a variant for the double lion *rwty*.[628]

A fragmentary stuccoed canvas pasted onto a papyrus of the 22nd Dynasty also shows the shrine with *ỉwꜥ nṯr* surmounted by Anubis.[629] A very similar variant of this decoration is present on the coffin of the 'overseer of the army' (*ỉmy-r mšꜥ*) Iahmes,[630] son of king Amasis and therefore chronologically closer to the Leiden naos. On the left side of the central structure with a *khekeru* frieze, there is a shrine with Anubis on top and the lion *ỉwꜥ nṯr* inside; on the right side, the deity *ḫsr-ḏw* has been replaced by *sḥr-ḏw*, 'He who drives away evil', whose name and iconography, however, indicate an identical function. In the burial chamber of Mutirdis there is a image of *sḥr-ḏw* on a shrine carrying the lion *ỉwꜥ nṯr*,[631] while in the sarcophagi from the Graeco-Roman Period of Ankhhapi son

627 Montet 1951, pl. 88.
628 Mysliwiec 1978a, 16.
629 Nelson 1986, fig. 3.
630 Hermitage 766: Leclant 1962, 111.
631 Assmann 1977, pl. 45.

of Tefnakht (CG 29303)[632] and Djedhor son of Iahmes (CG 29304)[633] there is a combination of Anubis and *sḥr-ḏw* on shrines with *iwꜤ nṯr*, facing each other but without any central architectonic structure.

The association of the shrine with Anubis and *iwꜤ nṯr* is probably a variant of a more ancient group composed of two superimposed shrines, of which the upper one has Anubis on top and the other a recumbent lion. This group has been analysed by Wolfgang Waitkus, who has noted that it appears near the entrance doors of the burial chamber of the tomb of Ramses III (KV 11) and of other tombs of the 19th-20th Dynasties in the Valley of the Queens.[634] The position of the shrines with Anubis and the lions on the Leiden naos is consistent with the position of similar shrines in the New Kingdom tombs. Clearly, they had to protect the entrance giving access to the deceased, in this case Osiris Hemag. Moreover, in the Leiden naos the motif of the shrines with Anubis and *sḥr-ḏw* and the lion *iwꜤ nṯr* has been newly interpreted in order to create a perfect visual symmetry. Here, both the shrines are indeed surmounted by Anubis, while the guardian-deity *sḥr-ḏw* has been removed from the top of the right shrine to be represented squatting immediately behind it. The fact that the sarcophagi of the Graeco-Roman Period show the more common variant, with both Anubis and *sḥr-ḏw* on shrines, confirms the originality and compositional refinement of the Leiden naos.

Other aspects should also be noted. Firstly, that *sḥr-ḏw* is the only deity represented on the lintel of the naos who also appears in the New Kingdom, being depicted in a pair of Theban tombs.[635] Secondly, that apart from Horus and Isis, the other deities appear for the first time in the sarcophagus usurped by Psusennes I (*sekhem*-sceptre and *mꜣꜣ-it=f* in the form of a falcon) or in the 26th Dynasty (*dwn-ḥr*, as a standing ibis-headed god), and are not to be seen on any other naos. Thirdly, that the sequence on the left of the central shrine with uraei – consisting of Anubis, *iwꜤ nṯr*, *dwn-ḥr*, the *sekhem*-sceptre, and Horus – also occurs on the coffin of Iahmes, son of king Amasis, though with a few differences in the iconography of Horus and *dwn-ḥr*. Nevertheless, in a more ancient document, the sarcophagus usurped by Psusennes I, the left sequence is composed of Anubis, *iwꜤ nṯr*, a squatting ibis-headed god called *dwn-ḥꜣt* ('Extended of brow'),[636] the *sekhem*-sceptre, and a squatting falcon-headed deity whose name seems to be read [...]*ds=sn*.[637] Even though *dwn-ḥꜣt* is usually depicted as a ram-headed or crocodile-headed deity, the similarity of his name with that of *dwn-ḥr* may have caused confusion; but it is also possible that the latter, unknown before the Saitic period, has simply to be regarded as a variant of the former, who is also present, among other sources, in the Coffin Texts,[638] in Chapter 144 of the Book of the Dead,[639] on the sarcophagus of Iahmes son of Amasis,[640]

632 Maspero 1908-1914, 101, pl. 11.
633 Maspero 1908-1914, 144-145.
634 Group M5 of Waitkus 1987, 59-60. See also Willems 1996, 145-147.
635 TT 58 and TT 158: Assmann 1983, 80, 6 and 156, 14.
636 Grimm 1979; Leitz 2002, VII, 526-527.
637 Montet 1961, pl. 88.
638 CT VII, 416a; 418a.
639 Lepsius 1842, pl. 60; Munro 1995, 200; Lapp 1997, 26.
640 Leclant 1962, fig. 17.

in the tomb of Mutirdis,[641] and on the Ptolemaic sarcophagus of Khaf.[642] The presence of Isis among the gods in the right sequence, just before the falcon *mꜢꜢ-it=f*, is peculiar, but can be justified by the dedication of the monument to an Osirian form and by the fact that it was used for balancing the presence of Horus in the left sequence.

The fact that the deities represented on the lintel appear almost exclusively on sarcophagi or inside tombs, and on no other naos, says something about the nature of the monument, which was evidently regarded as a burial place, a container for a divine body. Moreover, Isis, Horus, and all the apotropaic deities on the lintel look both towards the central shrine with uraei and to the cavity, preventing passage to any opponent of Osiris Hemag.

The decoration on the doorjambs has a strong resemblance to that on the naos Louvre D 29, which, like the Leiden naos, comes from Kom el-Ahmar and was dedicated by Amasis to an Osirian form. On both naoi, the doorjambs have been divided in registers surmounted by the *pt*-sign, each with standing deities looking towards the cavity which contained a statue of Osiris. The main difference consists in the number of registers, three on the Louvre naos and only two on the Leiden one. The couple of gods of the upper registers of the Louvre naos, with Hor-nedj-it-ef and Anubis on the left, and Thoth 'lord of Hermopolis' and Hor-khenty-irty on the right, have not been copied in the Leiden naos, since they were not in line with the religious themes of the monument. The decoration of the second register of the Louvre naos corresponds to the top register of the Leiden one and has Imsety and Duamutef on the left and, on the right, Hapy and Qebehsenuef. As far as I know, the Four Sons of Horus do not appear on the front of any other Egyptian naos. Their presence strongly stresses the funerary connotations of the recipient of these two monuments. In particular, it should perhaps be compared to a group of scenes such as for example the one in the burial chamber of Mutirdis, where they lead the rows of gods, one on the right and one on the left, assisting the rebirth of Osiris, who is represented lying prone on a lion couch inside a structure with uraei.[643]

In the lower register of the front of the Louvre naos, on the left are a goddess called Nekhbet and Hapi, the personification of the Nile inundation, and on the right Mwyt and Wadj-wer, the 'Great-green', all slightly leaning forward and holding a tray with a *was*-sign between two *hes*-vases. The Leiden naos omits the two male figures, showing only the first deity of each couple, that is Nekhbet and Mwyt, in the same attitude as on the Louvre shrine. Before the 26th Dynasty, these two goddesses are otherwise known only in sources from the Old Kingdom.[644] In Spell 205 of the Pyramid Texts, dealing with the food supplies for the king, one reads: 'the king has copulated (*nk*) with Mwyt... the king has united with (*dmḏ*) Nekhbet, he has copulated (*nk*) with the beautiful one (*nfrt*), for his fear is the lack of food...' In the pyramid temple of Sahura the two deities, depicted decisively fatter than those on the two naoi, lean forward and carry their offering tables.[645] Since there is no

641 Assmann 1977, 94, pl. 45.

642 Daressy 1917, 8.

643 Assmann 1977, 91, 94, pl. 45.

644 See Baines 1973, 9-14; Baines 1983, 110-111, 147. For a possible example of Mwyt in the Graeco-Roman Period, see a papyrus from Tebtynis: Osing/Rosati 1988, 163, pl. 20, 4, 31.

645 Borchardt 1913, pls. 29-30. For another example of Mwyt in the sun temple of Niuserra, see von Bissing 1956, pl. 5.

example for this pair of goddesses between the Old Kingdom and the reign of Amasis, John Baines has suggested that their figures on the naoi were copied from the relief of Sahura.[646] The re-adoption of these two figures on the Saite naos undoubtedly had to evoke an abundance of products and fertility, both very appropriate themes on a monument dedicated to Osiris. But, together with the epithet *ḫnty pr-ʿ3* and the representation of the *imy-wt* emblem in front of the king's *serekh*, their presence is certainly a further archaism in the decoration of the naos.[647] The reintroduction of old deities, epithets and motifs, drawn from various sources of different periods, was undoubtedly a deliberate choice by the commissioner and/or the Saite artisans involved in the creation of the shrine, but how all these themes were intended to function in relation to the king and the beneficiary of the monument – a rather 'new' Osirian form – remains a matter of speculation. It is perhaps possible to assume that, rather than for an actual ritual purpose, these themes and motifs were adjusted into a new cultural and Osirian context in order to attach the agency and legitimacy of older traditions to the naos.

3.4. Left wall

On the left side wall, the theme of the upper register is predominantly Osirian. It is notable that this is the only register where not all the deities are depicted looking towards the entrance of the naos. The five gods here represented create a homogeneous group: Isis and Nephthys, recognizable thanks to their hieroglyphic headdresses, stand with their arms hanging down their bodies, and turn their backs to the door, in order to look directly at three different forms of Osiris. To each form, identified by its name written in front of it, corresponds a different iconography. The first one, Osiris *nb ḏdw*, is represented as a human mummy, standing on a low base and without a crown. The second one, Osiris *itf3 wr*, is shown seated on a throne, wearing the white crown and a collar, and with the body wrapped in a garment but with prominent elbows and arms folded at different levels on the chest, the hands holding a flail and *heqa*-sceptre. The third Osiris, *nb r3-sṯ3w*, is equally seated, but wears a tightly fitting shroud and collar, with his hands in front of him holding a long *heqa*-sceptre and flail. His crown is damaged, but it seems to be the white or *atef* crown.

The first and the third of these Osiris figures are directly connected with place-names, while the second one is more enigmatic. The expression *itf3 wr*, the 'Great Saw' or 'Great Knife', appears for the first time in Spell 366 of the Pyramid Texts: 'O Osiris N, arise and lift yourself up! Your mother Nut has borne you, Geb has wiped your mouth for you, the Great Ennead protects you and has put your enemy under you. Lift up one who is greater than you – they say to him (= enemy) – in your (= beneficiary) name of (house of) the great saw (*f3 n=k wr ir=k i.n=sn ir=f m rn=k n itf3 wr*). Lift up one who is greater than you – they say – in your name of Ta-wer...'[648] *'Itf3 wr* is here written with the determinative of the primitive shrine, and therefore seems to denote a sanctuary, probably already connected

646 Baines 1973, 9-14.

647 For a discussion on archaism in ancient Egypt, see Brunner 1970; Brunner 1975; Schenkel 1977; Der Manuelian 1983; Der Manuelian 1994; Jansen-Winkeln 1998; Kahl 1999; Baines/Riggs 2001; Josephson 2001; Davis 2003; Morkot 2003; Jurman 2010.

648 On this passage, see Kuhlmann 1996, 133; Hays 2012, 128, 376.

with the god Osiris, who is however not directly mentioned. After this example, *ỉtfꜣ wr* occurs twice, clearly as the name of a deity, on a wooden coffin from Deir el-Bersha dating to the second millennium BC; on this monument the owner, Neferi, is said to be 'venerable before *ỉtfꜣ wr*', written without determinative, while in an offering formula to Thoth and the Great Ennead, he is granted 'glory' (*ꜣḫ*) on the land before *ỉtfꜣ wr*', written with the determinative of the seated god.[649] But it was starting from the New Kingdom that the name of *ỉtfꜣ wr* spread. Besides appearing as an independent name – as in the Tenth Hour of the Amduat[650] and in the tomb of Senenmut[651] – *ỉtfꜣ wr* started being directly associated with the name of Osiris and, in this form, he could be mentioned or depicted both on private and official monuments. In the Book of the Day, *ỉtfꜣ wr*, represented as a mummy, is clearly a figure of Osiris, since he appears in a row of gods together with Osiris Wennefer and *Ỉty*.[652] Osiris *ỉtfꜣ wr* occurs inside the Theban tomb of Kheruef (TT 192)[653] of the 18th Dynasty, where the owner is described as 'venerable before Osiris *ỉtfꜣ wr*'. But the god generally appears together with other Osirian forms, as in the tomb of Nakhtmin (TT 87)[654] of the reign of Thutmose III, in a tomb of the time of Ramses II at Saqqara,[655] and in Chapter 141/142 of the Book of the Dead on papyri,[656] on the right panel of the interior of the first shrine and on the left panel of the interior of the second shrine of Tutankhamun,[657] in the Osireion at Abydos,[658] as well as on a coffin of Ahaneferamun called Pakhar (Cairo JE 29670) of the 21st Dynasty.[659] Moreover, at least three private stelae from the Delta[660] and a model of a small limestone sarcophagus[661] present offering formulas dedicated to this Osirian form.

A statue base of the reign of Amenhotep III, most likely coming from his mortuary temple at Kom el-Heitan, is the first example of a direct and personal link between a king and the god; it is also the only surviving evidence, although very fragmentary, for the

---

649 Lacau 1906, 11, 17. *Ỉtfꜣ wr* might also occur in CT III, 393e, but the reading is uncertain.

650 Hornung 1987-1994, 717, no. 714, where the god appears as a mummy. See also the sarcophagus of Padikhonsu: Jamen 2016, 153 and fig. 61.

651 South wall of room A: 'Your son Horus has placed your enemies under you. He is burdened with you, for you are greater than he. He has lifted you upon himself in your name of Great Saw', written with the determinative of the seated god (Dorman 1991, 107, pl. 65).

652 Piankoff 1942, 6, pl. I; Müller-Roth 2008, 331, 337, pls. VII, XVIII.

653 Epigraphic Survey 1980, pl. 79.

654 Guksch 1995, 55, pl. 7.

655 Gohary 1991, pl. 54.

656 For the 18th Dynasty, see: a) pCairo CG 51189 of Iuia: Davis 1908, pl. X; b) pLondon BM EA 10477 of Nu: Lapp 1997, pl. 44; c) pLondon BM EA 10009 of Userhat: Naville 1836, 367; d) pTurin 8438 of Kha: Schiaparelli 2007, 52. For the 19th Dynasty: e) pBerlin 3002 of Nakhtamun: Munro 1997, pls. 16, 22. For the 21st Dynasty: f) pCairo JE 95838 of Gatseshen: Lucarelli 2006a, pl. 40; g) pLeiden T 3 of Tayuheryt: Niwinski 2009, 141; h) pLeiden T 7 of Paser: Niwinski 2009, 141; i) pLondon BM EA 10064 of Paennestitaui: Munro 2001, pl. 42; j) pLouvre E 6258 of Nodjmet: Niwinski 2009, 141, pl. 7.

657 Piankoff 1955, 110, 141, pl. 45. Particularly interesting is the example of the second shrine, where he is part of a group of thirty-one Osiris figures, represented squatting before Nephthys; another thirty-one squatting Osirian forms are depicted behind Isis.

658 Murray 1904, pl. IX.

659 Niwinski 2009, 141, pl. 1.

660 Stela of Ptahmes (18th Dynasty) in Giza: *wsỉr ỉtfꜣ wr nṯr ꜥꜣ* (el-Banna 1990, 7-19); stela of Tameret and Djehutymes (19th-20th Dynasty) from Bubastis: *wsỉr ỉtfꜣ wr nb tꜣ-ḏsr ḫnty ỉmntt nb ꜣbḏw* (Habachi 1957, 101-102, pl. XXXVIIIA; Bakr/Brandl 2014, 152-153); stela of Iyrey (20th Dynasty) from Qantir: *wsỉr ỉtfꜣ wr nb ḏt nṯr ꜥꜣ nb tꜣ-ḏsr ḫnty ỉmntt nb ꜣbḏw* (Habachi/Ghalioungui 1971, 65-66, figs. 3-4).

661 Cairo CG 48483 (18th Dynasty), with an offering formula to Osiris *ỉtfꜣ wr*, Anubis 'the great god, lord of the sacred land', and the gods and goddesses 'who are in Shen-Qebeh': Newberry 1930-1957, 369, pl. 29. The object belonged to a certain Ra, known thanks to other documents.

existence of three-dimensional images of this Osirian form during the New Kingdom.[662] In the inscriptions, the king declares himself 'beloved of Osiris the Great Saw, lord of the *heb-sed*, who resides in the *per-neser*' (*mry wsỉr ỉtfꜣ wr nb ḥb-sd ḥry-ib pr-nsr*). While the first epithet links Osiris *ỉtfꜣ wr* to the *sed* festival,[663] like a few other gods represented in the inscriptions on statues coming from the king's temple, the second one probably says something about the god's origin, associating him with the north of the country, with the archaic symbol of Lower Egypt.

His only representation in a temple ritual scene also comes from the Theban region. Inside the Chapel of Osiris (room 25) of the temple of Medinet Habu,[664] Ramses III offers Maat to Osiris *ỉtfꜣ wr* 'who resides in the temple' (*ḥry-ib ḥwt*), protected by a winged Isis 'the great, mother of the god' (*wrt mwt nṯr*). The god is shown standing on a base surmounted by a lotus flower with the Four sons of Horus. He wears the *atef* crown and holds the *ankh-was-djed* sceptre with his hands protruding from his shroud. Through his words, Osiris *ỉtfꜣ wr* gives the king the lifetime of Ra – that is eternity – in heaven (*ꜥḥꜥw n rꜥ m pt*).

However, it was after the New Kingdom that Osiris *ỉtfꜣ wr* started being directly and closely associated with the territory of Heliopolis and Kher-Aha, with which also Osiris Hemag had strong connections. A dyad (Cairo JE 92591), most likely of the Third Intermediate Period and found in the eastern sector of Ain Shams, shows Osiris *ỉtfꜣ wr* with the *atef*-crown and Isis seated side by side, the hand of the goddess on the shoulder of the god.[665] In two offering formulas, one to Osiris *ỉtfꜣ wr* 'the great god, lord of the sky' (*nṯr ꜥꜣ nb pt*) and one to Osiris *ỉtfꜣ wr* 'the great god, lord of the sky' and Isis 'the great, mother of the god', the deities grant the deceased, the 'chief of the storehouse of the house of Ra' Sewer, 'to enter and come forth, and not be detained from seeing Ra when he raises, that he may grant me to kiss the earth and to come forth in Heliopolis' (*di=sn ꜥḳ pr n šnꜥ mꜣꜣ rꜥ m wbn=f di=f n=i sn tꜣ pr* [*m*] *ỉwnw*). In a fragmentary stela[666] of a certain Padipep of the Late Period, Osiris *ỉtfꜣ wr* is mentioned in a list of gods of Heliopolis, such as Ra-Atum, Shu, Tefnet, Isis 'in the great temple' (*m ḥwt-ꜥꜣt*), Hathor-nebet-hetepet, Hapi 'father of the gods' (*ỉt nṯrw*) and 'all the gods of Kher-Aha' (*nṯrw nbw ḫr-ꜥḥꜣ*), while an offering table (Cairo CG 23144)[667] of the Graeco-Roman Period from Heliopolis presents two offering formulas, one for Atum 'lord of Heliopolis' (*nb ỉwnw*) and Horakhty, and the other one for Anubis, Geb, and Osiris *ỉtfꜣ wr*. In the same period, we encounter the only known priest of this Osirian form. The owner of the stela Louvre C 119 was *hem*-priest of Horus 'foremost of the houses' (*ḫnty prw*), a Heliopolitan form of the falcon god, of Osiris *ỉtfꜣ wr* – written with the determinative of the seated god – and of Isis 'who resides in Shen-Qebeh'.[668] In the papyrus Louvre I 3079, containing a glorification for Osiris, *ỉtfꜣ wr* again appears as a place-name: 'You come, and the young people who are in Heliopolis put your majesty in the temple of Sepa. *ỈIfꜣ wr* [written with the determinative of city] is inundated with your name and Kher-Aha is in adoration in seeing you, and

662 Bryan 1997, 69.
663 Bryan 1997, 57-58.
664 Epigraphic Survey 1963, pl. 480B.
665 Bickel/Tallet 2000, 130-131, 141-142.
666 Heiden 2002.
667 Kamal 1909, 111, pl. 26.
668 Spiegelberg 1929, 108, pl. VI; Kuentz 1931, 849; Guermeur 2005, 78-79.

Atum overthrows your enemies…'.[669] It is also notable that in the Saitic period, Osiris *itf3 wr*, besides being mentioned in Chapter 142 of the Book of the Dead,[670] occurs in the Theban tomb of Pediamenopet (TT 33), which also contains images of Osiris Hemag; more precisely, the god is quoted in an offering formula of the sarcophagus chamber.[671]

Though the expression *itf3 wr* can be attested from the Old Kingdom to the Graeco-Roman Period, what is hidden behind it remains uncertain. Does it evoke a particular moment or episode of Osiris' life or, rather, death? In the above-mentioned stela of Padipep, the owner has the title of 'the one who protects the body' (*nh ḥʿw*), which has been put in relation with the Osirian epithet *itf3 wr* by Désirée Heiden.[672] In this respect, one of the very rare occurrences of *itf3 wr* in the temple of Edfu is in relation with Horus 'who protects his father *itf3 wr*'.[673] The 'Great Saw' must refer to a weapon which had a special meaning for Osiris. Was it just something used against enemies to protect the god or, conversely, the weapon that killed him? If so, the instrument of destruction and death would no longer be something hateful, an abomination. On the contrary, the weapon would have been sacralised and, through a linguistic association with its victim, it would evoke the god's violent death, with the following dismemberment of his body and the dramatic injuries of his limbs, strewn far and wide.

Neither Osiris *itf3 wr* nor Osiris lord of Djedu are represented on other monolithic shrines; only Osiris lord of Ra-setau appears on a naos of Nekhthorheb from Abydos.[674] Even though groups of three, or even four Osiris figures are not seldom represented on Egyptian monuments,[675] the threefold distinction of the god as it appears on the Leiden naos does not occur anywhere else and must have a specific meaning for the fourth and most important Osiris of the naos, Osiris Hemag, who – although not shown on any of the outer faces – was present inside its walls. As far as I know, this is the only monolithic shrine presenting an Osirian triad whose components are clearly identifiable thanks to epithets. On a naos of Nekhthorheb from Bubastis, at least three Osiris figures are depicted, the first one seated on a throne, with the *atef*-crown and the crook and flail, the second one lying on a lion couch with hands crossed over his breast and protected by two kneeling goddesses, and the third one as a standing mummy with a white crown. In this case, however, it has been suggested that they might express three different phases of the life of Osiris.[676]

---

669 Goyon 1967, 107, 113. For another example of *itf3 wr* as a place-name, see a papyrus from Tebtunis, with the mention of *ḥwt sp3 itf3 wr*: Osing 1988, 145.

670 See pColon.Aeg. 10207 of Iahtesnacht, Saitic Period (Verhoeven 1993, 269, 102*, pl. 23) and pVatican 48832 of Pasherientaihet, Saitic Period (Gasse 2002, 249). For other examples of the god in the Graeco-Roman Period, see Chapter 141 of the Book of the Dead in pChicago OIM 9787 (Ryerson), Persian-Ptolemaic Period (Allen 1960, 227, pl. 49) and pTurin 1791 of Iufankh, Ptolemaic Period (Lepsius 1842, pl. 59); the Ptolemaic gate of the precinct of Mut at Karnak (Sauneron 1983, pl. 11); and the pGiessen 115, fragm. 2 (Faulkner 1958, 68).

671 Piankoff 1947, 82.

672 Heiden 2002, 199.

673 *Edfu* IV 87, 8-9. See also a ritual scene dedicated to the opening of the mouth of Osiris, where the king is 'the living image of *itf3 wr*' (*šsp ʿnḫ n itf3 wr*; *Edfu* IV 243, 4). Another possible allusion to this Osirian form comes from the second eastern Osirian chapel of the temple of Dendera (*Dendera* X 71, 5), where the king, represented in front of a standing Osiris, is said to be '*itf3 wr* (?), excellent of mouth (*3ḫ r3*), who leads the ritual for the Heliopolitan (= Osiris) (*sšm ḫs n iwny*)'.

674 Roeder 1914, 55.

675 See Coulon 2009. On the concept of triad in the Egyptian religion, see Te Velde 1971, 80-86; Griffiths 1974, 28-32; Griffiths 1996.

676 Spencer 2006, 11, 81, 103. See also Coulon 2009, 16 n. 73.

However, the Osirian triad on the Leiden naos has a preponderantly geographical value. It is hardly a coincidence that these three Osiris figures – plus the Isis and Horus in the lower registers of the left and right walls respectively – are the only gods on the naos whose names are followed by epithets, of which at least two are clearly referring to localities. This specification of their provenance was probably regarded as particularly important. This divine triad, in each of its three components, presents Osiris as a northern god. Osiris 'lord of Busiris' indicates the most popular and renowned Osiris of Lower Egypt. Osiris of Ra-setau and Osiris *ỉtfꜣ wr* are expressions of the religion scene in Memphis and the territory of Heliopolis and Kher-Aha, where *ỉtfꜣ wr* with its specific Osirian form was presumably located, and allude to a more circumscribed area of the Delta, with which Osiris Hemag had strong and privileged connections.[677] The presence of this Osirian triad might hint at a northern origin of Osiris Hemag, more precisely in the territory of Memphis and Heliopolis, and seems to contextualize a mythological event (that is the rebirth of the god expressed through the form Hemag) in a specific region of Egypt.

In the lower register of the left wall, the Osirian theme is also particularly significant. Of the nine deities represented, the second one is a Horus falcon on a pedestal which contains the image of a knife, in all probability a reminder of his protective role towards his father Osiris. The fifth deity is an image of Isis 'mistress of the two lands' in the guise of a vulture on a pedestal, followed by a second Horus falcon, likewise on a pedestal. Images of Isis as a vulture are quite unusual and are above all found in funerary contexts.[678] The most ancient one is perhaps shown in a pectoral from the tomb of Tutankhamun, with Isis as a vulture with an *atef*-crown facing Nephthys as a cobra, both protecting Osiris with their wings.[679] Another illustration is found on a sarcophagus of the Third Intermediate Period (Cairo CG 61030),[680] while a later example is very likely an image of a vulture on a base represented on the above-mentioned naos of Nekhthorheb in a row of gods, including three Osirian forms.[681] It is notable that in all these contexts, as well as on the Leiden naos, the goddess is associated with Osiris.

Two of the other six deities of the lower register – the crocodile-headed *ẖsf-m-tp-ʿ*, 'He who repels at the beginning', and Akh in the form of a crested ibis – appear for the very first time on the sarcophagus of Merenptah usurped by Psusennes I, as well as in the tomb of the latter. But at least three of them – *ꜣsb*, 'Radiant one', *ỉn-ḥr*, 'He who brings the face' (?), and *sḳd-ḥr*, 'Watchful of face' – are more ancient guardian-deities, who make their first appearance in the Coffin Texts.[682] Moreover, they are shown in Chapters 144 and 147 of the Book of the Dead and in the second or third shrine of Tutankhamun. The otherwise unattested deity *ʿnḫ-m-fdt*, 'He who lives on sweat', who seems to testify to a certain degree of (unintentional?) originality in the organization of the guardian-deities on this side wall of the naos, is probably also a variant of an identical deity named *ʿnḫ-m-*

677 Zecchi 1996, 85-87 (Memphis), 87-90 (Heliopolis and Kher-Aha).
678 Russmann 1997.
679 Catalogue Carter 261o, JE 61946: James 2000, 238-239.
680 Daressy 1909, 131, pl. 48.
681 Spencer 2006, 9, fig. 8b, pl. 12.
682 CT III, 260d (*ꜣsb*); IV 39j (*ꜣsb*); VII, 215e (*ꜣsb*), 288c (*ꜣsb*), 291d (*ỉn-ḥr*), 296gd (*sḳd-ḥr*), 499h (*ꜣsb*).

fnṯw, 'He who lives on worms',[683] known from the Coffin Texts[684] and in the New Kingdom, thanks to Chapters 144 and 147 of the Book of the Dead. In the following periods, this deity was depicted, together with many other deities of the Leiden naos, on the sarcophagus and tomb of Psusennes I,[685] on the sarcophagus of Ankhefenkhonsu,[686] in the 26th Dynasty on the sarcophagus of Iahmes[687] and in the tomb of Mutirdis,[688] and on a few sarcophagi of the Graeco-Roman Period.[689]

3.5. Right wall

The upper register of the right side wall bears the same number of gods as the upper register on the left side, with the difference that all of them look towards the front. The first of the row is an image of Shu, who is the only one to be identified with certainty thanks to the presence of his name in front of him. He is followed by a lion-headed goddess, whose name is no longer readable but who could possibly be an image of Tefnet, and by a ram-headed god, who might be Montu or Amun, because only the sign *mn* survives of his name. It is interesting to note that these first three deities of the row are the only ones on the Leiden naos, together with two Osirian forms in the upper register of the left side, to be represented as seated on a throne, perhaps in order to highlight their different divine status. Shu and Tefnet are depicted as two *ba*-birds with a sun disk on a dais on the other naos from Kom el-Ahmar (Louvre D 29), in a row of deities also including Ra-Horakhty, Atum, Geb, and Nut.[690] If the identification of the lion-headed goddess with Tefnet is correct, she and her companion Shu might be representatives, also on the Leiden naos, of Heliopolis, while the ram-headed god might be regarded as a Theban god.[691]

They are followed by two standing gods, presumably associated with funerary themes. The first one is a canine-headed god whose name is no longer readable but who might be Anubis; of the second one, only part of his figure and name, *is*[…], survives. He might be an image of Isdes,[692] who often appears in the guise of a canine-headed god just behind Tefnet in rows of gods, in particular in scenes in funerary contexts featuring the awakening of Osiris by his son Horus.[693] That the god before Isdes might be Anubis seems

---

683 Munro 1983, 215, 232-233; Leitz 2002, II, 142-143; Abdelrahiem 2006, 8-9.
684 CT VII, 437f.
685 Montet 1951, pls. 14, 84.
686 Cairo CG 41001bis: Moret 1913, 27, pl. III.
687 Leclant 1962, fig. 17.
688 Assmann 1977, 93, pl. 44.
689 For example, the sarcophagi Cairo CG 29303 and 29304 (Maspero 1908-1914, 99, 112, 131, 146, pls. 11, 13) and the sarcophagus of Khaf (Daressy 1917, 10).
690 In the following periods, Shu and Tefnet are represented in different guises on naoi of the reign of Nekhtnebef from Saft el-Henna: Roeder 1914, 84, 87, 91 (Cairo CG 70021); Yoyotte 1954, 81; von Bomhard 2008, 23-27 (Alexandria JE 25774 and Louvre D 37).
691 As far as I know, the only naos with images of Montu, and Montu-Ra, is Cairo CG 70021 of the reign of Nekhtnebef: Roeder 1914, 65, 78. For Amun or Amun-Ra on naoi, see Cairo CG 70040 of the Middle Kingdom (Roeder 1914, 135); Louvre D 29 of Amasis (Piankoff 1933, 165-168); Cairo CG 70021 (Roeder 1914, 66, 82, 86, 92, 95).
692 On this god, see Farouk 1999-2000, 11-15.
693 See the Cenotaph of Sety I at Abydos (Frankfort/de Buck/Gunn 1939, pl. 74); tomb and sarcophagus of Psusennes I (Montet 1951, pls. 12, 92); tomb of Sheshonq III (Montet 1960, pl. 30); sarcophagus of Iahmes (Leclant 1962, 111); tomb of Mutirdis (Assmann 1977, 93, pl. 41); sarcophagi of the Graeco-Roman Period Cairo CG 29303 and 29304 (Maspero 1908-1914, 101, 135, pl. 13) and of Khaf (Daressy 1917, 10).

to be corroborated by the fact that they can appear together since the Middle Kingdom. For example, Spell 155 of the Coffin Texts ends with the words: 'I know the souls of the New Moon (*psḏntyw*): they are Osiris, Anubis, and Isdes',[694] while in Chapter 18 of the Book of the Dead Isdes is represented as a squatting man behind Anubis.[695] Moreover, it is worth mentioning that on the sarcophagi of Anlamani (Khartum 1868) and Aspelta (Boston MFA 23729), contemporaries of the 26th Dynasty, Isdes acts as a protector of Osiris in the netherworld.[696]

As on the left side, the lower register is more crowded than the upper one, but the exact number of the deities represented here is uncertain, since the right edge is badly damaged. However, as we have seen, there were presumably at least seven gods, six of which are still visible. Also in this case, the names of many of the gods have disappeared and therefore their identities remain hypothetical.

While the gods Shu and Tefnet might evoke the ancestors of Osiris, the first god of the lower register represents his offspring. The presence of Horus 'the great god', just facing the door of the naos and depicted as the leader of a row of deities on the right side (from the viewpoint of someone looking at the front of the monument), is hardly a coincidence. As we will see, his pre-eminent position is rather reminiscent of that which he occupies in scenes of the awakening of Osiris, as for instance in the tomb of Mutirdis. Horus 'the great god' is followed by at least four deities, *šʿ*[*-tb*], *wnm-ḥwꜣt, nfr-nfrw* (or *ʿꜣ-ḫrw*), and a deity who might perhaps be identified as *nḥmmt*. Some of them are also known thanks to the Cenotaph of Sety I, Chapter 144 of the Book of the Dead, and the sarcophagus of Merenptah/Psusennes I; moreover, during the 26th Dynasty, they were all depicted on the sarcophagus of Iahmes and in the tomb of Mutirdis.

3.6. Rear wall

The upper register of the rear wall is the only one to show a strict consistency in the iconography of the deities, who are all portrayed standing and holding an *ankh*-sign in one hand and a staff in the other. The two rows of deities, one looking left and the other facing right, include five figures each, of which seven are male gods (*ḫssii, pḥrr* (or *pḥtr, pḥgr?*), *kkw,* [...]*wr* (?), *ʿbwy, ḫꜣbs,* and *ḥr=f-m-ḫꜣḫ*) and three are goddesses (Nephthys, *ḥr-mḥwnt* (?), and Maat). In these two groups, only the presence of the gods [...]*wr* and *pḥrr* is not clearly understandable, since it is not consistent with similar divine sequences present in other sources depicting the awakening of Osiris by his son Horus, nor with the sequence in the central room dedicated to Osiris in the temple of Ramses II at Abydos.[697] A possible explanation is that their inclusion in this context was just due to the initiative of local engravers. Even though nothing can be said of the figure of [...]*wr*, it should be noted that, apart from the two goddesses Maat and Nephthys, both represented in fully human form, all the other deities are differentiated one from the other by distinct animal

694 CT II 308-309b.

695 Vignette of the papyrus of Ani: Budge 1913, sheet 14, G; see also *Urk.* V, 126, 7.

696 Soukiassian 1982, 337.

697 Mariette 1880, pl. 19b.

heads. The canine-headed *pḥrr/pḥtr/pḥgr* might just be a local substitute, or variant, of the crocodile-headed deity called *ḥng-rꜣ*, who constantly appears in similar divine rows.[698]

The number of the gods in the lower register is no longer determinable. Since the row of deities facing right includes six divine figures, it is possible that the row facing left was also composed of the same number of images. However, of these figures, only *ỉr-rn=f-ḏs=f*, in a semi-sitting posture and grasping lizards with his upraised hands, is clearly recognisable thanks to the survival of his name.

3.7. Interpretation

For design, proportions, and above all decoration, there is no naos that parallels this unique monument. One of the main interests of the Leiden naos is that it allows us to understand the logic that governs the presence and arrangement of the deities on its outer surfaces. Divine figures on naoi have occasionally been interpreted as images of statues,[699] although this is by no means a rule applicable to all monolithic naoi.[700] The divine figures on the other naos from Kom el-Ahmar (Louvre D 29) might indeed be representations of cult statuary. One of its dedicatory texts expressly says that Amasis made it 'as his monument for the gods who are in the temple of Osiris Merty, so that their names may endure forever' (*ỉr.n=f m mnw=f n nṯrw ỉmyw ḥwt wsỉr-mrty rwḏ rn=sn ḏt*).[701] But on the Leiden naos there is nothing to suggest that the divine images represent statues. The standing figures, for example, are not provided with pedestals or back-pillars. More significantly, apart from the three Osirian forms, Horus the 'great god', and Isis 'mistress of the two lands', all the captions tell us just the gods' names, with no other specification. Moreover, Amasis does not establish any relationship with the gods of the naos. He is in direct contact only with the *ỉmy-wt* emblem on the roof and, of course, through the dedicatory text, with Osiris Hemag. Unlike the Louvre naos or other naoi of the Late Period with rows of gods, Amasis is not represented making offerings. When a sovereign is present, he becomes the point to which the gods turn their gaze. But in the Leiden naos, they all look toward the front, to the door which hides Osiris Hemag. So, no ritual is actually depicted and the theme is not a representation of terrestrial cult topography.

The arrangement of the decoration on the four outer walls, with their different gods in different guises, aims at creating a narrative in respect to Osiris Hemag. All over the naos, bodily difference is emphasized. Each deity is unlike the other. Even the three Osiris figures on the left wall are not identical. Visual equality is only adopted when gods are supposed to form a unity – such as the Four Sons of Horus or Nekhbet and Mwyt on the front, or the two squatting baboons on the rear – or for the same god, as the two Anubis canids on shrines on the front. The overall effect is that the onlooker is presented with multiple levels of meaning, which offer information on Osiris Hemag's nature and on what he is going to experience inside the monument. The gods of the naos reflect distinct themes, though all are connected with Osiris, his death, and above all his rebirth.

---

698 Leitz 2002, V, 227.
699 For example El-Sayed 1975, 133; Zivie-Coche 1991, 234.
700 Spencer 2006, 22, 31.
701 Piankoff 1933, 167.

The deities in the upper registers of the two side walls – the three Osiris figures, Isis, and Nephthys on the left, and Shu, Tefnet, the ram-headed Montu (or Amun), and perhaps the canine-headed god (Anubis?) on the right – enjoyed a national importance, with cults widespread throughout Egypt. In order to enhance their value, most of them are represented enthroned. These two registers were perhaps designed to convey a more specific geographical meaning. In particular, the three Osirian forms, all definitely more ancient than Osiris Hemag, are testimonials of important northern localities connected with Osiris Hemag himself, while Shu and Tefnet might represent Heliopolis and the ram-headed god the city of Thebes.

But what makes the Leiden naos different from all the other naoi is the presence all over its surfaces of deities who are usually called 'demons'. These, however, do not constitute a rather indistinct and anonymous troop. Even though some of them are no longer readable, all the figures are accompanied by their menacing names, actually epithets that refer to their potentially dangerous nature.

The gods' distribution over the different registers reflects differentiated tasks and purposes. First of all, the gods in the lower registers and the front appear under a great variety of iconographies. As we have seen, there are deities in full animal form on pedestals; some have human faces, others are animal-headed; some are depicted frontally, a small number is standing or in a semi-sitting position, many are squatting or kneeling on pedestals, occasionally armed with knives or holding lizards. These differences in physical appearances and postures convey the idea of a vast and multiform horde, assembled around Osiris Hemag in order to efficaciously carry out, if needed, his protection.

The origin of the majority of the deities in the right and left lower registers is different from that of the deities depicted on the other parts of the naos. While the first god on the right is Horus 'the great god', the divine row on the left is led by *ḫsf-m-tp-ʿ*, 'He who repels at the beginning', first known from the sarcophagus of Merenptah re-used by Psusennes I. But both registers include very ancient apotropaic deities, who appeared for the first time in the Book of Two Ways and other spells of the Coffin Texts, and subsequently in Chapter 144 of the Book of the Dead:[702] *ꜣsb* 'The radiant one';[703] *ỉn-ḥr* 'He who brings the face';[704] *sḳd-ḥr* 'Watchful of face';[705] *wnm-ḥwꜣt* 'Eater of excrements';[706] to these, one should perhaps add *ʿꜣ-ḫrw* 'Loud of voice'[707] (or more likely *nfr-nfrw*). Also the fourth deity on the left side wall, *ʿnḫ-m-fdt*, might actually be a variant of *ʿnḫ-m-fnṯw*, who is present in Spell 1109 of the Coffin Texts. Chapter 144 of the Book of the Dead and its variant Chapter 147 deal with the seven *ʿrrwt*-gates that the deceased must pass to have access to the afterlife. But in order to block the way to those not allowed to the netherworld, each gate is protected by three guardian-deities: an *iry-ʿꜣ* 'doorkeeper', a *sꜣw* 'watcher', and

702 For the re-use of the Book of Two Ways deities in Chapters 144-147 of the Book of the Dead, see Robinson 2003, 157-159. See also Bennet 2014; Quirke 2016, 553-555.

703 Spells 997, 1039, and 1149.

704 Spell 1041.

705 Spell 1044.

706 Spell 1102.

707 Spells 938, 1041, and 1152.

a *smỉ* 'herald'.[708] On the Leiden naos none of these categories is missing: the left register presents one herald (*ꜣsb*), two watchers (*ỉn-ḥr* and *sḳd-ḥr*), and perhaps a doorkeeper (*ʿnḫ-m-fdt/ʿnḫ-m-fnṯw*), while the right register has a doorkeeper (*wnm-ḥwꜣt*) and perhaps a watcher (*ʿꜣ-ḫrw*).

Peculiar as it may seem, the choice to represent these door-watchers on a monolithic shrine is perfectly in line with the idea of creating a protective shield against potentially dangerous intruders. The titles occasionally given to Chapters 144 ('Knowing the names of the keepers of the seven gates') and 147 ('Spell for knowing the gates of the house of Osiris, foremost of the west, and the gods who are in their caverns, to whom offerings are made on earth') refer to the *ʿrrwt*-gates as being those of Osiris and his realm. And here, on the Leiden naos, these deities are not at work for a common deceased, but for the god Osiris himself. It is also possible that their presence, which evokes the doors of the afterlife, aims at suggesting a transitional phase, a passage between Osiris' death and rebirth. Moreover, the presence of these deities in the left register along with two 'Horus' falcons and the vulture of Isis is perhaps due to an adaptation of their task to a more Osirian context. It is also interesting that here, unlike on other parts of the monument, both Horus and Isis are portrayed in full animal form and on pedestals, iconographies that are more in harmony with those of the rest of the troop.

The deities represented on the lintel of the front and in the lower register of the rear, as well as a small number in the lower registers of the right and left sides, seem to have a different origin. Apparently, they are not as ancient as those coming from Chapter 144 of the Book of the Dead, whose antiquity can be traced back as far as the Coffin Texts and, more specifically, the Book of Two Ways. With the exception of *ỉr-rn=f-ḏs=f*, known from the Middle Kingdom onwards, the names of the majority of these deities are indeed not attested before the New Kingdom or the beginning of the Third Intermediate Period. Nevertheless their origin, or at least that of a few of them, should be sought in royal contexts of the Ramesside period, that is in those deities represented, in groups of two or three, around the burial chamber of the tomb of king Ramses III (KV 11), or in tombs of members of the royal family in the Valley of the Queens, such as the tombs of queen Sitra, wife of Ramses I (QV 38), of an unnamed queen perhaps of the time of Sety I (QV 40), of Pareherwenemef (QV 42), Sethherkhepshef (QV 43), and Khaemwaset (QV 44), all sons of Ramses III, of queen (Dua-) Tentopet (QV 74), daughter of Ramses III and wife of Ramses IV, and of queen Tyti (QV 52), perhaps sister and wife of Ramses X.[709] Similar anonymous deities were also represented in wooden statuettes found in some royal tombs of the 18th (Horemheb), 19th (Ramses I and Sety I), and 20th (Ramses IX) Dynasties.[710] All these deities – whose complete sequence appears only in the tombs of Ramses III, Pareherwenemef, and queen Tyti – created a sort of impassable perimeter around the deceased, who was identified with Osiris. Moreover, the fact that the wooden statuettes were coated with a black varnish or simply painted

708 On these guardian-deities and their iconography, see also Munro 1987, 215; Guilhou 1999; Abdelrahiem 2006; Lucarelli 2006, 209-211; Lucarelli 2010a, 86-88.

709 These deities have been studied by Waitkus 1987.

710 See British Museum EA 2018, 50698, 50699, 50702, 50703, 50704, 61283: Waitkus 1987; Reeves/Wilkinson 1996, 132-135, 169; Russmann 2001, 159-161; Strudwick 2006, 188-189; Taylor 2010, 200-201.

black, suggests that they were also connected with the idea of regeneration, death, and resurrection.

Wolfgang Waitkus and other scholars,[711] following a theory by Jan Assmann,[712] have suggested that all these deities should be connected or regarded as forerunners of those of the nightly 'hour vigil' (*Stundenwachen*) of the Graeco-Roman period. Moreover, the religious themes expressed by these protective deities, who had to watch over Osiris' body, had antecedents in the private mortuary beliefs of the Middle Kingdom.[713]

Starting from the very beginning of the Third Intermediate Period, the protective role of all these gods was extended to other funerary and private contexts. The so-called vignette of Chapter 182 of the Book of the Dead – which appears only on the papyrus London BM EA 10010, belonging to Muthetepti, a priestess of Amun of Thebes, and dating to the 21st Dynasty[714] – has been interpreted by Rita Lucarelli[715] as a variant of the representation of the nightly vigil of the mummy of Osiris. The deceased/Osiris, labelled *sꜥḥ šps*y, the 'noble mummy', is lying on a funerary bed with three vases under it. The mummy is protected, on the left and right sides, by Isis, Nephthys, and the Four Sons of Horus, and, in the upper and lower registers, by a row of six protective guardians, represented under different guises and holding snakes, lizards, or knives.

But, starting from the 21st Dynasty, it was on the walls of tombs and, above all, of coffins, that the groups of guardian demons studied by Waitkus found their most congenial venue. The divine figures present in a specific Ramesside Theban context – the tomb of Ramses III and some tombs of the Valley of the Queens – were also taken up by Psusennes I for his tomb at Tanis, in the Delta. Here, they were represented on the external surfaces of the outer sarcophagus in pink granite,[716] made primarily for king Merenptah. In which way Psusennes I acquired this sarcophagus – originally the innermost of a nest of three stone sarcophagi, which enclosed other coffins – is at present unknown.[717] However, this royal sarcophagus must have been a source of inspiration for the decoration of the tomb itself, since some of these deities were also portrayed on the east wall of the vestibule.[718]

It is interesting that, though the majority of these divine names were known since the Middle or New Kingdoms, some others – *iwꜥ-nṯr*, *ḥsf-m-tp-ꜥ*, *sẖm* in the guise of a sceptre, *wnm-ḥwꜣꜣt* (instead of the longer variant *wnm-ḥwꜣꜣt-nt-pḥwy.fy*) – started to be connected with these deities in the usurped sarcophagus and tomb of Psusennes I himself. Equally interesting is the fact that, from the beginning of the Third Intermediate Period, these figurative themes also started to be used in private contexts, above all on sarcophagi. The first evidence of the transfer of some of these deities from the sarcophagus of Merenptah/Psusennes I to a private sphere is offered by a pair of

711 Waitkus 1987. See also, for example, Grajetzki 2004, 28; von Lieven 2007, I, 20; Lucarelli 2012, 86.

712 Assmann 1977, 14.

713 Willems 1988, 141-146; Willems 1996, 92; Willems 1997, 358-364; Grajetzki 2004, 28-29.

714 Lucarelli 2012. Since the vignette is inserted in between Chapter 182 and Chapter 151, Lucarelli has suggested that it should actually be connected with the latter, rather than the former.

715 Lucarelli 2012, 90. See also Quirke 2016, 562-564.

716 Montet 1951, pls. 84-88.

717 Verner 2012, 338-339 suggests that the sarcophagus might have been a gift to Psusennes I from the Theban priests of Amun.

718 Montet 1951, pl. 14.

sarcophagi of the 22nd Dynasty. The first one is that of Hornakht,[719] son of Osorkon II, discovered at Tanis, and both chronologically and geographically close to Psusennes I's tomb; here, as well as in Psusennes' case, the divine figures are accompanied by their names. In the second one, belonging to Horaawesheb (BM EA 6666)[720] and coming from Thebes, the deities are still anonymous, like in the so-called vignette of Chapter 182 of the 21st Dynasty. Next, these deities appear, accompanied by their names, on a restricted number of sarcophagi of the 25th and 26th Dynasties – Ankhefenkhonsu (Cairo CG 41001bis),[721] Rome V.O. 1000,[722] and Iahmes[723] – and of the Graeco-Roman Period, all from Saqqara: Panehemisis (Vienna AS 4),[724] Khaf,[725] Ankhhapi son of Tefnakht (Cairo CG 29303), Djedhor son of Iahmes (Cairo CG 29304), Ankhhapi son of Tanetbaanepet (Cairo CG 29301),[726] and Wennefer (Cairo CG 29310).[727]

These depictions are probably to be identified with the gods – whose names are now lost – represented in the burial chamber of the tomb of Ramose (TT 132) of the 25th Dynasty.[728] In the following dynasty they are depicted on the west and east walls of Chamber IV in the tomb of Mutirdis (TT 410).[729] Statuettes portraying some of these deities have also been found in the Theban tomb of Montuemhat.[730] These statuettes represent groups of two or three deities each, corresponding to the sequence of deities on the walls of New Kingdom Theban tombs or on the sarcophagi, and were located inside niches of the walls of the burial chamber, with the evident purpose of protecting the coffin. That the main task of all these deities was to safeguard Osiris, the Osirianized deceased, and his coffin is confirmed by the texts that introduce their figures on some sarcophagi of the Graeco-Roman Period. For example, on the sarcophagus of Djedhor son of Iahmes (CG 29304), they are said to make 'the protection of the Osiris, the overseer of the army Djedhor, true of voice, like Osiris, for ever'[731] (*ỉr=sn sꜣ ḥꜣ wsỉr ỉmy-r mšꜥ ḏd-ḥr mꜣꜥ-ḫrw mỉ wsỉr ḏt*) and to 'protect' his coffin 'like the one who is in the coffin',[732] an epithet for Osiris[733] (*stp=sn sꜣ=sn ḥꜣ ḏbꜣt n wsỉr ỉmy-r mšꜥ ḏd-ḥr mꜣꜥ-ḫrw mỉ ḏbꜣty*), or are invoked as the 'door-keepers of the doors' and 'guardians of the necropolis'[734] (*ỉryw-ꜥꜣ nw sbḫwt sꜣww nw ẖrt-nṯr*) and to act for Osiris himself, since they are 'the gods who make the protection of Osiris and of the Osirianized Djedhor[735] (*nṯrw ỉr sꜣ ḥꜣ wsỉr ỉr=ṯn sꜣ ḥꜣ wsỉr ỉmy-r mšꜥ ḏd-ḥr mꜣꜥ-ḫrw*).

---

719 Montet 1947, 60, pl. 51.
720 Taylor 2010, 202-203.
721 Moret 1913, pl. III.
722 Sist 2013, 73-83; Sist 2017, 509-514.
723 Hermitage 766: Leclant 1962, 111, fig. 17.
724 Leitz 2011.
725 Daressy 1917.
726 Maspero 1908-1914.
727 Maspero/Gauthier 1939.
728 Greco 2014. Very likely also in the tomb of Padiamenopet (TT 33): Traunecker/Régen 2016, 72.
729 Assmann 1977, pls. 44-45.
730 Leclant 1961, 116-132, pls. XXXIV-XLIII. See also the statuette published by Clère 1986, 99-106, and the statuette Bologna EG 347 (Picchi 2011, 199, 209, 324).
731 Maspero 1908-1914, 125, 127.
732 Maspero 1908-1914, 126, 128.
733 Zandee 1981-1982, 12-13. Or, in this case, should it be read as *ḏbꜣt nṯr*, the 'coffin of the god'?
734 Maspero 1908-1914, 145, 147.
735 Maspero 1908-1914, 144-145.

Like a few funerary monuments, the Leiden naos presents yet another category of deities connected to a different Osirian theme, concentrated prevalently along the upper register of the rear. Isdes and *šʿ(-bṯw)*, the last god of the upper register and the second one of the lower register on the right side, respectively, likewise belong to this group. Unlike the front and lower registers, where the guardian-deities tend to be clearly differentiated from each other through the adoption of distinct forms and postures, these deities constitute an orderly group. They are all standing, holding the *ankh*-sign in the hand nearest the centre of the register and the *was*-staff in the hand facing outwards; all the male gods wear the *shendyt* and the goddesses a long and tight dress. The only concession to diversity is presented by the differentiation of their animal or human heads, and, of course, by their names written above them. Also in this case, their iconography is directly inspired by more ancient attestations. They are part of a group of thirty-six divine beings who also include the Four Sons of Horus and important gods such as Isis, Thoth, Shu, Tefnet – all represented, with the exception of Thoth, in the other registers of the naos. They participate in the awakening of Osiris by his son Horus. This scene appears for the first time in the final transverse chamber (or 'sarcophagus chamber') of the cenotaph of Sety I at Abydos,[736] then, in the 20th Dynasty, on the ceiling of Hall H of the tomb of Ramses VI (KV 9)[737] and on the rear wall of the sarcophagus chamber of Ramses IX (KV 6),[738] and, in the 22nd Dynasty, in the tomb of Sheshonq III at Tanis (NRT 5).[739] This group of gods seems to disappear from the royal decorative repertory for more than a century, recurring again at the end of the 25th Dynasty both at el-Kurru in the Sudan, in the burial chambers of the Kushite pyramids of queen Qalhata (KU 5)[740] and of her son and last king of the dynasty, Tanutamun (KU 16),[741] and at Thebes, in the private tombs of Ramose (TT 132),[742] active during the reign of Taharqa, and Padiamenopet (TT 33, eastern wall of Room XIX),[743] whose main activity was probably under the reigns of Taharqa and Tanutamun. The tomb of Qalhata represents a breach of tradition, since it is the first example of the adoption of the scene of the awakening of Osiris for a woman – even though belonging to a royal family – rather than for a male king. One of the main differences between the Kushite version at el-Kurru and the other awakening scenes lies in the fact that, as in the tomb of Ramses IX, none of the thirty-six deities is named. In the following dynasty, the awakening scene of Osiris is still shown in a few private tombs of the Theban necropolis: in the tomb of Pabasa (TT 279),[744] and on the south wall of Chamber IV of the tomb of another woman, Mutirdis (TT 410) (Fig. IV.12),[745] which shows the best preserved scene of the period.

---

736 Frankfort/de Buck/Gunn 1939, pl. 74. Some of these deities are also visible in a fragmentary scene in the central shrine (chamber D of Mariette) of the temple of Ramses II at Abydos: Mariette 1880, pl. 19.

737 Piankoff 1954, pls. 183-185.

738 Guilmant 1907, pl. 93; Abitz 1990, 31, 33; Roberson 2013, pl. 3.

739 Montet 1960, pl. 30. See also Roulin 1998, 257-261.

740 Dunham 1950, pls. IX-X.

741 Dunham 1950, pls. XIX-XX. See also Albers 2003, 52-63.

742 Greco 2014, 173-199. The names of the gods have been lost.

743 Piankoff 1947, 87; Traunecker/Régen 2016, 72.

744 Assmann 1977, 90-92. See also Sheikholeslami 2010.

745 Assmann 1977, fig. 41, pl. 41.

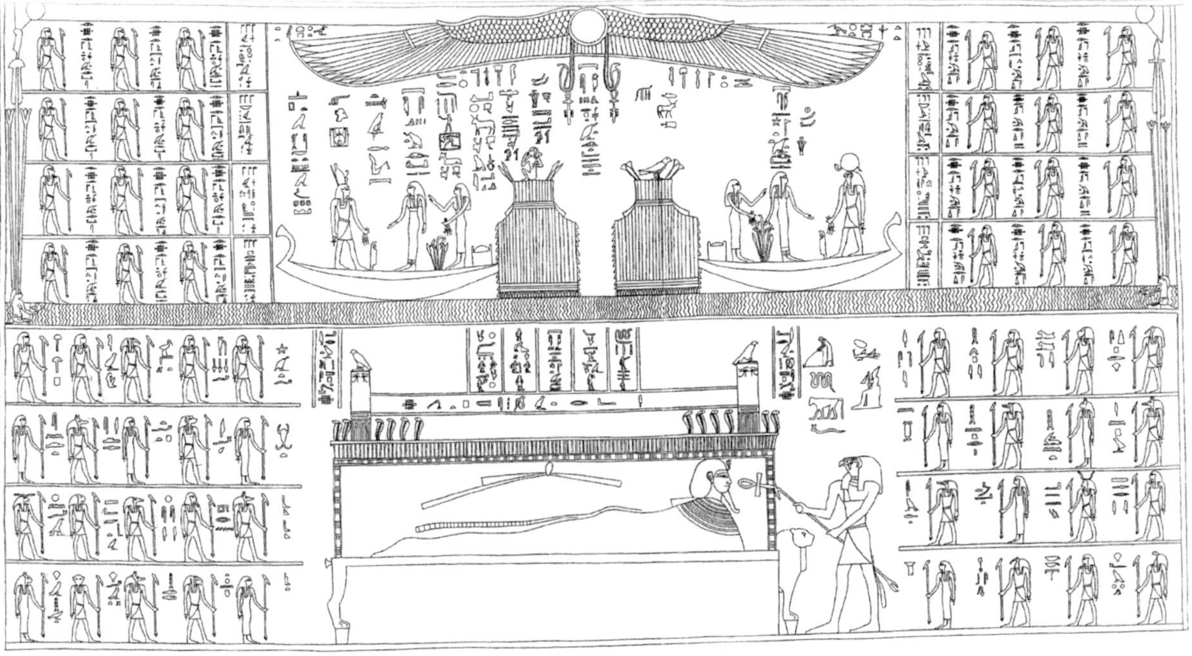

Fig. IV.12. Thebes, tomb of Mutirdis (TT 410), awakening scene. Reproduced after Assmann 1977, fig. 41.

Usually, the awakening scene of Osiris by his son Horus occupies the lower register of a bi-partite tableau, with a scene of the transit of the solar barques in the upper register.[746] At the centre, a mummiform Osiris is represented inside a shrine, lying prone on a lion bed with his head upraised and facing east and with a *uraeus* attached to his brow (in the tomb of Qalhata, the awakening figures lacks the *uraeus*). In the tomb of Ramses VI, the figure of Osiris is accompanied by the cartouches of the king, while the caption in the tomb of Tanutamun reads 'Osiris, ruler of the West' (*wsỉr ḥḳꜣ ỉmntt*). Above the god is a large *rs*-hieroglyph, 'awake' (not present in the Kushite version), while beneath the lion bed there are royal and divine emblems, such as crowns, clothing, sceptres, and weapons. In front of the shrine, which is surmounted by rearing *uraei*, Horus stands and extends a *was*-sceptre – alone or in combination with the *ḏd*-pillar and/or the *ankh*-sign – towards the nostrils of Osiris. It should be noted that in all the royal examples, as well as in Qalhata's tomb, Horus is human-headed, in order to stress his identification with the king, while in the private version of Mutirdis from the 26th Dynasty, he has the head of a falcon.[747]

The event of Osiris's awakening by his son Horus is attended by thirty-six deities, who are represented to either side of the shrine. The western group consists of twenty deities, arranged in four rows of five figures each; in the east, there are the other sixteen deities, arranged in four rows of four figures each.[748] In the tomb of Ramses IX, there are only twenty gods, arranged in two rows of five figures on either side. As on the Leiden naos,

746 Roberson 2013.

747 No image of the scenes in TT 33 and TT 279 has been published. The scene in TT 132 is unclear.

748 A later variant of the awakening scene, without the thirty-six deities, is located in room K2 of the temple of Hibis (Davies 1953, pl. 24). Here, the awakening of Osiris is performed not by Horus but Thoth, 'twice great, lord of Hermopolis, lord of the divine words, great god who resides in Hibis', who extends a *was*-staff towards Osiris, lying on his stomach inside a shrine, behind which there are Isis and Nephthys, whose words present Horus as the legitimate heir of his deceased father.

Fig. IV.13. Sarcophagus of Psusennes, detail. Reproduced after Montet 1951, pl. 90.

all the gods – male and female, and with human or animal heads – are standing, holding a *was*-sceptre in one hand and an *ankh*-sign in the other, and look towards the shrine with the lion bed.

It should be noted that in the tombs of Qalhata and Tanutamun, the awakening scenes are mirrored on the opposite wall by a similar scene, showing the mummy of the deceased/Osiris, covered with bandages, lying on her/his lion-bier inside a shrine flanked by the thirty-six gods. In this scene, Horus is not yet present. Evidently, the two different tableaus describe two different crucial moments of the burial ceremonies; the mummy, ready to be reborn but still motionless on its funerary bed, and the actual awakening of the deceased/Osiris by Horus.

The group of gods of the awakening scene also appears on the interior sides of the granite sarcophagus originally made for Merenptah in the 19th Dynasty and then usurped by Psusennes I in the 21st Dynasty.[749] Thirty deities are depicted in two rows along the long sides of the sarcophagus; at the foot-end there are five gods in front of an incense brazier, while at the head-end there is a hawk-headed Horus, extending a *was-ankh*-staff in front of the incense brazier, in the company of three other deities (Fig. IV.13).[750] Eighteen of these deities are also depicted in two rows, one of which is led by Horus holding a *was-ankh*-staff, on the west wall of the vestibule of Psusennes I's tomb.[751] A similar sequence also occurs on the Ptolemaic coffin of Khaf from Saqqara.[752] As pointed out by Roberson,[753] both the sarcophagi of Psusennes I and Khaf should indeed be regarded as three-dimensional variants of the two-dimensional awakening scenes depicted on the bi-partite tableau.[754] To these sources, one should also add the sarcophagus of the son of king Amasis, Iahmes.[755]

749 Montet 1951, pl. 92.
750 Montet 1951, pl. 90.
751 Montet 1951, pl. 11.
752 Daressy 1917, 5-11.
753 See also Manassa 2007, 148-149, 394-395.
754 Roberson 2013, 121-122.
755 Hermitage 766: Leclant 1962, fig. 17.

The scenes of the awakening of Osiris have been studied by Assmann[756] and Waitkus,[757] and, more recently, by Roberson. According to a theory by Assmann, followed by many scholars, the awakening of Osiris by Horus would take place in the Embalming Hall, as a precursor of the Graeco-Roman nightly 'hour vigil' (*Stundenwachen*) for Osiris. In this respect, it has been noted that the thirty-six deities who had to watch over Osiris' corpse – twenty on the west side and sixteen on the east side – might evoke the thirty-six decans, representing the passage of the night-time hours.[758]

However, the monument usurped by Psusennes I is particularly interesting, since it is the first example of the presence of these deities on a sarcophagus; it is also the first time that they appear together with the guardian-deities originally connected with Chapter 144 of the Book of the Dead or with the New Kingdom Theban tombs. Indeed, all these gods will then find one of their privileged locations on the walls of sarcophagi. Moreover, the usurped sarcophagus of Psusennes I seems to be a very good example of the different competences of these two different groups of deities. Both these divine groups surround the body of the deceased who is lying inside the sarcophagus. But while the guardian-deities are located on the outer sides of the sarcophagus, as if they were actually warding off any evil that might jeopardize the deceased's safety, the deities associated with the awakening scene and represented on the interior sides, are directly in contact with the deceased's body, and witness his resurrection by Horus. They not only protected the body, but also helped to revivify the god. During the 26th Dynasty, these two categories of deities also appeared together in the tomb of Mutirdis[759] and on the sarcophagus of the son of king Amasis, the 'overseer of the army' (*ỉmy-r mšʿ*) Iahmes,[760] which shows two rows of deities on each side, with the gods from the awakening scene in the lower registers and the other deities in the upper ones.

The presence of these divine groups on the Leiden monument has no parallels on any other monolithic naos. If the guardian-deities on the front and on the lower registers of the rear, right and left sides had the purpose to thwart any malevolent interference, the presence of the deities on the upper register of the rear aimed, if not at representing the awakening of Osiris scene, at least at evoking it. The fact that these deities are divided in two rows, represented back to back, does not just have an aesthetic reason, but reflects their original arrangement in two groups, to the west and east of the central figure of Osiris. Moreover, they create a sort of protective shield for Osiris and look towards the front. That is, like the figures of the awakening scenes, they all look towards Osiris' body, inside the niche, which is the focal point of the naos. Moreover, the shrine with *uraei* on the lintel of the naos resembles the shrine containing the corpse of Osiris in the awakening scenes. The fact that, on the naos, there are just ten gods, rather than thirty-six, is not necessarily a problem, since they could be representing a *pars pro toto*.[761] In

756 Assmann 1977, 92-93. See also Smith 1987, 25-26.

757 Waitkus 1987, 68-70.

758 Waitkus 1987, 68-69; Roberson 2013, 130-131, 133. See also Abitz 1979, 62-66; Quack 1999, 215; von Lieven 2007, vol. 1, 25.

759 They are probably to be identified with the gods (whose names are lost) represented in the tomb of Ramose (TT 132) of the 25th Dynasty: Greco 2014.

760 Leclant 1962, fig. 17.

761 For the *pars pro toto* principle, see Niwinski 1989, 19-24, 219-228.

this respect, the sculptors of the naos had a choice of thirty-six deities, some of them showing an identical aspect; they took them from both the east and west sides of the lion bed carrying the awakening Osiris. The uniformity of the pose of these figures is striking, because variety was a preferred principle on the naos and perhaps not only for aesthetic reasons. Each god, with the exception of the two goddesses Maat and Nephthys portrayed in fully human form, shows a different head: crocodile, lioness, ram, serpent, canine, antelope, and ibis. Despite the limited number of figures, ten deities in all, this is an exhaustive inventory, ensuring that every divine power is here in action.

If the niche of the naos, with Osiris Hemag's statue, may be regarded as an equivalent of the two-dimensional shrine with the god's body, the presence of Horus as the first god of the row of deities in the lower register on the right side wall might be relevant, since he might be playing the role of the standing falcon-headed Horus who awakes Osiris. As pointed out by Roberson,[762] in all the royal versions the double identification of the king with both Horus and Osiris is emphasized. The king is Osiris on his funerary bed, but also Horus, who puts in motion the awakening of his deceased father. The equation Horus/king is acknowledged by the royal titles of Horus and by the fact that his figure maintains human features. It is hardly a coincidence that in the royal sarcophagus of Merenptah usurped by Psusennes I, Horus, with the caption 'foremost of the gods' (*m-ḫnt nṯrw*), is depicted falcon-headed for the first time in this kind of scenes, and that Horus, in this specific context, has no royal titles but is accompanied by an inscription that identifies Psusennes I as Horus' father. In the sarcophagus of Amasis' son, the 'overseer of the army' Iahmes, with twenty-six deities in the lower registers of the two long sides, Horus' figure has been omitted. Instead, very appropriately, the falcon-headed iconography is present in the private versions of Mutirdis and Khaf, where, however, no epithet is bestowed on the god. If the naos of Leiden is to be read as a three-dimensional variant of the awakening scene, the presence of Horus as a falcon-headed god might indicate, as in the usurped sarcophagus of Psusennes I, that in this context it is the god himself who acts for Osiris. The fact that the god is here accompanied by the epithet 'great god' (*nṯr ꜥꜣ*) corroborates this hypothesis. As a consequence, the Osiris statue would have been placed inside the niche with its head looking towards Horus, rather than in the other direction. It should also be stressed that Horus is followed by the lion-headed Sha, 'He who cuts to pieces', in my opinion a variant of Sha-betjw, who actually belongs to the thirty-six gods of the awakening scenes. His presence on this part of the naos might seem out of place. However, Sha is the only deity who is represented while moving. He raises an arm behind Horus' shoulders. The two gods are therefore linked by that gesture. And their presence just at the beginning of the lower right row of deities makes sense if one considers their position as if they were located just in front or next to the door of the naos, with Horus occupying a similar position as in the awakening scenes and with Sha as a reminder of the event occurring inside the naos, that is the awakening of Osiris Hemag.

Moreover, the great majority of the deities of the naos appear in contexts preserving an awakening scene of Osiris by Horus. Therefore, it is very likely that the naos shares with these monuments a similar group of themes concerning Osiris' death and resurrection. It

762 Roberson 2013, 133-135.

does not seem possible to establish if the Saite artisans who created Amasis' naos had a direct source of inspiration at their disposal and borrowed all the sequences of deities and the theme of Osiris' awakening from a specific monument. The Delta provenance of the naos and its royal 'nature' would argue in favour of a Lower Egyptian royal antecedent; in this case the only possibilities would be the tombs of Psusennes I, with his usurped sarcophagus, and Sheshonq III at Tanis. However, owing to its unique variations, a direct link to a single monument cannot be taken for granted. The actual methods of transmission of religious themes and types of decoration may have varied from case to case, and may as well have depended on the mediation of a papyrus template or one – or even more – pattern books.[763] From these sources, the Saite artisans may have gleaned their divine figures, aiming at creating a new and three-dimensional version of the theme of the Osirian awakening, purposely adapted to a monolithic naos.

Unfortunately, our knowledge of the religious meaning of the naos is restricted by the lack of information on its architectonic context, so many important questions remain unanswered. What was its original location? And how did it relate to other religious buildings, in particular to the other naoi installed by Amasis? Who had access to it? And, above all, how was the naos used?

The decoration of the naos expresses religious ideas in vogue from the New Kingdom, through the Third Intermediate and Saite Periods, to the Graeco-Roman Period. However, the Leiden naos is the first instance where these ideas, lying behind the construction of a narrative told in images, are not related to a deceased man, woman, or king, but to the deceased god par excellence, Osiris. The only other examples where similar deities are gathered together for Osiris, or any other god, are the Osirian chapels in the temple of Hathor at Dendera, in the Graeco-Roman Period. In particular, the Leiden naos might be regarded as a forerunner – by a few centuries – of some of the themes expressed in the third eastern and western Osirian chapels. Several deities, a few of them appearing also on the Leiden naos, are represented on the walls of the third eastern chapel, with the intent of protecting the awakening of Osiris.[764] Other deities carrying out an apotropaic function are also depicted in the second western chapel.[765] This might suggest that the regeneration of Osiris Hemag was celebrated during the festivals that took place in the month of Khoiak. Images of Osiris lying on beds are indeed usually associated with the 'mysteries' of Khoiak, at least from the reign of Sety I at Abydos.[766] The special link of Osiris Hemag, evoking the theme of the Osirian awakening, with the festivals of Khoiak is confirmed by the fact that, at Dendera,[767] the 'house of *hemag*' and the epithet and verb *hemag* occur almost exclusively in the inscriptions of the Osirian chapels, and above all by the presence on their walls of images of this form of the god.

Unlike other Osirian forms appearing at Dendera, Osiris Hemag is depicted on both the west walls of the third eastern and western chapels. In the eastern chapel the god, representated as a naked and ithyphallic Osiris of Behbeit el-Hagar (Fig. IV.7), appears

763 See Der Manuelian 1994, 55; von Lieven 2007, 205-217; Roberson 2013, 121-122.
764 *Dendera* X, pls. 94-95.
765 *Dendera* X, pls. 192-203. See also Lucarelli 2010a, 88-89.
766 Eaton 2006, 75-101.
767 On the Festivals of Khoiak at Dendera, see Chassinat 1966-1968; Cauville 1988; Pizzarotti 2012. On the connection of the Festivals of Khoaik and the 'hour vigil' (*Stundenwachen*), see Pries 2011, 17-26.

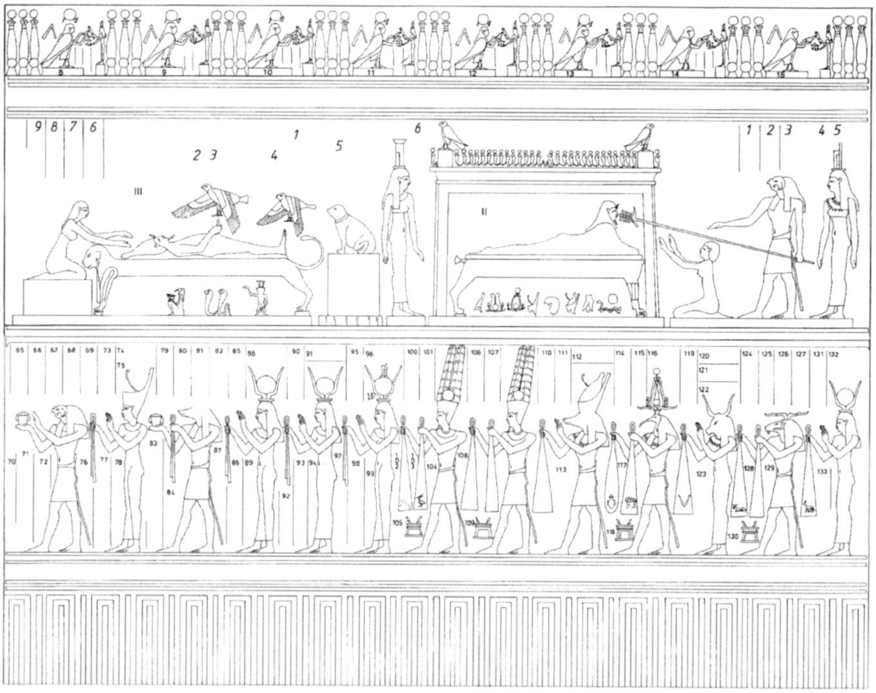

Fig. IV.14. Dendera, Hathor temple, third western Osiris chapel, east wall. Reproduced after *Dendera* X, pl. 237.

in a row of Osiris images of the Delta – Memphis, Sile, Heliopolis – while on the opposite wall there are Osirian forms from the south: Dendera, Ombos, Edfu, and el-Kab.[768] But the relevance of Osiris Hemag is above all visible inside one of the most important areas of the whole Osirian complex, the third western chapel, where he appears as one of the three local forms of the god. Here, the various Denderite Osirian forms[769] are exclusively accompanied by Osirian forms from his most important cult-centres – Abydos and Busiris – likewise represented on their own lion beds. The north wall features a central scene with a mummified and ithyphallic Osiris of Dendera – named 'the one who presides over the god's hall, who resides in Iunet (*ḫnty sḥ-nṯr ḥry-ib iwnt*) – on his lion bed, surrounded by Anubis, Heqet, Hor-nedj-it-ef, Isis, Nephthys, and Thoth.[770] This scene is flanked, on the right and left, by two other 'bed scenes', one with the mummified and ithyphallic Sokar-Osiris, 'the great god in Djedu' (*nṯr ꜥꜣ m ḏdw*), and the other with the mummified Ptah-Sokar-Osiris, both accompanied by Isis and Nephthys.[771]

On the west wall, the rather elaborate scene described above (Fig. IV.8) with a naked and ithyphallic Osiris Hemag on his lion bed, is located next to the falcon-headed Sokar-Osiris, 'the great god, who resides in Djedu' (*nṯr ꜥꜣ ḥry-ib ḏdw*), ithyphallic, with an *atef*-crown, lying mummiform on a lion bed and with Isis and Nephthys to either side.[772] It is striking that the decoration is arranged in such a way that Sokar-Osiris of Busiris is in front of Osiris of Abydos, 'who presides over the West, the great god, lord of the horizon of Abydos' (*ḫnty imntt nṯr ꜥꜣ nb ꜣḫt ꜣbḏw*), depicted on the opposite wall as a mummy

768 Cauville 1997, 113-121, 239. On the Osirian chapels at Dendera, see also Cauville 1988.
769 Cauville 1997, 199-203.
770 *Dendera* X, pls. 235, 255.
771 *Dendera* X, pls. 236, 254, 259.
772 *Dendera* X, pls. 239, 257-258, 264.

wearing the white crown, lying on a lion bed and holding his erect phallus, with Isis hovering above it and Hathor and the frog goddess Heqet at his sides (Fig. IV.14).[773] But it is hardly a coincidence that, in front of Osiris Hemag, there is a scene similar to the scenes of the awakening of Osiris by his son Horus: the god, whose name is rather curiously not specified, lies mummiform with his head upraised on a lion bed, under which are divine and royal emblems. He is inside a shrine surmounted by rearing uraei and two falcons on rectangles recalling the variant with *serekhs* of the awakening scenes of the royal versions. Behind the god there is an image of a standing Nephthys, while in front of him there is the falcon-headed Horus 'who protects his father, son of Osiris, the great god who resides in Iunet' (*ḥr nḏ-it=f sꜣ wsir nṯr ꜥꜣ ḥry-ib iwnt*), followed by Isis 'the great, the god's mother' (*wrt mwt-nṯr*) and in the act of extending a *djed-was*-staff towards the nostrils of Osiris.[774] The upper registers of the west and east walls of the third western Osirian chapel create a connective symmetry between all these Osirian forms. The two main Egyptian Osiris forms of the north (Djedu) and south (Abydos) are one in front of the other; in this context, the other two Osiris images might be regarded as Denderite forms of the god, with Osiris Hemag, one of the most significant types of the resurrecting Osiris, being represented opposite a nameless Osiris, very similar to the Osiris of the more ancient awakening scenes.

Roberson[775] has pointed out that the earliest version of the awakening of Osiris by Horus, that of Sety I, was not in a tomb, but rather in a temple designed to function ritually as a tomb, a cenotaph, for Osiris and, therefore, the text and scene should be interpreted as part of a temple ritual for the cult of the god's statue in connection with the mortuary ceremonies and interment of his image. The Leiden naos shares with the Cenotaph of Sety I the fact that it is neither a tomb nor a sarcophagus. This monument, though having minor dimensions, may have been intended in a rather similar way. A naos is for hiding: inside its walls, the statue of Osiris Hemag was enshrined and preserved. In this specific case, it is also a symbolic burial place, a tomb or a sarcophagus, which provides a magical protection for Osiris. And the texts of the Graeco-Roman Period appropriately insist on the secrecy surrounding this Osirian form: Osiris Hemag is the one 'whose image is sacred in the two sanctuaries of Egypt' (*ḏsr sštꜣ m itrty bꜣḳt*)[776] and 'whose plans are hidden in the shrines' (*imn sẖrw m sẖmw*),[777] while the temple of *hemag* keeps his 'secret' (*štꜣ*) 'form' (*irw*)[778] or 'relic' (*iẖt*).[779]

But a naos has also to be opened: it implies a certain amount of human activity around it, however sporadic and occasional. To open its doors – of which unfortunately nothing can be said – means to reveal the statue representing the god in the act of coming to a

773 *Dendera* X, pl. 253.

774 *Dendera* X, pls. 237, 252, 262.

775 Roberson 2013, 133.

776 No other example of this epithet is attested; however, Osiris is occasionally the one 'whose image is sacred' in the Graeco-Roman temples: *ḏsr sštꜣ* (*Edfu* II 68, 11; *Kom Ombo* n. 150), *ḏsr sštꜣ m iw wꜥb* (Bénédite 1893, 121, 11), *ḏsr sštꜣ=f m ẖnt ḥwt nbw* (*Dendera* X 230, 3), *ḏsr sštꜣ=f m ẖnw mꜥnḏt* (*Dendera* X 25, 3), *ḏsr sštꜣ m spꜣwt* (*Edfu* III 142, 2), *ḏsr sštꜣ m tꜣ-rr* (*Dendera* II 152, 16; IX 86, 4).

777 *Dendera* X 160, 18-161, 1. For similar epithets ascribed to Osiris, see also *Dendera* X 398, 7-8 (*imn sẖrw m ḥwwt-nṯr*) and *Kom Ombo* n. 150 (*imn sẖrw=f m ẖnw st štꜣt*).

778 *Edfu* V 110, 8-9; *Dendera* X 282, 11.

779 *Médamoud*, 157.

new life, taking care of this image, and making it the protagonist of rituals concerning aspects of Osiris' resurrection. In this respect, the gods and goddesses represented, with their power to prevent any evil, ensure that nothing goes wrong and are part of the ritual. The theme of the awakening of Osiris has never been so clearly expressed in a monolithic shrine. It is not surprising that this monument was specially created for Osiris Hemag, who is sexually active in order to generate his son and heir Horus, the awakener, and who perfectly embodies a reborn god who has successfully gone through the most critical phase of his existence.

4. Naoi at Kom el-Ahmar

Kom el-Ahmar is located about 5 km east of the modern town of Minuf, in the central Delta province of Minufiyeh. As we have seen, some information on the village was first provided by two French travellers from Marseilles – Pascal Coste and Jean-Jacques Rifaud – who visited the site in the 1820s and drew the *kom* rising above the fields.[780] In 1822 the so-called Athribis stela,[781] celebrating king Merenptah's victory over the Lybians in his 5th year of reign, was found at the site, which was moved to the Cairo Museum in 1927. The site does not seem to have drawn the attention of Georges Daressy, who did not make any mention of the presence of blocks when he surveyed the area in 1911.[782]

A renewed interest in Kom el-Ahmar arose after nearly 90 years thanks to Jean Yoyotte's article *Le grand Kôm el-Ahmar de Menûfiyah et deux naos du Pharaon Amasis*, published in 2001, and, more recently, to the EES Minufiyeh Archaeological Survey led by Joanne Rowland, a project that aims at understanding the distribution of the archaeological sites in the area. An initial ground survey at Kom el-Ahmar was carried out in 2005,[783] when, also thanks to the collaboration of the villagers, the team was able to identify a few blocks, some of them re-used in modern buildings. The Minufiyeh Archaeological Survey returned to Kom el-Ahmar in 2006 and 2007,[784] when other blocks were recovered, and in 2008 and 2009.[785]

The main issue about these blocks – some of them with the cartouches of king Amasis – and the naoi found at the site concerns their original location. In this respect, according to Jean Yoyotte[786] and Joanne Rowland,[787] the village of Kom el-Ahmar might still be covering the foundations of a temple complex which housed all these monuments. Sylvain Dhennin has recently questioned this hypothesis.[788] He has pointed out that the naos Louvre D 29 is dedicated to an Osirian form of Mefekat (*mfkꜣt*), or Fekat, a locality of the Western Delta probably to be connected with the site of Kom Abu Billo (Terenouthis), which was included in the *sepat* 'Southern shield', *i.e.* the Prosopite nome.[789] Moreover, the inscriptions on the fragmentary corner of a naos found by Joanne Rowland refer

780 Yoyotte 2001, 54-83. See also above, Chapter I.
781 PM IV, 67; KRI IV, 19-22; Sourouzian 1989, 69-72.
782 Daressy 1912.
783 Rowland/Wilson 2006, 11-13; Rowland/Billing 2006, 3-6.
784 Rowland 2007, 69-71. See also Rowland/Billing 2009, 7-9; Billing/Rowland 2015.
785 Rowland *et al.* 2009, 36-37, 48. See also Rowland/Strutt 2012, 328-345.
786 Yoyotte 2001, 80-81.
787 Rowland/Billing 2009, 8; Billing/Rowland 2015, 108-110.
788 Dhennin 2014, 14-15; Dhennin 2016, 61-62.
789 On this Egyptian province, see Dhennin 2012.

to a 'great house in granite' (*pr wr m mꜣṯ*) that was made for 'Hathor who resides in the *set-weret*' (*ḥt-ḥr ḥry-ib st-wrt*) and 'the gods who are in the Upper Mansion' (*nṯrw imyw ḥwt-ḥry-tp*). Both the *pr wr* and the *ḥwt-ḥry-tp*, the 'Upper Mansion', are mentioned together in a passage of the so-called 'Rituel de Mefky',[790] preserved on a basalt block in Cairo (JE 45936). On this basis, according to Sylvain Dhennin, both these naoi would have been together in a cultic context dedicated to Hathor at Mefekat, where a temple already existed before the Ptolemaic Period.[791] The naoi would have been transported to Kom el-Ahmar only after Mefekat was abandoned. As for the naos of Leiden AM 107 dedicated to Osiris Hemag, it would have reached its new destination after having been removed from another locality, perhaps Sais.

In my opinion, there are, instead, strong elements that indicate that all three of these naoi originally stood in the same place. First of all, in case they came from more than one site, one should explain why so many moveable monoliths that originally belonged to the same king – the three naoi, but also other blocks with Amasis' name – had Kom el-Ahmar as their final destination.

Moreover, both the Louvre naos and the Leiden one suffered *damnatio memoriae*. Since this practice does not seem to have been systematically applied to the monuments of Amasis all over Egypt, but only in a limited number of places, it is more probable that these two shrines shared the misfortune of being in the same location. Besides, it should be noted that the three granite naoi have interesting characteristics in common. The two Amasis naoi now in Europe and the fragmentary one with a dedication to Hathor all have a similar decoration, consisting of the combination of a dedicatory text with registers showing rows of deities. Moreover, the decorations on the fronts of the Louvre and Leiden naoi are clearly variants of each other and are not present on any other monolithic shrine. More interestingly, in the dedicatory inscriptions, all three of these examples present, as we have already seen, a peculiar writing for the word *mnw* 'monument', with the bilateral sign *mn* followed by the phonetic complement *n*. Yet, in all the other known dedicatory texts from Amasis' reign not originating from Kom el-Ahmar – the naos from Athribis, the obelisk from Mensha/Ptolemais (CG 17029),[792] the Apis sarcophagus in the Serapeum,[793] and the offering-table (CG 23110)[794] of unknown provenance – the word is spelled as usual, with the bilateral *mn* and three *nw*-vases. All this suggests that these naoi were chronologically and geographically united, and were conceived and also created in the same environment, within a restricted span of time.

Since the hypothesis that Mefkat has to be identified with ancient Kom el-Ahmar, rather than with ancient Kom Abu Billo, does not seem sustainable,[795] I would assume – if Sylvain Dhennin's hypothesis is correct – that also the Leiden naos was set up by Amasis in Mefekat (Kom Abu Billo). However, it should be noted that no other document corroborates the existence of Osiris Hemag's worship at this site. New archaeological evidence would be required to rule out the possibility that all the Saite monuments found

790 Daressy 1916, 228-229.
791 Dhennin 2014, 13-14.
792 Kuentz 1932, 59-60, pl. XV.
793 Gunn 1926, 82-84.
794 Kamal 1909, 91, pl. XXV.
795 Dhennin 2014, 15.

Fig. IV.15. Louvre D 29 (© Musée du Louvre / Christian Larrieu).

at Kom el-Ahmar were indeed commissioned by Amasis for a local temple, and were not moved here from elsewhere. In order to understand the context in which these blocks have been discovered, the Minufiyeh Archaeological Survey has carried out core drilling and geophysical surface surveys. In particular, the data offered by the magnetometer survey indicate that on the low ground around the *kom*, in the same area where the Leiden and Louvre naoi were found before being transported to Europe, there might be a sub-surface structure, possibly the remains of a sacred area or building.

But there are many other problems yet to be resolved. At present, no inscribed document from Kom el-Ahmar presents a place-name that might be identified as the name of the supposed ancient site, which would have laid in the Prosopite province, the fourth of Lower Egypt.[796] Moreover, it is not clear if the five – inscribed and uninscribed – blocks recorded by the Minufiyeh Archaeological Survey are fragments of just one naos, or of two or even more shrines. At least three naoi were present at the site, two dedicated to different Osirian forms and one to the goddess Hathor. The fact that Amasis commissioned more than one monolithic shrine suggests that, in the Saite period, the ancient Kom el-Ahmar would have been a rather significant site. The scanty archaeological data combined with the information obtained from Coste and Rifaud indicates that the king may have set up all these monuments in the same area, of which no reconstruction is presently possible.

The clustering of several monolithic shrines in a single sacred space was not unusual. As in the case, for example, of Nekhthorheb's naoi at Bubastis,[797] not only the number, but also the original arrangement of the shrines remains at present a matter of speculation. It is equally unknown whether there was one main naos and two (or more) secondary ones, or whether their disposition did not reflect a hierarchic subdivision. They may simply have been standing in separate adjacent sanctuaries; otherwise, in the case of more than three naoi, one shrine may have been located at the centre, with the other shrines to the sides or – as has been suggested for Tell Tebilla in the eastern Delta[798] – around it inside separate sanctuaries. It is also plausible that their disposition echoed that executed by Amasis at Mendes, with the shrines contained in an open-air court (Fig. III.14). At present, there is no way to ascertain if any of these interpretations is correct. The religious and ritual connections among these monuments also remain an open question. Did any single naos fulfil an independent function? Or were they in harmony with each other, being part of a coherent and unitary religious discourse?

Compared to the Leiden naos, the naos Louvre D 29 is more 'traditional' in shape, with an arched roof and a niche which is taller than it is wide (Fig. IV.15). However, this shrine, too, presents some original elements. Its form recalls that of a small temple with a cavetto cornice, torus moulding, and a frieze of uraei that – unlike that in the naos of Athribis – runs around all four faces.

The decorative scheme of the front closely resembles the one on the Leiden naos. On the lintel, Isis and Nephthys take the place of the *imy-wt* emblem in front of the royal *serekh*. The jambs present a few significant differences, first of all the number of registers: three on the Louvre naos, and only two on the Leiden one. In the upper register on the left, there are Horus-who-protects-his-father (*ḥr-nḏ-it=f*) and Anubis. On the right there are Thoth 'lord of Khemenu' (*nb ḫmnw*) and Horus Khenty(-en)-irty (*ḥr-ḫnty-irty*), a form of the falcon god associated with Letopolis, not far away from the fourth Lower Egyptian province. These four gods on the front allude to the function and themes of the naos. Anubis may evoke the funerary nature of the recipient of the monument, Thoth of Khemenu/Hermopolis evokes the Hermopolitan Ogdoad and the creative cycle also present in the upper register of the rear, while the two Horus forms clearly emphasize the

796 See Yoyotte 2001, 81-83; Dhennin 2016, 61.
797 Rosenow 2006, 45, figs. 22-24.
798 Mumford 2004, 274-276, fig. 5.

protective role played by the son Horus for his father Osiris. In this respect, in Chapter 17 of the Book of the Dead, Horus Khenty-en-irty is said to be a protector of Osiris and is mentioned together with Horus-who-protects-his-father as the 'twin progeny' (*ṯ3w=f*) of the god. The second register of the front is dedicated to the Four Sons of Horus, two on each side; their distribution is identical to the one of the Leiden naos – Hapy and Qebehsenuef on the right and Imsety and Duamutef on the left – but their iconography is different, being represented as standing male figures with one arm bent over the chest just above the waist, the hand holding a flail. The lower register is also different from the one in Leiden, since here the goddesses *nẖbt* and *mwyt* are followed by Hapi and Wadj-wer (*w3ḏ-wr*), respectively, both holding a platter with a *was*-sign between two *hes*-vases like the goddesses.

The upper register of the left wall presents deities of the Heliopolitan cycle: a standing lion-headed Ra-Horakhty,[799] with one hand on his chest and the other holding an *ankh*-sign; Atum, enthroned and with the double crown; Shu and Tefnet, depicted as human-headed birds,[800] with the solar disk and placed on the same base; Geb, seated and wearing the white crown; and Nut, seated and wearing the red crown. Members of the Heliopolitan Ennead are also present in the first part of the second register: Osiris (*wsỉr*), as a standing god wearing a tripartite wig, *shendyt*, and holding the *was*-staff in one hand and the *ankh*-sign in the other; Isis and Nephthys, both standing with the *was*-staff and the *ankh*-sign; and a standing falcon-headed Horus 'in the *hut-aat*' (*ḥr-m-ḥwt-ʿ3t*).[801] The divine row ends with two goddesses: a lion-headed Bastet 'secret of form' (*b3stt št3 ỉrw*),[802] with two plumes on her head and squatting on a base, and an otherwise unattested goddess named *šbtyt*, the 'curly one'.[803] In the lower register the row of gods is led by Ptah 'who is on the *set-weret*' (*ḥry st-wrt*), seated inside a chapel; Maat; an ibis-headed god defined as 'lord of Khemenu', evidently an image of Thoth; and finally four images of Hathor, all squatting on a base and with the solar disk between cow horns on their heads, identified as 'The Golden one, she has come' (*nbwt-ỉỉ-tỉ*);[804] 'Lady of Anet' (*nbt ʿnt*),[805] a locality in the vicinity of Memphis; Nebet-hetepet (*nbt-ḥtpt*);[806] and 'Lady of the sycamore' (*nbt nht*).[807]

The upper register of the right wall opens with an image of a falcon with solar disk on a *djed*-pillar, followed by a standing Ptah. This group, placed within a shrine, is labelled 'Ptah *djed*' (*ptḥ ḏd*). The row of gods continues with two animal images: the falcon Sokar 'in Biket' (*skr m bỉkt*)[808] and the beetle Khepрer, both on pedestals. Then there are two images of Osiris as standing mummies with white crowns – 'Osiris lord of the horizon' (*wsỉr nb*

799 Images of Ra-Horakhty in the guise of a lion-headed god are rare; see the temple of Hibis (Davies 1953, 2, VI) and *Edfu* III 224, 17, pl. 72.

800 In the temple of Hibis (Davies 1953, 5, V), Shu and Tefnet appear as two human-headed birds – one male, one female – on a *djed*-pillar.

801 Leitz 2002, V, 273. For the Saite period, see also Goyon 1972, X, 5. This form of Horus appears also on a naos of the Late Period (Cairo CG 70021).

802 No other example of Bastet with this epithet is known: Leitz 2002, II, 171.

803 Leitz 2002, VI, 239.

804 Leitz 2002, IV, 182 quotes only the Louvre naos for this form of Hathor, but she appears also on a Ptolemaic block from Mefekat: Dhennin 2012, 14.

805 Leitz 2002, IV, 27.

806 Leitz 2002, IV, 111-112.

807 Leitz 2002, IV, 79-81.

808 There are only four known examples of this form of Sokar; the Louvre D 29 is the only one dated to the Late Period: Leitz 2002, VI, 668.

ꜣḫt)[809] and 'foremost of the West' (*ḫnty imntt*) – and Shentayt. The second register presents three falcons on pedestals: Sema-tawy (*smꜣ-tꜣwy*) and the 'lord of Sakhebu' (*nb sꜣḫbw*),[810] both with solar disks on their heads, and the 'lord of Khem' (Letopolis) (*nb ḫm*), with the double crown. These are followed by Sopdu as a falcon with the white crown crouching on a pedestal; Amun, seated on a throne and wearing two high plumes; Khonsu, with the side lock of hair; and another image of Amun as a recumbent lion on a tall pedestal. The lower register has a more aggressive nuance and includes Horus 'mighty of arm' (*ḥr ṯmꜣ-ꜥ*), holding a harpoon; Neith 'lady of Sais' (*nt nbt sꜣw*), kneeling on a pedestal and grasping a bow; Wadjet of Dep (*wꜣḏt dp*); the lion Mahes (*mꜣi-ḥsꜣ*), depicted with a lotus with two plumes on his head and devouring a captive; and the Upper and Lower Egyptian Meret-goddesses (*mrt šmꜥw* and *mrt mḥw*),[811] with their typical hairdo and making a gesture of adoration with their arms aloft and the palms of the hands upwards.

The upper register of the rear wall is occupied by the eight gods of Khemenu – Heh and Hehet, Keku and Keket, Nun and Nunet, Amun and Amunet – representing the Hermopolitan creative cycle. The themes of creation and fertility are also emphasized in the second register, showing Hor-Khenty-khety (*ḥr-ḫnty-ḫty*) in the form of a crocodile-headed god, and 'Horus son of Isis of Gebtyu' (*ḥr sꜣ ꜣst gbtyw*),[812] represented with double feather crown, wrapped body, erect phallus, and an arm extended to hold a flail. In front of him, there is a small image of the goddess Maat. These are followed by Amun, depicted as a human-headed bird on a pedestal, ithyphallic and with a double feather crown. The epithet of the god – written with the bilateral sign *ḥꜣ*, followed by the *p*, the phallus, and the *f* – might be read 'who hides his image' (*ḥꜣp sšmw=f*).[813] In the last part of the divine row the themes of the descent of Horus from Osiris, of the legitimacy of his rule, and of his filial relation with his father, already evoked in the epithet 'Horus son of Isis of Gebtyu', are reiterated by means of two other Horus forms: 'Horus who loves his father' (*ḥr mr-it=f*)[814] and 'Hor-sema-tawy upon his great throne' (*ḥr smꜣ-tꜣwy ḥr st=f wrt*). In the lower register, Mefekat, the locality of the Osiris who is beneficiary of the naos, is recalled. The first image is that of a *djed*-pillar, labelled 'Osiris *djed*' (*wsir ḏd*);[815] then there is a mummy, lying on a pedestal or bed and called 'Sokar the equipped one,[816] foremost of Mefekat' (*skr ꜥpr ḫnty mfkꜣt*); this is followed by 'Isis, the sister' and 'Nephthys, the sister'; and finally there are six

---

809 In the Saite Period, besides Osiris in the Louvre naos, this epithet is bestowed on Ra (Corteggiani 1979, 119, 124; Assmann 1983, 38, 16) and Sokar (Goyon 1972, XVII, 23). See also Leitz 2002, III, 565-566.

810 A locality in the western Delta: Montet 1954, 28-32; Sauneron 1983a, 1-11, 13. See also Leitz 2002, III, 726.

811 Leitz 2002, III, 330-331.

812 Leitz 2002, V, 285.

813 The only other example of this epithet is, once again, bestowed on Amun and is dated to the Graeco-Roman Period: Leitz V, 23.

814 There is only one other example of this form of Horus: Leitz 2002, III, 335.

815 The form Osiris *djed* is rather rare. In his statue from Taremu/Leontopolis of the late 25th or early 26th Dynasty (Brooklyn Musem 64.146: Bothmer 1970, pl. 6), Padimahes bears the title of '*hem-netjer* priest of Osiris *djed*'. On the naos Verona 30297 of the Late Period (Clère 1973, 103, pl. 15), he appears again as a *djed*-pillar, but inside a large structure with rounded top – perhaps a coffin – and between two kings with one raised arm, one wearing the white crown and the other the red crown. See also Leitz 2002, II, 569.

816 Or should it be intended as 'Sokar (*m*) *ꜥpr*', denoting a mythological place or sanctuary in the territory of Memphis? See Leitz VI, 666.

standing mummies, the first three identified as 'the gods of the horizon' (*nṯrw ꜣḫt*),[817] the last three as 'the gods of the two caverns' (*nṯrw ḳrrty*).[818]

The decoration of the naos Louvre D 29 evokes the creative cycles of Hermopolis and Heliopolis.[819] Besides Hermopolis, the only other Upper Egyptian site mentioned on the naos is Coptos. The other toponyms refer to Lower Egypt – Dep, Sais – with a prevalence for the south-west or south of the Delta: Letopolis, the territories of Memphis and Heliopolis, Sakhebu and Mefekat. This last site is also connected with the recipient of the naos: 'Osiris-*mryt*, the [great ?][820] god, foremost of Fekat' (*wsỉr mryt nṯr* [*ꜥꜣ ?*] *ḫnty fkꜣt*), who was worshipped there together with the goddess Hathor – the main local deity – and Horus-sema-tawy.[821]

In the two naoi of Amasis dedicated to Osiris, the relations established between the king and the represented gods on the one side, and between these deities and the recipients of the shrines on the other, are substantially different. As we have seen, in the Leiden naos the majority of the deities are functional to the rebirth of Osiris Hemag. That they are conceptually and literally close to Osiris Hemag, kept inside the niche, is reflected by their distribution on the walls of the monument, with (almost) all the deities – including those on the rear – looking towards the doors in perfect symmetry, which efficiently emphasises their actual presence around Osiris Hemag's image. The arrangement of the gods on the Louvre naos is instead asymmetric and more conventional, with all the figures in perfect rows, those on the side walls looking towards the doors, but those on the back all facing left. All these gods are represented here because they evoke themes in connection with Osiris' nature and/or because they have a geographical relation to him, since they are said to reside in the temple of Osiris.

It is interesting that neither of the two recipients is represented on the naos; Amasis is also physically absent. However, unlike the Leiden naos, on the Louvre shrine the king, through the dedicatory text, creates a connection not only with the recipient but also with all the other deities. The dedicatory texts on all the side walls run above the upper registers and continue down behind the three registers. The left and right side walls have the same inscription, with the king declaring that 'he has made as his monument for his father Osiris' (*ỉr.n=f m mnw=f n ỉt=f wsỉr*) a 'great naos in granite' (*kꜣr ꜥꜣ m mꜣṯ*) 'on which are placed the name of the gods who follow him. That he may act, (the one who has been) given life!' (*wd rn n nṯrw ỉmyw ḫt=f ḥr=f ỉr=f dỉ ꜥnḫ*). On the rear it is said that the king 'has made (this) as his monument for the gods who are in the temple of Osiris-*mryt*, so that their name is enduring forever. That he may act, (the one who has been) given life and all the stability and power, all the health and joy on the seat of Horus, forever' (*ỉr.n=f m mnw=f n nṯrw ỉmy ḥwt wsỉr mryt rwḏ rn=sn ḏt ỉr=f dỉ ꜥnḫ dḏ wꜣs nb snb nb ꜣw ỉb=f ḥr st ḥr ḏt*). That the deities represented on the naos are the same as those who, according to the dedicatory text, reside within the temple of Osiris is corroborated by the fact that they, in their turn, interact with the king. Before each register there is indeed a column of hieroglyphs in which the gods reward Amasis by granting him the means by which he is able to rule: 'Words spoken: may

817 This is the only example of these gods for the 26th Dynasty: Leitz 2002, IV, 454.

818 Leitz 2002, IV, 548.

819 Spencer 2006, 22.

820 The *netjer*-sign is followed by a lacuna, with part of a small sign at the top. Jansen-Winkeln 2014, 420 suggests the presence of a *t*-sign, but it might be what remains of the top part of the biliteral *ꜥꜣ*, 'great'.

821 Dhennin 2012a. See also Dhennin 2011 and Dhennin 2014.

these give all life and dominion to the Horus Semen-maat' (*ḏd mdw dỉ nn ꜥnḫ wꜣs nb n ḥr smn-mꜣꜥt*). In the second and third register, 'all life and dominion' are replaced by 'stability' (*ḏd*) and 'health' (*snb*) respectively. Unlike the Leiden naos, where the king and the gods are not directly connected with each other, but both act for the benefit of Osiris Hemag, in the Louvre naos there is a complementary and circular beneficial action which passes through Osiris-*mryt*, with the king and the gods being donors and recipients at the same time.

The reading and interpretation of the first epithet of the Osiris of the naos Louvre D 29 – written *mryt* with the determinative of the canal – is rather problematic. Jean Yoyotte read the epithet of the Osiris of Mefekat as 'Osiris-de-la-rive' (*mryt*),[822] which should be associated with the place-name *mryt* mentioned in the so-called 'Rituel de Mefky'.[823] However, as Sylvain Dhennin[824] has pointed out, in private documents of the 25th-26th Dynasties the epithet of Osiris of Mefekat can be written differently as *mry*[825] or *mrty*[826], and it is possible that it should be connected with the Osiris *mrty*, the 'well-beloved', who also played a key role in the chapel of Osiris lord of the eternity-*neheh* (*nb nḥḥ*) of the time of Amasis at Thebes.[827]

The other two fragments with rows of deities found at Kom el-Ahmar, probably part of naoi, are also in red granite. Nothing can be said with certainty about their architectural form, but they must have shared a similar decoration with the naos Louvre D 29, with hieroglyphic texts very likely running along the top and the lateral sides, thus framing the deities arranged in different registers. One fragment,[828] almost certainly the lower corner of a naos, preserves the bottom register with the last three deities of the divine row – three baboons, one standing and two on a sledge – and the last part of the dedicatory text: [...*prt-ḫrw*] *n rꜥ nb ỉr=f dỉ ꜥnḫ ḏd wꜣs ꜣwt-ỉb ḏt*, '[... invocation offerings] every day. That he may act, (the one who has been) given life, stability, power, and joy forever'.

The fragmentary upper corner of a naos[829] in red granite for Hathor is even more interesting. Unlike the two naoi made for Osiris, this one has an internal decoration of a *kheker*-frieze and its exterior rear wall is simply polished, not decorated. The external left side wall preserves the last part of the divine row of the upper register, with four standing gods – Geb, Nut, Wadjet, and Shesmetet – looking towards the missing front of the shrine; since traces of a throne are still visible just before Geb, these four deities must have been preceded by one or more seated divine figures. The dedicatory text presents a similar arrangement to those on the naos Louvre D 29 and, very likely, also on the naos with the three baboons; the text runs above the upper register and runs down behind the deities. One might suggest that another vertical inscription was also running in front of the gods. What survives of the text says that a king, very likely Amasis, made as 'his monument' (*mnw=f*) a 'great house in granite' (*pr wr m mꜣṯ*) for 'his mother Hathor who resides in the *set-weret*' (*mwt=f ḥt-ḥr ḥry-ỉb st-wrt*) and the gods who are in the Upper Mansion (*nṯrw*

822 Yoyotte 2001, 68. See also Koemoth 2009, 43.
823 Daressy 1916, 224, 226.
824 Dhennin 2012a, 70.
825 Stela Musée d'Yverdon 83.2.1: Chappaz 1986, pl. II.
826 Stela Montgeron 2007.4: Dhennin 2012a, pls. V-VI.
827 Traunecker 2010, 181-185. On this important Osirian form, see also Cauville 1983, 83; Koemoth 2009.
828 Rowland 2007, 70-71, fig. 4; Rowland/Billing 2009, 7-8; Jansen-Winkeln 2014, 761; Billing/Rowland 2015, 105-106, fig. 4.
829 Rowland 2007, 70; Rowland/Billing 2009, 7-8; Jansen-Winkeln 2014, 761; Billing/Rowland 2015, 107.

imyw ḥwt-ḥry-tp)'. It is plausible that a similar, if not identical, text was also present on the right side wall.

The choice of a different terminology in the dedicatory texts was probably significant. All three naoi stress the filial relationship between donor and recipient and specify that the 'monument' (*mnw*) was made of 'granite' (*mꜣṯ*). While in both naoi for Osiris the monument is a 'great naos' (*kꜣr ꜥꜣ*), in the dedicatory text for Hathor this is defined as a 'great house' (*pr wr*).[830] The expression *per-wer* might, of course, be a generic definition of the naos, but at the same time the possibility cannot be ruled out that the differentiation between the terms *kꜣr*, actually a 'naos', and *pr-wr* had a topographical and cultic value. In the temple of Hathor at Dendera, for example, the *per-wer* is the chapel located on the central axis, at the rear of the main temple, just behind the barque sanctuary. It is also worth noting that in no other Egyptian monument the goddess Hathor is said to be the one 'who resides in the *set-weret*' (*ḥry-ib st-wrt*). This epithet is attested only twice in the Graeco-Roman Period in the temple of Edfu, once for Isis[831] and once for Sesheta-weret,[832] while a similar title – *ḥryt st-wrt*, 'she who is in the *set-weret*' – is bestowed to Hathor only at Dendera.[833] It is therefore possible that this epithet had a definite meaning at a local level. The *st-wrt*, the 'great place', might indeed have denoted, in this context, either the sanctuary which housed the naos or the whole temple complex.[834] Even more uncertain is how to interpret the place-name *ḥwt-ḥry-tp*, where the other deities (*nṯrw*) are said to be. Was this a chapel, temple, or sacred area at Mefekat or in the nearby ancient Kom el-Ahmar? In this case the naos, unlike the other two monuments for Osiris, would mention a local religious institution. Another interesting characteristic about the fragmentary naos for Hathor is the fact that, unlike the two naoi for Osiris, its outer rear wall was polished but does not present any decoration. Was the monument never completed? Or was the rear wall left purposely undecorated? If so, was this connected to its original position and to its relation with the other naoi?

Another very interesting red granite fragment from Kom el-Ahmar, bearing the cartouches of Amasis,[835] preserves six columns of a hieroglyphic text. Nothing can be said on the origin of this block; however, the arrangement of the text indicates that it was part of a building within the temple area, rather than a portion of a further naos. The signs of the two columns on the left are orientated to the right, while the signs of the other columns face left. The cartouche of the king is repeated in at least three columns, twice with his throne name and once unreadable. The surviving text surely refers to a building: '[...] may you make this house beautiful and enduring', [...] *ir=ṯ pr pn nfr rwḏ*; the text continues with the expression *ir.n=ṯ* or *ir.n(=i) n=ṯ* [...], 'you have made' or '(I) make for you [...]'; then, the following line preserves *di=ṯ n=f wꜣs nb ḫr* [...], 'may you give him all

830 The name *pr wr* is followed by the determinative of the archaic Upper Egyptian shrine of Nekhbet, which was important at the coronation of the king and at his *sed* festival.

831 *Edfu* I 490, 9-10.

832 *Edfu* IV 430.

833 Leitz 2002, V, 440-441.

834 On the use of the term *st-wrt*, see: Spencer 1984, 108-114.

835 Rowland/Wilson 2006, 11-13, fig. 5; Rowland/Billing 2006, 4-5; Rowland/Billing 2009, 7; Jansen-Winkeln 2014, 426; Billing/Rowland 2015, 104-105, fig. 3.

the power from [...]'. The use of the second person feminine suffix pronoun suggests a goddess, very likely Hathor herself.

Like the locality of Mefekat, the territory of Kom el-Ahmar may also have been particularly involved in the cult of Hathor during the Late Period. Moreover, during the reign of Amasis Osiris was a preponderant figure in the religious policy of the king, above all with an emphasis on the theme of the rebirth of the god, as for example at Ayn el-Muftella, with images of a naked awakening Osiris,[836] or in the decoration of the naos of Athribis for Kem-wer.

In the creation of the two naoi for Osiris and the one for Hathor, the men who conceived and designed these monuments must have looked intentionally for significant elements of originality, both in the decoration and in religious motifs and epithets. The Leiden naos is unlike any other Egyptian monolithic shrine. Many of the divine figures, names, and epithets on the Louvre naos – such as the lion-headed Ra-Horakhty, Bastet *št3 ỉrw*, *šbtyt,* Sokar *m bỉkt*, Sokar *ʿpr ḫnty mfk3t*, Osiris *nb 3ḫt*, Osiris *djed*, Horus *s3 3st gbtyw*, Horus *mr-ỉt=f*, Amun *ḥ3p sšmw=f*, and *nṯrw 3ḫt* – are very rare or attested nowhere else. Even though fragmentary, also the dedicatory text of the naos for Hathor is peculiar.

In case the naoi were made at (or for) Mekekat, Osiris Hemag may have joined Hathor and Osiris Merty in their own locality, in order to express ideas and themes connected with the god's awakening. However, future investigations at Kom el-Ahmar may provide new archaeological data revealing the importance of the site during the Late Period. In this case, Osiris Merty and Hathor may have come from the fairly close Mefekat, while Osiris Hemag may have migrated to Kom el-Ahmar from Sais or the territory of Memphis and/or Heliopolis, as the presence of three Osirian forms on the left side wall of the Leiden naos seems to indicate. At present, one may perhaps only suggest that, wherever these monolithic shrines were originally located, they stood on the same site. The naos for Hathor may have been the main shrine, which gathered together other naoi dedicated to Osirian forms. The goddess may have been at the centre of the local religious beliefs, and the naoi may have created a ritual landscape for the cult of Hathor, together with Osirian forms representing different aspects of the god's nature. And in particular, the peculiar Leiden naos of Osiris Hemag may have been involved in rituals of the Osirian 'mysteries' celebrated in the month of Khoiak, with its recipient well representing the final awakening of the god.

836 Room 121 (second chapel of Djedkhonsuiuefankh, reign of Amasis): Labrique 2007, 1062, 1065.

List of figures

Figs. I.1-5. The Leiden naos, as drawn and lithographed by the museum's assistant T. Hooiberg for Leemans 1839-, livraison 7 (Leiden 1845), pls. XXXV-XXXVI.

Figs. I.6-10. The Leiden naos, as represented in Boeser 1915, pls. I-V.

Fig. I.11. Drawing by Pascal Coste, labelled *Basse Egypte / Province de Menoufie / Ruines d'une ville égyptienne / actuellement village de Coum-Larma / du 26 novembre 1821 / P.C.* Reproduced from Yoyotte 2001, 63, fig. 2.

Fig. I.12. Drawing by Jean-Jacques Rifaud, as lithographed for Rifaud 1830, pl. 109, fig. 2. Reproduced from Yoyotte 2001, 71.

Figs. I.13-17. The Leiden naos, as displayed today in the galleries of the National Museum of Antiquities in Leiden (photographs by Robbert-Jan Looman).

Fig. II.1. Detail of front, centre of lintel: shrine with row of uraei. Author's photograph.

Fig. II.2. Detail of front, lintel, right of centre: Anubis and lion. Author's photograph.

Fig. II.3. Detail of front, lintel, left of centre: Anubis and lion. Author's photograph.

Fig. II.4. Detail of front, lintel, right side: Seherdju, Isis, and Maaitef. Author's photograph.

Fig. II.5. Detail of front, lintel, left side: Dewenhor, Sekhem, and Horus. Author's photograph.

Fig. II.6. Detail of front, right jamb, upper register: Hapy and Qebehsenuef. Author's photograph.

Fig. II.7. Detail of front, left jamb, upper register: Imsety and Duamutef. Author's photograph.

Fig. II.8. Detail of front, right jamb, lower register: Muyt. Author's photograph.

Fig. II.9. Detail of front, left jamb, lower register: Nekhbet. Author's photograph.

Fig. II.10. Detail of left side, upper register: Isis and Nephthys. Author's photograph.

Fig. II.11. Detail of left side, upper register: Osiris, lord of Djedu. Author's photograph.

Fig. II.12. Detail of left side, upper register: Osiris, the Great Saw. Author's photograph.

Fig. II.13. Detail of left side, upper register: Osiris, lord of Ra-setjau. Author's photograph.

Fig. II.14. Detail of left side, lower register: Khesefemtepa and Horus. Author's photograph.
Fig. II.15. Detail of left side, lower register: Aseb and Ankhemfedet. Author's photograph.
Fig. II.16. Detail of left side, lower register: Isis and Horus. Author's photograph.
Fig. II.17. Detail of left side, lower register: Akh, Inher, and Seqedher. Author's photograph.
Fig. II.18. Detail of right side, upper register: Shu and Tefnet. Author's photograph.
Fig. II.19. Detail of right side, upper register: ram-headed god. Author's photograph.
Fig. II.20. Detail of right side, upper register: canine-headed god and Isdes. Author's photograph.
Fig. II.21. Detail of right side, lower register: Horus and Sha. Author's photograph.
Fig. II.22. Detail of right side, lower register: turtle-headed god. Author's photograph.
Fig. II.23. Detail of right side, lower register: antelope-headed god. Author's photograph.
Fig. II.24. Detail of right side, lower register: hippopotamus-headed goddess. Author's photograph.
Fig. II.25. Detail of rear, upper register, right half: Khesesi. Author's photograph.
Fig. II.26. Detail of rear, upper register, right half: Nephthys. Author's photograph.
Fig. II.27. Detail of rear, upper register, right half: Pehrer. Author's photograph.
Fig. II.28. Detail of rear, upper register, right half: Heremhunet and Keku. Author's photograph.
Fig. II.29. Detail of rear, upper register, left half: Abuy and Maat. Author's photograph.
Fig. II.30. Detail of rear, upper register, left half: Khabes and Herefemkhakh. Author's photograph.
Fig. II.31. Detail of rear, lower register, right half: hippopotamus goddess and frontal face male. Author's photograph.
Fig. II.32. Detail of rear, lower register, right half: Medes and standing male. Author's photograph.
Fig. II.33. Detail of rear, lower register, right half: semi-sitting male and Irrenefdjesef. Author's photograph.
Fig. II.34. Detail of rear, lower register, left half: two squatting deities. Author's photograph.
Fig. II.35. Detail of rear, lower register, left half: two baboons. Author's photograph.
Fig. II.36. Detail of left wall, dedication text: *mnw*. Author's photograph.
Fig. II.37. Detail of rear, dedication text: *kꜣr* and *mꜣṯ*. Author's photograph.
Fig. II.38. Detail of rear, dedication text: *ḥmꜣg*. Author's photograph.
Fig. II.39. Detail of right side, lower registre: face of Inher. Author's photograph.
Fig. II.40. Detail of right side, upper registre: face of Osiris the Great Saw. Author's photograph.
Fig. II.41. Line drawing of front including roof (drawn by Giuliano Carapia).
Fig. II.42. Line drawing of left side (drawn by Giuliano Carapia).
Fig. II.43. Line drawing of right side (drawn by Giuliano Carapia).
Fig. II.44. Line drawing of rear (drawn by Giuliano Carapia).
Fig. III.1. Naos Cairo CG 70010. Reproduced from Roeder 1914, pl. 8.
Fig. III.2. Naos Cairo CG 70011 including base. Reproduced from Habachi 1982, fig. 5..
Fig. III.3. Naos at Tell Nabasha, as found by Petrie. Photograph by Petrie (© Egypt Exploration Society).
Fig. III.4. Naos at Tell Nabasha, as found by Petrie. Photograph by Petrie (© Egypt Exploration Society).
Fig. III.5. Naos at Tell Nabasha, present-day situation, looking south. Photograph by the Tell Nabasha Project.

Fig. III.6. Naos at Tell Nabasha, present-day situation, looking west. Photograph by the Tell Nabasha Project.
Fig. III.7. Naos fragments from Abydos. Reproduced from Petrie 1902, pl. LXVIII.
Fig. III.8. Leiden naos, left wall, damaged cartouche in dedication text. Author's photograph.
Fig. III.9. Naos Brussels E 5818, corner (© KMKG – MRAH).
Fig. III.10. Naos Brussels E 5818, rear (© KMKG – MRAH).
Fig. III.11. Fragment of Osiris chapel from Coptos, now London UC 14468 (courtesy of the Petrie Museum of Egyptian Archaeology, UCL).
Fig. III.12. Sfinx of Amasis, now in Rome, Musei Capitolini, MC 0035 (Photo: Archivio Fotografico dei Musei Capitolini).
Fig. III.13. Offering table of Amasis, now in Baltimore, Walters Art Gallery, 22.122 (Photo: the Walters Art Museum, Baltimore).
Fig. III.14. Reconstruction of court with shrines in the Banebdjed temple at Mendes. Reproduced from Arnold 1999, fig. 42.
Fig. III.15. Naos of Athribis, left side, upper register. Reproduced from Habachi 1982, 228, fig. 7.
Fig. III.16. Naos of Athribis, right side, upper register. Reproduced from Habachi 1982, 232, fig. 10.
Fig. III.17. Naos of Athribis, rear, upper register. Reproduced from Habachi 1982, 233, fig. 12.
Fig. IV.1. Cairo JE 36997bis, block-statue of Amunmes with depiction of Osiris Hemag (Karnak Cachette Database – Fonds B.V. Bothmer, CLES, © Brooklyn Museum, CLES – IFAO).
Fig. IV.2. Sa el-Hagar, SCA reg.no. 985, block with depiction of Osiris Hemag. Photograph by Penelope Wilson.
Fig. IV.3. Behbeit el-Hagar, temple walls depicting Osiris Hemag. Reproduced from Favard-Meeks 2003, 103, fig. 5.
Fig. IV.4. Hibis temple, double representation of Osiris Hemag. Reproduced from Davies 1953, pl. 3.
Fig. IV.5. Dendera, Hathor temple, chapel of Sokar, north wall. Reproduced after *Dendera* II, pl. CXXVII.
Fig. IV.6. Dendera, Hathor temple, chapel of Sokar, south wall. Reproduced after *Dendera* II, pl. CXXXV.
Fig. IV.7. Dendera, Hathor temple, third eastern Osiris chapel, detail of west wall. Reproduced after *Dendera* X, pl. 107.
Fig. IV.8. Dendera, Hathor temple, third western Osiris chapel, west wall. Reproduced after *Dendera* X, pl. 239.
Fig. IV.9. Sarcophagus Louvre E 5534 (© Musée du Louvre / Christian Décamps).
Fig. IV.10. Sais, naos of Amasis for Osiris. Photograph by Penelope Wilson.
Fig. IV.11. Sarcophagus of Psusennes, detail. Reproduced after Montet 1951, pl. 88.
Fig. IV.12. Thebes, tomb of Mutirdis (TT 410), awakening scene. Reproduced after Assmann 1977, fig. 41.
Fig. IV.13. Sarcophagus of Psusennes, detail. Reproduced after Montet 1951, pl. 90.
Fig. IV.14. Dendera, Hathor temple, third western Osiris chapel, east wall. Reproduced after *Dendera* X, pl. 237.
Fig. IV.15. Naos Louvre D 29 (© Musée du Louvre / Christian Larrieu).

Abbreviations

ASAE	Annales du Service des Antiquités de l'Egypte
BCE	Bulletin de liaison du groupe international d'étude de la céramique égyptienne
BIFAO	Bulletin de l'Institut Français d'Archéologie Orientale du Caire
BMSAES	British Museum Studies in Ancient Egypt and Nubia
BSFE	Bulletin de la Societé française d'égyptologie
CdE	Chronique d'Egypte, Bulletin périodique de la Fondation Egyptologique Reine Elisabeth
CT	De Buck, A., 1935-1961: The Egyptian Coffin Texts, I-VII, Chicago
Deir Chelouit	Zivie, C., 1982-1986: Le temple de Deir Chelouit, Cairo
Dendera	Chassinat, E./Daumas, F./Cauvile, S., 1934-: Le temple de Dendara, Cairo
Dendera, Mammisis	Daumas, F., 1959: Les mammisis de Dendara, Cairo
DHA	Dialogues d'histoire ancienne
EA	Egyptian Archaeology
Edfu	Chassinat, E., 1897-1934: Le temple d'Edfou, I-XIV, Paris
ENiM	Égypte Nilotique et Méditerranéenne
GM	Göttinger Miszellen
JANER	Journal of Ancient Near Eastern Religions
JARCE	Journal of the American Research Center in Egypt
JEA	Journal of Egyptian Archaeology
JNES	Journal of Near Eastern Studies
JSSEA	Journal of the Society of the Study of Egyptian Antiquities
KMT	KMT. A Modern Journal of Ancient Egypt
Kom Ombo	De Morgan, J., 1895-1909: Catalogue des monuments et inscriptions de l'Égypte antique, II-III, Vienna
LÄ	Helck, W./Otto, E./Westendorf, W. (eds.), 1972-: Lexikon der Ägyptologie, I-VII, Wiesbaden
MDAIK	Mitteilungen des Deutschen Archäologischen Instituts Abteilung Kairo
Médamoud	Drioton, E., 1926: Rapport sur les fouilles de Médamoud (1925), les inscriptions, Cairo
MIFAO	Mémoires publiés par les membres de l'Institut français d'Archéologie égyptienne

OMRO	Oudheidkundige Mededelingen uit het Rijksmuseum van Oudheden te Leiden
Opet	De Wit, C., 1958: Les inscriptions du temple d'Opet à Karnak, Brussels
PM	Porter, B./Moss, R.L.B., 1927-: Topographical bibliography of Ancient Egyptian hieroglyphic texts, reliefs, and paintings, I-VIII, Oxford
RdE	Revue d'Égyptologie
Rec.Trav.	Recueil de travaux relatifs à la philologie et à l'archéologie égyptienne et assyrienne
RHR	Revue de l'Histoire des Religions
SAK	Studien zur altägyptischen Kultur
SCO	Studi Classici e Orientali
Tôd II	Thiers, Chr., 2003: Les inscriptions du temple ptolémaïque et romain, II. Le second vestibule, la salle des déesses, les cryptes et la salle des offrandes, Cairo
Urk. II	Sethe, K., 1904-1910: Hieroglyphische Urkunden der griechisch-römischen Zeit, I-III, Leipzig
Urk. V	Grapow, H., 1915-1917: Religiöse Urkunden, nebst Übersetzung, Leipzig
Urk. VIII	Sethe, K./Firchow, O., 1957: Thebanische Tempelinschriften aus griechisch-römischen Zeit, Berlin
ZÄS	Zeitschrift für aegyptische Sprache und Altertumskunde

Bibliography

Abdelrahiem, M., 2006: Chapter 144 of the Book of the Dead from the temple of Ramesses II at Abydos, SAK 34, 1-16.

Abitz, F., 1979: Statuetten in Schreinen als Grabbeigaben in den ägyptischen Königsgräbern der 18. und 19. Dynastie, Wiesbaden.

Abitz, F., 1990: Der Bauablauf und die Dekoration des Grabes Ramses' IX., SAK 17, 1-40.

Albers, F.J., 2003: The pyramid tombs of Tanutamen, last Nubian pharaoh, & his mother, Queen Qalhata, KMT 14.2, 52-63.

Albert, F., 2013: Le Livre des Morts d'Aset-Ouret, Vatican City.

Allen, T.G., 1960: The Egyptian Book of the Dead documents in the Oriental Institute Museum at the University of Chicago, Chicago.

Alliot, M., 1933: Rapport sur les fouilles de Tell Edfou (1932), Cairo.

Altenmüller, B., 1975: Synkretismus in den Sargtexten, Wiesbaden.

Amélineau, E., 1904: Les nouvelles fouilles d'Abydos, 1897-1898, Paris.

Arnold, D., 1992: Die Tempel Ägyptens. Götterwohnungen, Baudenkmäler, Kultstätten, Zurich.

Arnold, D., 1999: Temples of the last pharaohs, New York/Oxford.

Arslan, E.A. (ed.), 1997: Iside. Il mito, il mistero, la magia, Milan.

Arveiller-Dulong, V./Nenna, M.D., 2011: Les verres antiques du Musée du Louvre, III: Parures, instruments et éléments d'incrustation, Paris.

Assmann, J., 1977: Das Grab der Mutirdis, Mainz.

Assmann, J., 1983: Sonnenhymnen in thebanischen Gräbern, Theben 1, Mainz.

Assmann, J., 1991: Das Grab des Amenemope TT 41, Mainz.

Aufrère, S.H., 1982-1983: Caractères principaux et origine divine des minéraux, RdE 34, 3-21.

Aufrère, S.H., 1984: Etudes de lexicologie et d'histoire naturelle, IV-VI, BIFAO 84, 1-21.

Aufrère, S.H., 1991: L'univers minéral dans la pensée égyptienne, I-II, Cairo.

Aufrère, S.H., 1993: Le cosmos, le minéral, le végétal, et le divin, Bulletin du Cercle Lyonnais d'Egyptologie 7, 7-24.

Aufrère, S.H., 1997: L'univers minéral dans la pensée égyptienne: essai de synthèse et perspectives, Archéo-Nil 7, 113-144.

Aufrère, S.H., 1999: L'univers des minéraux et des métaux précieux dans l'Égypte ancienne, in: A. Caubet (ed.), Cornaline et pierres précieuses: la Méditerranée, de l'antiquité à l'Islam: actes du colloque organisé au musée du Louvre par le Service culturel les 24 et 25 novembre 1995, Paris, 357-371.

Aufrère, S.H., 2000: Le propylône d'Amon-Rê-Montou à Karnak-Nord, Cairo.

Baines, J., 1973: The destruction of the pyramid temple of Sahure, GM 4, 9-14.

Baines, J., 1983: Fecundity figures. Egyptian personification and the iconology of a genre, Warminster.

Baines, J., 1988: An Abydos list of gods and an Old Kingdom use of texts, in: J. Baines (ed.), Pyramid studies and other essays presented to I.E.S. Edwards, London, 124-133.

Baines, J./Riggs, C., 2001: Archaism and kingship: a late royal statue and its Early Dynastic model, JEA 87, 103-118.

Bakr, M.I./Brandl, H., 2014: Egyptian antiquities from the Eastern Delta, Cairo/Berlin.

Beaud, R., 1990: L'offrande du collier-ousekh, in: S. Groll (ed.), Studies in Egyptology presented to Miriam Lichtheim, Jerusalem, 46-61.

Beinlich, H., 1991: Das Buch vom Fayum: zum religiösen Eigenverständnis einer ägyptischen Landschaft, Wiesbaden.

Bell, L., 2008: The Ancient Egyptian "Books of Breathing," the Mormon "Book of Abraham," and the development of Egyptology in America, in: S.E. Thompson/P. Der Manuelian (eds.), Egypt and beyond. Essays presented to Leonard H. Lesko upon his retirement from the Wilbour Chair of Egyptology at Brown University, June 2005, Providence, 21-39.

Bénédite, G., 1893: Le temple de Philae, Paris.

Bennet, Z., 2014: What's in a name? Transforming our perception of the function of the demonic entities in the ancient Egyptian Book of Two Ways, Rosetta 15.5, 1-18.

Bergmann, E.R. von, 1883: Der Sarkophag des Panehemisis, Jahrbuch der Kunsthistorischen Sammlungen des österreichischen Kaiserhauses, I, 1-40.

Berlandini, J., 1995: Ptah-demiurge et l'exaltation du ciel, RdE 46, 9-41.

Bianchi, R.S., 1979: Ex-votos of Dynasty XXVI, MDAIK 35, 15-22.

Bianchi, R.S., 1983: Those ubiquitous glass inlays from pharaonic Egypt, part I, Journal of Glass Studies 25, 29-35.

Bickel, S./Tallet, P., 2000: Quelques monuments privés héliopolitains de la Troisième Période Intermédiaire, BIFAO 100, 129-144.

Billing, N./Rowland, J., 2015: Recently discovered blocks in the central Delta village of Kom el-Ahmar, Minuf, in: P. Kousoulis/N. Lazaridis (eds.), Proceedings of the Tenth International Congress of Egyptologists, University of the Aegean, Rhodes 22-29 May, 2008, Leuven, 101-110.

Bissing, F.W. von/Kees, H., 1923: Das Re-Heiligtum des Königs Ne-Woser-Re (Rathures), II, Leipzig.

Bissing, F.W. von, 1938: Das Grab des Petamenophis in Theben, ZÄS 74, 2-26.

Bissing, F.W. von, 1956: La chambre des trois saisons du sanctuaire du roi Rathourès [V^{e} dynastie], ASAE 53, 219-238.

Blöbaum, A.I., 2006: "Denn ich bin ein König, der die Maat liebt". Herrscherlegitimation im spätzeitlichen Ägypten. Eine vergleichende Untersuchung der Phraseologie in den offiziellen Königsinschriften vom Beginn der 25. Dynastie bis zum Ende der makedonischen Herrschaft, Aachen.

Bolla, M., 2007: Arte e cultura dell'antico Egitto nel Museo Archeologico di Verona, Montepulciano.

Bolshakov, A., 2010: Persians and Egyptians: cooperation in vandalism?, in: S.H. D'Auria, Offerings to the discerning eye. An Egyptological medley in honor of Jack A. Josephson, Leiden/Boston, 45-53.

Borchardt, L., 1913: Das Grabdenkmal des Königs Sa^{3}hu-Re^{c}, II, Leipzig.

Borghouts, J.F., 1971: The magical texts of papyrus Leiden I 348, OMRO 51, Leiden.

Boeser, P.A.A., 1907: Catalogus van het Rijksmuseum van Oudheden te Leiden: Egyptische afdeeling, Leiden.

Boeser, P.A.A. 1915: Beschreibung der aegyptischen Sammlung des niederländischen Reichmuseums der Altertümer in Leiden, VII: die Denkmäler der saïtischen, griechisch-römischen, und koptischen Zeit, The Hague.

Bomhard, A.-S. von, 2008: The naos of the decades, Oxford.

Bosticco, S., 1952: Musei Capitolini. I monumenti egizi ed egitizzanti, Rome.

Bothmer, B.V., 1970: Apotheosis in Late Egyptian sculpture, Kêmi 20, 37-48.

Bothmer, B.V., 1988: The great naos at Mendes and its sculpture, in: E.C.M. van den Brink (ed.), The archaeology of the Nile Delta. Problems and priorities. Proceedings of the seminar held in Cairo, 19-22 October 1986, on the occasion of the fifteenth anniversary of the Netherlands Institute of Archaeology and Arabic Studies in Cairo, Amsterdam, 205-220.

Botti, G., 1949: Alcune nuove accessioni del Museo Egizio di Firenze, Aegyptus 29, 118-125.

Bourguet, P. du/Gabolde, L., 2008: Le temple de Deir el-Médîna, Cairo.

Brandl, H., 2008: Untersuchungen zur steinernen Privatplastik der Dritten Zwischenzeit. Typologie, Ikonographie, Stilistik, I-II, Berlin.

Bresciani, E., 1967: Una statua della XXVI dinastia con il cosiddetto «abito persiano», SCO 16, 273-280.

Bruhn, K.-Ch., 2010: "Kein Tempel der Pracht". Architektur und Geschichte des Amasis-zeitlichen Tempels auf Agurmi, Oase Siwa, Ammoniaca I, Wiesbaden.

Brunner, H., 1970: Zum Verständnis der archaisierenden Tendenzen in der ägyptischen Spätzeit, Saeculum 21, 151-161.

Brunner, H., 1975: Archaismus, in: LÄ I, 386-395.

Bruwier, M.-C., 1998: L'Égypte au regard de J.-J. Rifaud 1786-1852: lithographies conservés dans les collections de la Société royale d'Archéologie, d'Histoire et de Folklore de Nivelles et du Brabant wallon, Nivelles.

Bruwier, M.-C./Claes, W./Quertinmont, A., 2014: "La Description de l'Egypte" de Jean-Jacques Rifaud (1813-1826), Brussels.

Bryan, B.M., 1997: The statue program for the mortuary temple of Amenhotep III, in: S. Quirke (ed.), The temple in Ancient Egypt. New discoveries and recent research, London, 57-81.

Budge, E.A.T.W., 1912: The Greenfield Papyrus in the British Museum. The funerary papyrus of Princess Nesitanebtashru, daughter of Painetchem II and Nesi-Khensu, and priestess of Amen-Ra at Thebes, about B.C. 970, London.

Budge, E.A.T.W., 1913: The Book of the Dead. The papyrus of Ani, scribe and treasurer of the temples of Egypt, about B.C. 1450, London/New York.

Buhl, M.-L., 1959: The late Egyptian anthropoid stone sarcophagi, Copenhagen.

Burton, J., 1825: Excerpta hieroglyphica, London.

Calverley, A.M., 1938: The temple of King Sethos I at Abydos, III: the Osiris complex, London/Chicago.

Cantilena, R./Rubino, P., 1989: La collezione egiziana del Museo Archeologico Nazionale di Napoli, Naples.

Capart, J., 1924: Un fragment de naos saïte, Brussels.

Castle, E., 1993: The dedication formula *ỉr.n.f m mnw.f*, JEA 79, 99-120.

Cauville, S., 1983: La théologie d'Osiris à Edfou, Cairo.

Cauville, S., 1988: Les mystères d'Osiris à Dendera. Interprétation des chapelles osiriennes, BSFE 112, 23-36.

Cauville, S., 1997: Dendara. Les chapelles osiriennes, 2: commentaire, Cairo.

Chappaz, J.-L., 1986: Une stèle de Basse Époque au musée d'Yverdon, BIFAO 86, 92-98.

Chassinat, E., 1966-1968: Le mystère d'Osiris au mois de Khoiak, I-II, Cairo.

Clère, J., 1950: Le système des décades du calendrier du Louvre (Louvre D 37), JNES 9, 143-152.

Clère, J., 1973: Trois fragments épigraphiques à Vérone, Oriens Antiquus 12, 99-105.

Clère, J., 1986: Deux groupes inédits de génies-gardiens du quatrième prophète d'Amon Mentemhat, BIFAO 86, 99-106.

Colin, F., 1998: Les fondateurs du sanctuaire d'Amon à Siwa (désert libyque). Autour d'un bronze de donation inédit, in: W. Clarysse/A. Schoors/H. Willems (eds.), Egyptian religion, the last thousand years, studies dedicated to the memory of Jan Quaegebeur, Louvain, 329-356.

Colin, F./Labrique, F., 2002: *Semenekh Oudjat* à Bahariya, in: F. Labrique, Religions méditerranéennes et orientales de l'Antiquité, Cairo, 45-78.

Corteggiani, J.-P., 1979: Une stèle héliopolitaine d'époque saite, in: Hommages à la mémoire de Serge Sauneron, 1927-1976, I, Cairo, 115-153.

Coulon, L., 2003: Un aspect du culte osirien à Thèbes à l'époque saïte. La chapelle d'Osiris Ounnefer "maître des aliments", Égypte Afrique & Orient 28, 47-60.

Coulon, L./Defernez, C., 2004: La chapelle d'Osiris Ounnefer Neb-Djefaou à Karnak. Rapport préliminaire des fouilles et travaux 2000-2004, BIFAO 104, 135-190.

Coulon, L., 2009: Une trinité d'Osiris thébains sur un relief découvert à Karnak, in: C. Thiers (ed.), Documents de théologie thébaines tardives (*D3T* 1), Montpellier, 1-18.

Coulon, L. (ed.), 2010: Le culte d'Osiris au Ier millénaire av. J.-C. Découvertes et travaux récents. Actes de la table ronde internationale tenue à Lyon, Maison de l'Orient et de la Méditerranée (université Lumière-Lyon 2), les 8 et 9 juillet 2005, Cairo.

Coulon, L., 2011: Les *uraei* gardiens du fétiche abydénien. Un motif osirien et sa diffusion à l'époque saïte, in: D. Devauchelle (ed.), La XXVIe dynastie. Continuités et ruptures. Actes du colloque international organisé les 26 et 27 novembre 2004 à l'Université Charles-de-Gaulle-Lille 3, Paris, 85-108.

Coulon, L., 2016: Les statues d'Osiris en pierre provenant de la cachette de Karnak et leur contribution à l'étude des cultes et des formes locales du dieu, in: L. Coulon, La cachette de Karnak. Nouvelles perspectives sur les dècouvertes de Georges Legrain, Cairo, 505-563.

Cruz-Uribe, E., 1988: Hibis Temple Project, I: translation, commentary, discussions and sign list, San Antonio, Texas.

Daressy, G., 1906: Statues des divinités, Cairo.

Daressy, G., 1909: Cercueils des cachettes royales, Cairo.

Daressy, G., 1912: A travers les koms du Delta, ASAE 12, 169-213.

Daressy, G., 1916: Une inscription d'Achmoun et la géographie du nome libyque, ASAE 16, 221-246.

Daressy, G., 1917: Fragments de deux cercueils de Saqqarah, ASAE 17, 1-20.

Dasen, V., 1993: Dwarfs in Ancient Egypt and Greece, Oxford.

Daumas, F., 1956: La valeur de l'or dans la pensée égyptienne, RHR 149, 1-17.

Daumas, F., 1980: Quelques textes de l'atelier des orfèvres dans le temple de Dendara, in: Livre du Centenaire, MIFAO 104, Cairo, 109-118.

Davies, N. de Garis, 1953: The temple of Hibis in El Khargeh Oasis, III: the decoration, New York.

Davis, T.M., 1908: The funeral papyrus of Iouiya, London.

Davis, W., 2003: Archaism and modernism in the relief of Hesy-Ra, in: J. Tait (ed.), "Never had the like occurred": Egypt's view of its past, London.

Davoli, P., 2001: Saft el-Henna. Archeologia e storia di una città del Delta orientale, Imola.

Defernez, C., 2004: Karnak. La chapelle d'Osiris Ounnefer Neb-Djefaou, BCE 22, 35-47.

Defernez, C., 2011: Les témoignages d'une continuité de la culture matérielle saïte à l'époque perse: l'apport de l'industrie céramique, in: D. Devauchelle (ed.), La XXVIe dynastie. Continuités et ruptures. Actes du colloque international organisé les 26 et 27 novembre 2004 à l'Université Charles-de-Gaulle-Lille 3, Paris, 109-126.

Derchain, P., 1990: L'atelier des orfèvres à Dendara et les origines de l'alchimie, CdE 65, 219-242.

Dhennin, S., 2011: Térénouthis – Kôm Abou Billou: une ville et sa nécropole, BIFAO 111, 105-127.

Dhennin, S., 2012: Djekâper et Nikiou, anciennes métropoles sur le territoire de la Minufiya, BIFAO 112, 111-128.

Dhennin, S., 2012a: Une stèle de Mefkat (Montgeron 2007.4), RdE 63, 67-78.

Dhennin, S., 2014: Mefkat, Térénouthis, Kôm Abou Billou: nouvelles recherches archéologiques à l'ouest du Delta, BSFE 189, 8-25.

Dhennin, S., 2016: (Per-)Inbou, Per Noubet et Onouphis. Une question de toponymie, in: S. Dhennin/C. Somaglino (eds.), Décrire, imaginer, construire l'espace. Toponymie égyptienne de l'Antiquité au Moyen Âge, Cairo, 49-68.

Dorman, P.F., 1991: The tomb of Senenmut. The architecture and decoration of tombs 71 and 353, New York.

Dunham, D., 1950: The royal cemeteries of Kush, I: El Kurru, Cambridge.

Dunham, D., 1955: The royal cemeteries of Kush, II: Nuri, Boston.

DuQuesne, T., 2000: Milk of the jackal: some reflections on Hezat, Anubis and the *ỉmywt*, Cahiers Cariéens d'Égyptologie 1, 53-60.

DuQuesne, T., 2005: The jackal divinities of Egypt, I: from the Archaic Period to Dynasty X, London.

Eaton, J.K., 2006: The festivals of Osiris and Sokar in the month of Khoiak: the evidence from Nineteenth Dynasty royal monuments at Abydos, SAK 35, 75-101.

Effland, U., 2006: Funde aus dem Mittleren Reich bis zur Mamlukenzeit aus Umm el-Qaab, MDAIK 62, 131-150.

Effland, U./Effland, A., 2013: Abydos. Tor zur ägyptischen Unterwelt, Darmstadt/Mainz.

Egberts, A., 1995: In quest of meaning. A study of the Ancient Egyptian rites of consecrating the *Meret*-chests and driving the calves, I-II, Leiden.

El-Banna, E., 1989: À propos des aspects héliopolitains d'Osiris, BIFAO 89, 101-126.

El-Banna, E., 1990: Un titre nouveau: "le gardien de volailles du temple de Rê", GM 116, 7-19.

El-Sadeek, W., 1984: Twenty-Sixth Dynasty necropolis at Gizeh: an analysis of the tomb of Thery and its place in the development of the Saite funerary art and architecture, Vienna.

El-Sayed, R., 1975: Documents relatifs à Sais et ses divinités, Cairo.

El-Sayed, R., 1982: La déesse Neith de Sais, Cairo.

Emery, W.B., 1967: Preliminary report on the excavations at North Saqqâra 1966-67, JEA 53, 141-145.

Engsheden, Å., 2014: Le naos de Sopdou à Saft el-Henneh (CG 70021), paléographie, Cairo.

Ensoli Vittozzi, S., 1990: Musei Capitolini, la collezione egizia, Milan.

Epigraphic Survey, 1963: The Epigraphic Survey, Medinet Habu, VI: the temple proper, part II: the Re chapel, the royal mortuary temple complex and adjacent rooms, with miscellaneous material from the pylons, the forecourts, and the first hypostyle hall, Chicago.

Epigraphic Survey, 1980: The Epigraphic Survey, the tomb of Kheruef: Theban tomb 192, Chicago.

Étienne, M., 2009: Les portes du ciel, visions du monde dans l'Égypte ancienne, Paris.

Fakhry, A., 1942: Bahria Oasis I, Cairo.

Faltings, D., *et al.*, 2000: Zweiter Vorbericht über die Arbeiten in Buto von 1996 bis 1999, MDAIK 56, 131-179.

Farag, S./Wahbah, G./Farid, A., 1977: Reused blocks from a temple of Amasis at Philae, Oriens Antiquus 16, 315-324.

Farid, A., 1980: Re-used blocks from a temple of Amasis at Philae, the final results, MDAIK 36, 81-103.

Farouk, H.A., 1999-2000: Der Gott Ides, ASAE 75, 11-15.

Faulkner, R.O., 1958: Giessen University Library papyrus no. 115, JEA 44, 66-74.

Faulkner, R.O., 1973-1978: The Ancient Egyptian Coffin Texts, I-III, Warminster.

Favard-Meeks, C., 1991: Le temple de Behbeit el-Hagara, Hamburg.

Favard-Meeks, C., 2003: Les constructions de Nectanébo II à Behbeit el-Hagara, in: N. Kloth/K. Martin/E. Pardey (eds.), Es werde niedergelegt als Schriftstück, Festschrift für Hartwig Altenmüller zum 65. Geburtstag, Hamburg, 97-108.

Favard-Meeks, C., 2009: Les couronnes d'Andjéty et le temple de Behbeit el-Hagara, in: I. Régen/F. Servajean (eds.), Verba manent. Recueil d'études dédiées à Dimitri Meeks, Montpellier, 137-143.

Frankfort, H./Buck, A. de/Gunn, B., 1939: The cenotaph of Seti I at Abydos, London.

Freed, R.E., 1983: A divine tour of Ancient Egypt (6 October – 8 December), Memphis.

Gaber, H., 2015: Le catalogue des dieux de la chapelle de Ptah-Sokar du temple de Séthi Ier à Abydos: une elaboration memphite des chapitres 141 et 142 du LdM, in: DHA 41/1, 245-255.

Gabolde, M./Galliano, G. (eds.), 2000: Coptos, l'Égypte antique aux portes du desert. Lyon, musée des Beaux-Arts, 3 février – 7 mai 2000, Paris.

Gasse, A., 2001: Le livre des morts de Pacherientaihet au Museo Gregoriano Egizio, Vatican City.

Gauthier, H., 1915: Le livre des rois d'Égypte, IV: de la XXVe dynastie à la fin des Ptolémées, Cairo.

Gauthier, H., 1922: A travers la Basse Égypte, ASAE 22, 199-208.

Gauthier, H., 1923: A travers la Basse Égypte, ASAE 23, 68-72, 165-182.

Goddio, F./Fabre, D., 2015: Osiris, mystères engloutis d'Égypte, Paris.

Goelet, O., 1982: Two aspects of the royal palace in the Egyptian Old Kingdom (Ph.D. dissertation, Columbia University), New York.

Gohary, S., 1991: The tomb-chapel of the royal scribe Amenemone at Saqqara, BIFAO 91, 195-205.

Gourlay, Y.J.-L., 1979: Les Seigneurs et les *Baou* vivants à Chedenou, in: Hommages à la mémoire de Serge Sauneron, 1927-1976, I, Cairo, 363-380.

Goyon, J.-C., 1967: Le ceremonial de glorification d'Osiris du papyrus du Louvre I. 3079 (colonnes 110 à 112), BIFAO 65, 89-156.

Goyon, J.-C., 1972: Confirmation du pouvoir royal au Nouvel An (Brooklyn Museum Papyrus 47.218.50), Cairo.

Goyon, J.-C., 1975: Textes mythologiques, II: Les révélations du mystère des quatre boules, BIFAO 75, 349-399.

Gozzoli, R.B., 2000: The statue BM EA 37891 and the erasure of Necho II's names, JEA 86, 67-80.

Gozzoli, R.B., 2009: The writing of history in Ancient Egypt during the first millennium BC (ca. 1070-180 BC), Trends and Perspectives, London.

Gozzoli, R.B., 2017: Psammetichus II. Reign, documents and officials, London.

Graefe, E., 2011: Le «*Tempelbauprogramm*» du roi Amasis, in: D. Devauchelle (ed.), La XXVIe dynastie, continuités et ruptures. Actes du colloque international organisé les 26 et 27 novembre 2004 à l'Université Charles-de-Gaulle-Lille 3, Paris, 159-164.

Grajetzki, W., 2004: Harageh, an Egyptian burial ground for the rich around 1800 BC, London.

Greco, C., 2014: The forgotten tomb of Ramose (TT 132), in: E. Pischikova/J. Budka/K. Griffin, Thebes in the first millennium BC, Cambridge, 173-199.

Green, C.I., 1987: The temple furniture from the Sacred Animal Necropolis at North Saqqâra 1964-1976, London.

Griffith, F.L./Thompson, H., 1904: The Demotic Magical Papyrus of London and Leiden, I, London.

Griffiths, J.G., 1974: Triune conceptions of deity in Ancient Egypt, ZÄS 100, 28-32.

Griffiths, J.G., 1996: Triads and trinity, Cardiff.

Grimm, A., 1979: *Dwn-ḥꜣt* und *Rs-ḥr* als Namen eines Torwächters in der Unterwelt. Zu zwei Beinamen des Sobek und zur Bezeichnung krokodilköpfiger Gottheiten, GM 31, 27-34.

Gubel, E. (ed.), 1991: Van Nijl tot Schelde/Du Nil à l'Escaut. Bank Brussel Lambert, Koningsplein 6, 1000 Brussel, 5 april – 9 juni 1991, Brussels.

Guermeur, I., 2005: Les cultes d'Amon hors de Thèbes. Recherches de géographie religieuse, Turnhout.

Guilhou, N., 1999: Génies funéraires, croquet-mitaines ou anges gardiens? Étude sur les fouets, balais, palmes et épis en guise de couteaux, in: S. Aufrère (ed.), Encyclopédie religieuse de l'univers végétal, Montpellier, 365-417.

Guilhou, N., 2009: Lézards et geckos dans l'Égypte ancienne, IVe Rencontres archéozoologiques de Lattes, UMR 5140, CNRS, Université Paul-Valéry Montpellier 3, 26 juin 2009 [= www.archeo-lattes.cnrs.fr/IMG/pdf/Guilhou_2009.pdf].

Guilmant, F., 1907: Le tombeau de Ramsès IX, Cairo.

Guksch, H., 1995: Die Gräber des Nacht-Min und des Men-Cheper-Ra-seneb, Theben Nr. 87 und 79, Mainz.

Gunn, B., 1926: Inscribed sarcophagi in the Serapeum, ASAE 26, 82-91.

Habachi, L., 1943: Sais and its monuments, ASAE 42, 369-407.

Habachi, L., 1957: Tell Basta, Cairo.

Habachi, L./Ghalioungui, P., 1971: The «House of Life» of Bubastis, CdE 46, 59-71.

Habachi, L., 1977: Tavole d'offerta, are e bacili da libagione, 22001 – 22067, Turin.

Habachi, L., 1982: Athribis in the XXVIth Dynasty, BIFAO 82, 213-235.

Haeny, G., 1985: A short architectural history of Philae, BIFAO 85, 197-233.

Halbertsma, R.B., 2003: Scholars, travellers and trade. The pioneer years of the National Museum of Antiquities in Leiden, 1818-40, London.

Hansen, D.P., 1967: The excavation at Tell el Rub'a, JARCE 6, 5-16.

Harris, J., 1961: Lexicographical studies in Ancient Egyptian minerals, Berlin.

Hays, H.M., 2012: The organization of the Pyramid Texts. Typology and disposition, Leiden.

Heiden, D., 2002: Die Stele des *Pꜣ-dj-Pp*, SAK 30, 187-201.

Heise, J., 2006: Erinnern und Gedenken. Aspekte der biographischen Inschriften der ägyptischen Spätzeit, Göttingen.

Herbin, F.R., 1994: Le livre de parcourir l'éternité, Leuven.

Hill, M., 1991: Pascal-Xavier Coste (1787-1879): a French architect in Egypt (PhD. thesis), Massachusetts.

Hornung, E., 1979-1980: Das Buch von den Pforten des Jenseits, Geneva.

Hornung, E., 1987-1994: Texte zum Amduat, Geneva.

Hornung, E./Bryan, B.M., 2002: The quest for immortality. Treasures of Ancient Egypt, Washington.

Iwaszczuk, J., 2013: *Jmn ḫnty jpwt.f* from the Middle Kingdom to the mid-Eighteenth Dynasty, Études et Travaux XXVI, 303-323.

Jacobi, D. (ed.), 1998: Pascal Coste, toutes les Egypte, Marseilles.

Jamen, F., 2016: Le cercueil de Padikhonsou au musée des Beaux-Arts de Lyon (XXIe dynastie), Wiesbaden.

James, T.G.H., 2000: Tutankhamon, Vercelli.

Jansen-Winkeln, K., 1985: Ägyptische Biographien der 22. und 23. Dynastie, Wiesbaden.

Jansen-Winkeln, K., 1998: Drei Denkmäler mit archaisierender Ortographie, Orientalia 67, 155-172.

Jansen-Winkeln, K., 2009: Inschriften der Spätzeit, III: Die 25. Dynastie, Wiesbaden.

Jansen-Winkeln, K., 2014: Inschriften der Spätzeit, IV: Die 26. Dynastie, Band 1: Psametik I. –Psametik III., Wiesbaden.

Jelinkova-Reymond, E., 1956: Les inscriptions de la statue guérisseuse de Djed-Hor-"le Sauveur", Cairo.

Josephson, J.A., 2001: Archaism, in: D.B. Redford (ed.), The Oxford Encyclopedia of Ancient Egypt, I, Oxford, 109-113.

Junge, F., 1987: Elephantine XI: Funde und Bauteile, Mainz.

Junker, H., 1910: Die Stundenwachen in den Osirismysterien nach den Inschriften von Dendera, Edfu und Philae, Vienna.

Jurman, C., 2006: *Bw ẖrj ḥm=f* – The place where His Majesty dwells. Some remarks about the localisation of royal palace, residence and central administration in the Late Period Egypt (M.Phil. dissertation, University of Birmingham), Birmingham.

Jurman, C., 2010: The trappings of kingship, remarks about archaism, rituals and cultural polyglossia in Saite Egypt, Aegyptus and Pannonia IV, 73-118.

Kahl, J.K., 1999: Siut – Theben: zur Wertschätzung von Traditionen im alten Ägypten, Leiden/Boston/Cologne.

Kahn, D., 2007: Note on the time-factor in Cambyses' deeds in Egypt as told by Herodotus, Transeuphratène 34, 103-112.

Kamal, A., 1904: Fragments de monuments provenant du Delta, ASAE 5, 193-200.

Kamal, A., 1909: Tables d'offrandes, Cairo.

Kaper, O.E., 2003: The Egyptian god Tutu. A study of the sphinx-god and master of demons with a corpus of monuments, Leuven.

Kees, H., 1915: Eine Liste memphitischer Götter im Tempel von Abydos, Rec.Trav. 37, 57-76.

Kemp, B., 1968: The Osiris temple at Abydos, MDAIK 23, 138-155.

Kitchen, K.A., 1993: Towards a reconstruction of Ramesside Memphis, in: E. Bleiberg/R. Freed (eds.), Fragments of a shattered visage. The proceedings of the international symposium on Ramesses the Great, Memphis, 87-104.

Klotz, D., 2006: Adoration of the ram. Five hymns to Amun-Re from Hibis temple, New Haven.

Klotz, D., 2010: Two studies on the Late Period temples at Abydos, BIFAO 110, 127-163.

Klotz, D./LeBlanc, M., 2012: An Egyptian priest in the Ptolemaic court: Yale Peabody Museum 264191, in: C. Zivie-Coche/I. Guermeur (eds.), «Parcourir l'éternité», hommages à Jean Yoyotte, Turnhout, 645-698.

Köhler, U., 1975: Das Imiut: Untersuchungen zur Darstellung und Bedeutung eines mit Anubis verbundenen religiösen Symbols, Wiesbaden.

Köhler, U., 1980: Imiut, in: LÄ III, 149-150.

Koemoth, P., 1998: review of M. Zecchi, A study of the Egyptian god Osiris Hemag, Imola 1996, Bibliotheca Orientalis 55, 755-758.

Koemoth, P., 2009: Osiris-*mrjtj* (le) bien-aimé. Contribution à l'étude d'Osiris sélénisé, Geneva.

Kousoulis, P. (ed.), 2011: Ancient Egyptian demonology. Studies on the boundaries between the demonic and the divine in Egyptian magic, Leuven.

Kuentz, C., 1931: Le chapitre 106 du Livre des Morts. À propos d'une stèle de Basse Époque, BIFAO 30, 817-880.

Kuentz, C., 1932: Obélisques, Cairo.

Kuhlmann, K.P., 1996: Serif-style architecture and the design of the Archaic Egyptian palace, in: M. Bietak (ed.), House and palace in Ancient Egypt, Vienna, 117-138.

Kurth, D., 1994: Treffpunkt der Götter. Inschriften aus dem Tempel des Horus von Edfu, Zurich/Munich.

Labrique, F., 2004: Le catalogue divin de 'Ayn el-Mouftella: jeux de miroir autour de "celui qui est dans ce temple", BIFAO 104, 327-357.

Labrique, F., 2005: Un culte d'Osiris-arbre dans le monument saïte de Mouftella (oasis de Bahariya) ?, DHA supplement 1, 213-223.

Labrique, F., 2007: Ayn El Mouftella: Osiris dans le Château de l'Or (Mission IFAO à Bahariya, 2002-2004), in: J.-C. Goyon/C. Cardin, Proceedings of the Ninth International Congress of Egyptologists, Grenoble, 6-12 septembre 2004, Leuven/Paris/Dudley, 1061-1070.

Labrique, F., 2013: Lieux et épiclèses locales à Bahariya, d'apres l'épigraphie monumentale d'époque tardive, in: M. Dospel/L. Suková, Bahriya Oasis. Recent research into the past of an Egyptian oasis, Prague, 253-267.

Lacau, P., 1906: Sarcophages antérieurs au Nouvel Empire, Cairo.

Ladynin, I.A., 2006: The Elephantine stela of Amasis: Some problems and prospects of study, GM 211, 31-56.

Lapp, G., 1997: The papyrus of Nu, London.

Leahy, A., 1984: The date of Louvre A.93, GM 70, 45-58.

Leahy, A., 1984a: Saite royal sculpture: a review, GM 80, 59-76.

Leahy, A., 1987: Multiple adverbial predicates in Ancient Egyptian, in: J.D. Ray, Lingua sapientissima: a seminar in honor of H.J. Polotsky by the Fitzwilliam Museum, Cambridge and the Faculty of Oriental Studies, Cambridge, 57-64.

Leahy, A., 1988: The earliest dated monument of Amasis and the end of the reign of Apries, JEA 74, 183-199.

Leahy, A., 1996: The adoption of Ankhnesneferibre at Karnak, JEA 82, 145-165.

Leclant, J./Meulenaere, H. De, 1957: Une statuette égyptienne a Délos, Kêmi 14, 33-42.

Leclant, J., 1961: Montouemhat quatrième prophète d'Amon, prince de la ville, Cairo.

Leclant, J., 1962: Les genies-gardiens de Montouemhat, in: FS Struve, Drevnij mir. sbornik statej V.V. Struve, Moscow, 104-129.

Leclère, F., 2003: La ville de Saïs à la Basse Époque, Egypte Afrique & Orient 28, 13-38.

Leclère, F., 2008: Les villes de Basse Égypte au Ier millénaire av. J.-C., Cairo.

Leemans, C., 1838: Lettre à M. François Salvolini sur les monumens égyptiens portant des légendes royales dans les Musées d'Antiquités de Leide, de Londres, et dans quelques collections particulières en Angleterre, Leiden.

Leemans, C., 1839-: Aegyptische Monumenten van het Nederlandsche Museum van Oudheden te Leyden, Leiden.

Leemans, C., 1840: Description raisonnée des monumens égyptiens du Musée d'Antiquités des Pays-Bas à Leide, Leiden.

Leitz, C., 1995: Altägyptische Sternuhren, Leuven.

Leitz, C. (ed.), 2002: Lexikon der ägyptischen Götter und Götterbezeichnungen, I-VIII, Leuven/Paris/Dudley.

Leitz, C., 2011: Der Sarg des Panehemisis in Wien, Wiesbaden.

Leitz, C., 2012: Geographisch-osirianische Prozessionen aus Philae, Dendara und Athribis. Soubassementstudien II, Wiesbaden.

Leitz, C., 2014: Die Gaumonographien in Edfu und ihre Papyrusvarianten. Ein überregionaler Kanon kultischen Wissens im spätzeitlichen Ägypten, I-II, Wiesbaden.

Leprohon, R.J., 1997: Gatekeepers of this and the other world, JSSEA 24, 77-91.

Lepsius, R., 1842: Das Todtenbuch der Ägypter nach dem hieroglyphischen Papyrus in Turin, Leipzig.

Lesko, L., 1972: The Ancient Egyptian Book of the Two Ways, Berkeley/Los Angeles/London.

Lichtheim, M., 1980: Ancient Egyptian literature, III: the Late Period, Berkeley.

Lieven, A. von, 2007: Grundriß des Laufes der Sterne. Das sogenannte Nutbuch, I-II, Copenhagen.

Lillesø, E.K., 1987: A seated man wearing a cloak (Naples no. 237), JEA 73, 230-234.

Limme, L., 1979: Stèles égyptiennes, Brussels.

Lloyd, A.B., 1982: The inscription of Udjahorresnet, a collaborator's testament, JEA 68, 166-180.

Lloyd, A.B., 1986: Herodotus book II, commentary 99-182, Leiden.

Logan, T.J., 1990: The origins of the *Jmy-wt* fetish, JARCE 27, 61-69.

Lollio Barbieri, O./Parola, G./Toti, M.P., 1995: Le antichità egiziane di Roma imperiale, Rome.

Lucarelli, R., 2006: Demons in the Book of the Dead, in: B. Backes/I. Munro/S. Stöhr (eds.), Totenbuch-Forschungen, gesammelte Beiträge des 2. Internationalen Totenbuch-Symposiums 2005, Wiesbaden, 203-212.

Lucarelli, R., 2006a: The Book of the Dead of Gatseshen. Ancient Egyptian funerary religion in the 10th century BC, Leiden.

Lucarelli, R. 2010: Demons (benevolent and malevolent), in: J. Dieleman/W. Wendrich (eds.), UCLA Encyclopedia of Egyptology, Los Angeles, 1-10.

Lucarelli, R., 2010a: The guardian-demons of the Book of the Dead, BMSAES 15, 85-102.

Lucarelli, R., 2011: Demonology during the Late Pharaonic and Greco-Roman Periods in Egypt, JANER 11, 109-125.

Lucarelli, R., 2012: The so-called vignette of Spell 182 of the Book of the Dead, in: R. Lucarelli/M. Müller-Roth/A. Wütrich (eds.), Herausgehen am Tage, gesammelte Schriften zum altägyptischen Totenbuch, Wiesbaden, 80-91.

Lucarelli, R., 2013: Review of P. Kousoulis, Ancient Egyptian demonology: studies on the boundaries between the demonic and the divine in Egyptian magic, Leuven 2011, Magical, Ritual and Witchcraft 8.1, 99-105.

Luft, U., 1998: A different world – religious conceptions, in: R. Schulz/M. Seidel (eds.), Egypt: the world of the pharaohs, Cologne, 416-431.

Macadam, M.F., 1946: Gleanings from the Bankes manuscripts, JEA 32, 57-64.

Malaise, M., 1972: Inventaire préliminaire des documents égyptiens en Italie, Leiden.

Manassa, C., 2007: The Late Egyptian underworld: sarcophagi and related texts from the Nectanebid period, Wiesbaden.

Manuelian, P. Der, 1983: Prolegomena zur Untersuchung saitischer "Kopien", SAK 10, 221-245.

Manuelian, P. Der, 1994: Living in the past. Studies in archaism of the Egyptian Twenty-sixth Dynasty, London.

Mariette, A., 1880: Abydos, description des fouilles, II: temple de Séti (supplement), temple de Ramsès, temple d'Osiris, petit temple de l'ouest, Paris.

Marlar, M., 2007: Excavations of the temple of Osiris at Abydos reported on behalf of the University of Pennsylvania Museum – Yale University – Institute of Fine Arts, New York University Expedition to Abydos, in: J.-C. Goyon/C. Cardin (eds.), Proceedings of the Ninth International Congress of Egyptologists, II, Leuven, 1251-1260.

Martin, G.T., 1979: The tomb of Hetepka and other reliefs and inscriptions from the Sacred Animal Necropolis, North Saqqâra 1964-1973, London.

Maspero, G., 1908-1914: Sarcophages des époques persane et ptolémaïque, Cairo.

Maspero, G./Gauthier, H., 1939: Sarcophages des époques persane et ptolémaïque, Cairo.
Masson, A./Millet, M./Boraik, M./Thiers, C., 2009: Centre franco-égyptien d'étude des temples de Karnak, rapport 2008, Luxor.
Meeks, D., 1979: Les donations aux temples dans l'Égypte du Ier millénaire avant J.-C., in: J. Lipinska (ed.), State and temple economy in the Ancient Near East, II, Leuven, 605-688.
Meeks, D., 2001: Demons, in: D. Redford (ed.), The Oxford Encyclopedia of Ancient Egypt, I, Oxford, 375-378.
Meijer, M.P., 2010: Gods galore. The sanctuary of the Hibis temple (MA thesis Egyptology), Leiden.
Meulenaere, H. De, 1968: La famille du roi Amasis, JEA 54, 183-187.
Meulenaere, H. De, 1975: Amasis, in: LÄ I, 181-182.
Meulenaere, H. De/MacKay, P., 1976: Mendes II, Warminster.
Mond, R./Myers, O.H., 1940: Temples of Armant, a preliminary survey, London.
Montet, P., 1938: Trois gouverneurs de Tanis d'après les inscriptions des statues 687, 689 et 700 du Caire, Kêmi 7, 123-159.
Montet, P., 1947: La necropole royale de Tanis, 1: les constructions et le tombeau d'Osorkon II à Tanis, Paris.
Montet, P., 1950: Études sur quelques prêtres et fonctionnaires du dieu Min, JNES 9, 18-27.
Montet, P., 1951: La necropole royale de Tanis, 2: les constructions et le tombeau de Psousennès à Tanis, Paris.
Montet, P., 1952: Ptah pathèque et les orfèvres, Revue archéologique 40, 1-11.
Montet, P., 1954: Nouveaux documents relatifs à l'Horus-Rê de Sakhebou, Kêmi 13, 28-32.
Montet, P., 1960: La necropole royale de Tanis, 3: les constructions et le tombeau de Chechanq III à Tanis, Paris.
Moret, A., 1913: Sarcophages de l'époque bubastite à l'époque saïte, I-II, Cairo.
Morkot, R., 2003: Archaism and innovation in art from the New Kingdom to the Twenty-sixth Dynasty, in: J. Tait, "Never had the like occurred": Egypt's view of its past, London, 79-99.
Moussa, A.M., 1987: A sandstone block bearing the Horus name of King Amasis from Memphis, ASAE 66, 147-148.
Müller, H.W., 1955: Ein Königsbildnis der 26. Dynastie mit der «Blaue Krone» in Museo Civico zu Bologna, ZÄS 80, 46-68.
Müller-Roth, M., 2008: Das Buch vom Tage, Fribourg.
Mumford, G., 2004: A preliminary reconstruction of the temple and settlement at Tell Tebilla (East Delta), in: G.N. Knoppers/A. Hirsch (eds.), Egypt, Israel and the Ancient Mediterranean world. Studies in honor of Donald B. Redford, Leiden, 267-286.
Munro, I., 1987: Untersuchungen zu den Totenbuch-Papyri der 18. Dynastie: Kriterien ihrer Datierung, London/New York.
Munro, I., 1995: Das Totenbuch des Bak-su (pKM 1970.37/pBrocklehurst) aus der Zeit Amenophis' II, Wiesbaden.
Munro, I., 1997: Das Totenbuch des Nacht-Amun aus der Ramessidenzeit (pBerlin P. 3002), Wiesbaden.
Munro, I., 2001: Das Totenbuch des Pa-en-nesti-taui aus der Regierungszeit des Amenemope (pLondon BM 10064), Wiesbaden.
Munro, I. 2011: Die Totenbuch-Papyri des Ehepaars Ta-scheret-en-Aset und Djed-chi aus der Bes-en-Mut Familie (26. Dynastie, Zeit des Königs Amasis), Wiesbaden.
Murray, M.A., 1904: The Osireion at Abydos, London.
Mysliwiec, K., 1978: Le naos de Pithom, BIFAO 78, 171-195.
Mysliwiec, K., 1978a: Studien zum Gott Atum, I: die heiligen Tiere des Atum, Hildesheim.
Mysliwiec, K., 1988: Royal portraiture of the Dynasties XXI-XXX, Mainz am Rhein.
Naville, E., 1886: Das aegyptische Totenbuch der XVIII. bis XX. Dynastie, Berlin.
Naville, E., 1890: The mound of the Jew and the city of Onias: Belbeis, Samanood, Abusir, Tukh el Karmus, London.
Needler, W., 1969: Acquisition by contribution: latest finds from the Egypt Exploration Society, Rotunda, The Bulletin of the Royal Ontario Museum 2/4, 22-32.
Nelson, M., 1986: Les récentes découvertes au Ramesséum, BSFE 106, 7-30.

Newberry, P.E., 1930-1957: Funerary statuettes and model sarcophagi, Cairo.

Nielsen, N./Gasperini, V./Mamedow, M., 2016: Preliminary report of the first season of the Tell Nabasha Project, autumn 2015, Ägypten und Levante 26, 65-74.

Niwinski, A., 1989: Studies on the illustrated Theban funerary papyri of the 11th and 10th Centuries B.C., Göttingen.

Niwinski, A., 2009: The so-called chapters BD 141-142 and 148 on the coffins of the 21st Dynasty from Thebes with some remarks concerning the funerary papyri of the period, in: B. Backes/M. Müller-Roth/S. Stöhr, Ausgestattet mit den Schriften des Thot, Festschrift für Irmtraut Munro zu ihrem 65. Geburtstag, Wiesbaden, 133-154.

O'Connor, D., 2009: Abydos, Egypt's first pharaohs and the cult of Osiris, London.

Osing, J./Rosati, G., 1988: Papiri geroglifici e ieratici da Tebtynis, Firenze.

Osing, J., 1998: Hieratische papyri aus Tebtunis, I, Copenhagen.

Otto, E., 1967: Ancient Egyptian art: the cults of Osiris and Amon, New York.

Otto, E., 1968: Eine Darstellung der "Osiris-Mysterien" in Theben, in: W. Helck, Festschrift für Siegfried Schott zu seinem 70. Geburtstag am 20. August 1967, Wiesbaden, 99-105.

Pantalacci, L., 1983: *Wnm-ḥwꜣꜣt*: génèse et carrière d'un génie funéraire, BIFAO 83, 297-311.

Pasquali, S., 2008: Le dépot extra-sépulcral trouvé par Fl. Petrie à Gîza-sud, RdE 59, 357-368.

Perdu, O., 1990: Neshor à Mendès sous Apriès, BSFE 118, 38-49.

Perdu, O., 2002: Recueil des inscriptions royales saïtes, I: Psammétique I, Paris.

Perdu, O., 2012: Sphinx à l'effigie d'Amasis, in: Le crépuscule des pharaons, chefs-d'oeuvre des dernières dynasties égyptiennes. Musée Jacquemart-André, 23 mars – 23 juillet 2012, Paris, 182-183.

Pernigotti, S., 1980: La statuaria egiziana nel Museo Civico Archeologico di Bologna, Bologna.

Petrie, W.M.F., 1888: Tanis Part II, Nebesheh (Am), and Defenneh (Tahpanhes), London.

Petrie, W.M.F., 1892: Ten years' digging in Egypt 1881-1891, London.

Petrie, W.M.F., 1896: Koptos, London.

Petrie, W.M.F., 1902: Abydos I, London.

Petrie, W.M.F., 1903: Abydos II, London.

Petrie, W.M.F., 1905: A history of Egypt, from the XIXth to the XXXth Dynasties, London.

Petrie, W.M.F., 1909: The palace of Apries (Memphis II), London.

Petrie, W.M.F., 1910: Meydum and Memphis (III), London.

Piankoff, A., 1933: Le naos D 29 du Musée du Louvre, RdE 1, 161-179.

Piankoff, A., 1942: Le Livre du Jour et de la Nuit, Cairo.

Piankoff, A., 1942a: Le Livre du Jour dans la tombe (no. 132) de Ramose, ASAE 41, 151-158.

Piankoff, A., 1947: Les grandes compositions religieuses dans la tombe de Pédéménope, BIFAO 46, 73-93.

Piankoff, A., 1954: The Tomb of Ramesses VI, New York.

Piankoff, A., 1955: The shrines of Tut-ankh-amon, New York.

Piankoff, A., 1957: Mythological papyri, New York.

Picchi, D., 2011: L'Egitto esibito: in visita con Georg Zoëga alle dimore veneziane di fine Settecento, in: E.M. Dal Pozzolo/R. Dorigo/M.P. Pedani, Venezia e l'Egitto, Milan, 195-200, 209, 324.

Pillet, M., 1923: Le naos de Senousret I, ASAE 23, 143-158.

Pizzarotti, S., 2012: Rituels et fêtes dans le temple. Les "mystères d'Osiris" du mois de Khoïak, Egypte Afrique & Orient 67, 31-40.

Posener, G., 1936: La premiére domination perse en Égypte, recueil d'inscriptions hiéroglyphiques, Cairo.

Postel, L./Régen, I., 2005: Annales héliopolitaines et fragments de Sésostris Ier réemployés dans la porte de Bâb al-Tawfiq au Caire, BIFAO 105, 229-293.

Pries, A., 2011: Die Stundenwachen im Osiriskult. Eine Studie zur Tradition und späten Rezeption von Ritualen im Alten Ägypten, Wiesbaden.

Quack, J.F., 1999: Frühe ägyptische Vorläufer der Paranatellonta?, Südhoffs Archiv 83, 212-223.

Quack, J.F., 2000: Ein neuer funerärer Text der Spätzeit (pHohenzollern-Sigmaringen II), ZÄS 127, 74-87.

Quirke, S., 2016: Birth tusks: the armoury of health in context – Egypt 1800 BC, London.

Rammant-Peeters, A., 1983: Les pyramidions égyptiens du Nouvel Empire, Leuven.

Ratié, S., 1968: Le papyrus de Neferoubenef, Cairo.

Ray, J.D., 1976: The archive of Hor, London.

Razanajao, V., 2009: La demeure de Min, maître d'Imet. Un monument de Tell Farâoun réinterprété, ENiM 2, 103-108.

Redford, D.B., 2010: City of the ram-man. The story of ancient Mendes, Princeton/Oxford.

Reeves, N./Wilkinson, R., 1996: The complete Valley of the Kings: tombs and treasures of Egypt's greatest pharaohs, London.

Régen, I., 2006: Aux origines de la tombe *js*. Recherches paléographiques et lexicographiques, BIFAO 106, 245-314.

Rifaud, J.-J., 1830: Voyage en Egypte, en Nubie et lieux circonvoisins depuis 1805 jusqu'en 1827, Paris.

Ritner, R.K., 1994: Denderite temple hierarchy and the family of Theban High Priest Nebwenenef: block statue OIM 10729, in: D.P. Silverman (ed.), For his ka. Essays offered in memory of Klaus Baer, Chicago, 205-226.

Roberson, J.A., 2013: The awakening of Osiris and the transit of the solar barques. Royal apotheosis in a most concise book of the underworld and sky, Fribourg.

Robinson, P., 2003: "As for them who know them, they shall find their paths": Speculation on ritual landscapes in the "Book of the Two Ways", in: D. O'Connor/S. Quirke (eds.), Mysterious lands, London, 139-159.

Roeder, G., 1914: Naos, Leipzig.

Rondot, V., 1989: Une monographie bubastite, BIFAO 89, 249-270.

Rondot, V., 1990: Le naos de Domitian, Toutou et les sept flèches, BIFAO 90, 303-337.

Rosenow, D., 2006: The Nekhthorheb temple, in: N. Spencer, A naos of Nekhthorheb from Bubastis. Religious iconography and temple building in the 30th Dynasty, London, 43-46.

Rosenow, D., 2008: The naos of 'Bastet, Lady of the Shrine', from Bubastis, JEA 94, 247-266.

Roulin, G., 1998: Les tombes royales de Tanis: analyse du programme decoratif, in: P. Brissaud/C. Zivie-Coche, Tanis. Travaux récents sur le Tell Sân el-Hagar, Paris, 193-275.

Roullet, A.M., 1972: The Egyptian and egyptianizing monuments of imperial Rome, Leiden.

Rowland, J./Billing, N., 2006: The EES Delta survey: Minufiyeh 2005, EA 28, 3-6.

Rowland, J./Wilson, P., 2006: The EES Delta survey – report for 2004-2005, JEA 92, 1-13.

Rowland, J., 2007: The Delta survey: Minufiyeh province, 2006-7, JEA 93, 65-77.

Rowland, J./Billing, N., 2009: Saite shrines at Kom el-Ahmar, Minuf, EA 34, 7-9.

Rowland, J./Edinborough, K./Phillipps, R./el-Senussi, A., 2009: The Delta survey: Minufiyeh province, 2008-9, JEA 95, 35-49.

Rowland, J./Strutt, K.D., 2012: Geophysical survey and sub-surface investigations at Quesna and Kom el-Ahmar (Minuf), governorate of Minufiyeh: an integrated strategy for mapping and understanding the sub-surface remains of mortuary, sacred and domestic contexts, in: G.A. Belova/S.V. Ivanov (eds.), Achievements and problems of modern Egyptology: international conference, Moscow, September 20 – October 2, 2009, Moscow, 328-345.

Rummel, U., 2010: Iunmutef. Konzeption und Wirkungsbereich eines altägyptischen Gottes, Berlin.

Russmann, E.R., 1997: Vulture and cobra at the King's brow, in: E. Goring/N. Reeves/J. Ruffle (eds.), Chief of seers. Studies in memory of Cyril Aldred, London, 266-284.

Russmann, E.R., 2001: Eternal Egypt. Masterworks of ancient art from the British Museum, London/New York.

Ruszczyc, B., 1976: Le temple d'Amasis à Tell Atrib, Études et Travaux 9, 117-127.

Ryhiner, M.-L., 1986: L'offrande du lotus dans les temples égyptiens de l'époque tardive, Brussels.

Sander-Hansen, C.E., 1937: Die religiösen Texte auf dem Sarg der Anchnesneferibre, Copenhagen.

Sandman-Holmberg, M., 1940: The god Ptah, Lund.

Sauneron, S., 1952: Rituel de l'embaumement (Pap. Boulaq III, Pap. Louvre 5.158), Cairo.

Sauneron, S., 1962: Une allusion inattendue à la «matière divine», Kêmi 16, 38-39.

Sauneron, S., 1983: La porte ptolémaïque de l'enceinte de Mout à Karnak, Cairo.

Sauneron, S., 1983a: Villes et légendes, Cairo.

Schenkel, W., 1977: Zur Frage der Vorlagen spätzeitlicher "Kopien", in: J.Assmann/E. Feucht/R. Grieshammer (eds.), Fragen an die altägyptische Literatur. Studien zum Gedenken an Eberhard Otto, Wiesbaden, 417-441.

Schiaparelli, E., 1887: Museo Archeologico di Firenze, antichità egizie, Rome.

Schiaparelli, E., 2007: La tomba intatta dell'architetto Kha nella necropoli di Tebe, Turin.

Schneider, H.D./Raven, M.J., 1981: De Egyptische Oudheid, The Hague.

Schneider, H.D., 1992: Beeldhouwkunst in het land van de farao's, Amsterdam.

Selim, A.-K., 1991: Les obélisques égyptiens: histoire et archéologie, I-II, Cairo.

Sethe, K., 1924: Aegyptische Lesestücke zum Gebrauch im akademischen Unterricht. Texte des Mittleren Reiches, Leipzig.

Seton-Williams, M.V., 1969: The Tell el-Farâ'in expedition, 1968, JEA 55, 5-22.

Sheikholeslami, C.M., 2010: The night and day hours in Twenty-Fifth Dynasty sarcophagi from Thebes, in: L. Bareš/F. Coppens/K. Smoláriková (eds.), Egypt in transition. Social and religious development of Egypt in the first millennium BCE, Prague, 376-395.

Sist, L., 2001: Due frammenti lignei con figurazione magica, in: M.G. Amadasi Guzzo/M. Liverani/P. Matthiae (eds.), Da Pyrgi a Mozia. Studi sull'archeologia del Mediterraneo in memoria di Antonia Casca, Rome, 533-544.

Sist, L., 2013: Osservazioni sul sarcofago del Museo del Vicino Oriente della Sapienza decorato con sfilata "demoniaca", in: I. Baglioni, Monstra. Costruzione e percezione delle entità ibride e mostruose nel Mediterraneo antico, I (Egitto, Vicino Oriente antico, area storico-comparativa), Rome, 73-83.

Sist, L., 2017: A 25th Dynasty Theban coffin in the Museo del Vicino Oriente at Sapienza Università di Roma, in: A. Amenta/H. Guichard, Proceedings First Vatican Coffin Conference, 19-22 June 2013, Vatican City, 509-514.

Smith, M., 1985: Lexicographical notes on demotic texts II, Enchoria 13, 103-114.

Smith, M., 1987: Catalogue of the demotic papyri in the British Museum, III: the mortuary texts of papyrus BM 10507, London.

Smith, M., 1993: The liturgy of the opening of the mouth for breathing, Oxford.

Smith, M., 2005: Papyrus Harkness (MMA 31.9.7), Oxford.

Smith, M., 2009: Traversing eternity. Texts for the afterlife from Ptolemaic and Roman Egypt, Oxford.

Soghor, Ch.L., 1967: Inscriptions from Tell el Rub'a, JARCE 6, 16-23.

Soukiassian, G.., 1982: Une version des veillées d'Osiris, BIFAO 82, 333-348.

Sourouzian, H., 1989: Les monuments du roi Merenptah, Cairo.

Speleers, L., 1923: Recueil des inscriptions égyptiennes des Musées Royaux du Cinquantenaire à Bruxelles, Brussels.

Spencer, N., 2006: A naos of Nekhthorheb from Bubastis. Religious iconography and temple building in the 30th Dynasty, London.

Spencer, N., 2008: Kom Firin I: the Ramesside temple and the site survey, London.

Spencer, N., 2010: Kom Firin after the New Kingdom, in: S. Ikram/A. Dodson, Beyond the horizon. Studies in Egyptian art, archaeology and history in honour of Barry J. Kemp, Cairo, 506-537.

Spencer, N., 2010a: Sustaining Egyptian culture? Non-royal initiatives in Late Period temple building, in: L. Bareš/F. Coppens/K. Smoláriková (eds.), Egypt in transition. Social and religious development of Egypt in the first millennium BCE, Prague, 441-490.

Spencer, P., 1984: The Egyptian temple. A lexicographical study, London.

Spencer, P., 2007: The Egypt Exploration Society – the early years, London.

Spiegelberg, W., 1929: Die Stele 119C des Louvre, Kêmi 2, 107-112.
Stadler, M.A., 2003: Der Totenpapyrus des Pa-Month ((P. Bibl. nat. 149), Wiesbaden.
Steindorff, G., 1946: Catalogue of the Egyptian sculptures in the Walters Art Gallery, Baltimore.
Sternberg-el Hotabi, H., 1994: Die 'Götterliste' des Sanktuars im Hibis-Tempel von El-Chargeh. Überlegungen zur Tradierung und Kodifizierung religiösen und kulttopographischen Gedankengutes, in: M. Minas/J. Zeidler (eds.), Aspekte spätägyptischer Kultur. Festschrift für Erich Winter zum 65. Geburtstag, Mainz am Rhein, 239-254.
Stewart, H.M., 1983: Egyptian stelae, reliefs and paintings from the Petrie Collection, III: The Late Period, with a supplement of miscellaneous inscribed material, Warminster.
Stricker, B.H., 1939: Le naos vert de Memphis, ASAE 39, 215-220.
Strudwick, N., 2006: Masterpieces of Ancient Egypt, London.
Szpakowska, K., 2009: Demons in Ancient Egypt, Religion Compass 3/5, 799-805.
Takàcs, G., 2008: Etymological dictionary of Egyptian, III, Leiden.
Taylor, J.H./Strudwick, N.C., 2005: Mummies: death and the afterlife in Ancient Egypt, Santa Ana.
Taylor, J.H., 2010: Journey through the afterlife. Ancient Egyptian Book of the Dead, London.
Teeter, E., 1997: The presentation of Maat: ritual and legitimacy in Ancient Egypt, Chicago.
Thausing, G./Goedicke, H., 1971: Nofretari – eine Dokumentation der Wandgemälde ihres Grabes, Graz.
Thiers, Ch., 1997: Un naos de Ptolémée II Philadelphe consacré à Sokar, BIFAO 97, 253-268.
Thiers, Ch., 2012: Un montant de naos au nom d'Amasis consacré au dieu Ptah, in: C. Zivie-Coche/I. Guermeur (eds.), «Parcourir l'éternité», hommages à Jean Yoyotte, Turnhout, 981-989.
Topozada, Z., 2003: Amasis à Memphis: details sur le culte memphite d'Osiris et d'Isis, in: Z. Hawass (ed.), Egyptology at the dawn of the twenty-first century. Proceedings of the Eight International Congress of Egyptologists Cairo, 2000, Cairo/New York, 527-533.
Traunecker, C., 2008: Le palais funéraire de Padiamenopé redécouvert (TT 33), Egypte Afrique & Orient 51, 15-48.
Traunecker, C., 2010: La chapelle d'Osiris «seigneur de l'éternité-*neheh*» à Karnak, in: L. Coulon, Le culte d'Osiris au Ier millénaire av. J.-C. Découvertes et travaux récents. Actes de la table ronde internationale tenue à Lyon, Maison de l'Orient et de la Méditerranée (université Lumière-Lyon 2), les 8 et 9 juillet 2005, Cairo, 155-194.
Traunecker, C./Régen, I., 2013: The funerary palace of Padiamenope at Thebes, EA 43, 32-34.
Traunecker, C., 2014: The "Funeral Palace" of Padiamenope: tomb, palace of pilgrimage, and library. Current research, in: E. Pischikova/J. Budka/K. Griffin (eds.), Thebes in the first millennium BC, Cambridge, 205-234.
Traunecker, C./Régen, I., 2016: La tombe du prêtre Padiamenopé (TT 33): éclairages nouveaux, BSFE 193-194, 52-83.
Vandier, J., 1961: Le Papyrus Jumilhac, Paris.
Varille, A., 1934: Quelques données nouvelles sur la pierre bekhen des anciens Égyptiens, BIFAO 34, 93-102.
Varille, A., 1956: La grande porte du temple d'Opet à Karnak, ASAE 53, 79-118.
Velde, H. te, 1971: Some remarks on the structure of Egyptian divine triads, JEA 57, 80-86.
Velde, H. te, 1975: Dämonen, in: LÄ I, 980-984.
Verhoeven, U., 1993: Das saitische Totenbuch der Iahtes-nacht, P. Colon. Aeg. 10207, Bonn.
Verner, M., 2012: Temple of the world. Sanctuaries, cults, and mysteries of Ancient Egypt, Cairo.
Vernus, P., 1975: Inscriptions de la Troisième Période Intermédiaire (II), BIFAO 75, 67-72.
Vernus, P., 1978: Athribis. Textes et documents relatifs à la géographie, aux cultes, et à l'histoire d'une ville du Delta égyptien à l'époque pharaonique, Cairo.

Vivian, C., 2012: Americans in Egypt, 1770-1915: explorers, consuls, travelers, soldiers, missionaries, writers and scientists, Jefferson.
Volokhine, Y., 2000: La frontalité dans l'iconographie de l'Égypte ancienne, Geneva.
Waitkus, W., 1987: Zur Deutung einiger apotropäischer Götter in den Gräbern im Tal der Königinnen und im Grabe Ramses III, GM 99, 51-82.
Walle, B. Van de, 1953: La tortue dans la religion et la magie égyptiennes, La Nouvelle Clio 5, 177-178.
Werning, D., 2011: Das Höhlenbuch. Textkritische Edition und Textgrammatik, I-II, Wiesbaden.
Wiedemann, A., 1880: Geschichte Aegyptens von Psammetich I. bis auf Alexander den Grossen, Leipzig.
Wiedemann, A., 1884: Ägyptische Geschichte, Gotha.
Willems, H., 1988: Chests of life. A study of the typology and conceptual development of Middle Kingdom standard class coffins, Leiden.
Willems, H., 1996: The coffin of Heqata (Cairo JdE 36418). A case study of Egyptian culture of the early Middle Kingdom, Leuven.
Willems, H., 1997: The embalmer embalmed. Remarks on the meaning of the decoration of some Middle Kingdom coffins, in: J. van Dijk (ed.), Essays on Ancient Egypt in honour of Herman te Velde, Groningen, 343-372.
Wilson, P., 1997: A Ptolemaic lexikon. A lexicographical study of the texts in the temple of Edfu, Leuven.
Wilson, P., 1998: Fieldwork, 1997-8: the survey of Sais, 1997, JEA 84, 2-4.
Wilson, P., 2006: The survey of Saïs (Sa el-Hagar), 1997-2002, London.
Yoyotte, J., 1954: À propos du naos des décades, JNES 13, 79-82.
Yoyotte, J., 1954a: Prêtres et sanctuaires du nome héliopolite à la Basse Époque, BIFAO 54, 83-115.
Yoyotte, J. 1961: Études géographiques, I: La «cité des acacias» (Kafr Ammar), RdE 13, 71-105.
Yoyotte, J., 1972: Pétoubastis III, RdE 24, 216-223.
Yoyotte, J., 1987: Tanis. L'or des pharaons, Paris.
Yoyotte, J., 1998: A la recherché d'un explorateur marseillais disparu: Jean-Jacques Rifaud, in: D. Jacobi (ed.), Pascal Coste, toutes les Egypte, Marseilles, 10-12, 14, 23, 28, 48, 191, 203, 216-218, 221-234.
Yoyotte, J., 2001: Le grand Kôm el-Ahmar de Menûfîyah et deux naos du pharaon Amasis, BSFE 151, 54-83.
Yoyotte, J., 2003: Jean-Jacques Rifaud (1786-1852), un singulier voyageur qui vint mourir à Genève, in: Voyages en Égypte de l'antiquité au début du XXe siècle (Catalogue de l'exposition, Musée d'art et d'histoire Genève, 16 avril – 31 août 2003), Geneva, 87-97.
Zago, M., 2010: Tebe magica e alchemica. L'idea di biblioteca nell'Egitto romano: la collezione Anastasi, Limena.
Zandee, J., 1981-1982: Eine doppelt überlieferter Text eines Hymnus an die Nachtsonne aus dem Neuen Reich, JEOL 27, 3-22.
Zecchi, M., 1996: A study on the Egyptian god Osiris Hemag, Imola.
Zecchi, M., 2010: Sobek of Shedet. The crocodile god in the Fayyum in the Dynastic Period, Todi.
Ziegler, C., 1990: The Louvre: Egyptian antiquities, London.
Zivie, A., 1975: Hermopolis et le nome de l'ibis: recherches sur la province du dieu Thot en Basse Egypte, Cairo.
Zivie, A., 1998: Pascal Coste Égyptologue, in: D. Jacobi (ed.), Pascal Coste, toutes les Égypte, Marseilles, 163-188.
Zivie-Coche, C., 1991: Giza au premier millénaire. Autour du temple d'Isis Dame des Pyramides, Boston.
Zivie-Coche, C., 2004: Tanis. Travaux récents sur le Tell Sân El-Hagar, 3: statues et autobiographies de dignitaires. Tanis à l'Époque Ptolémaïque, Paris.

Indices

1. Deities

Akh 30, 52
Amun 33-34, 36-37, 39, 53, 75, 87, 95, 109, 123, 126, 128, 143, 147
Amun-Ptah 98
Amun-Ra 24, 39, 97-98, 104, 114, 123
Amunet 143
Anubis 23, 25, 39, 51, 94, 101-102, 112-117, 119-120, 123-126, 136, 141
Anuket 56
Atum 73, 87, 91-92, 104, 110, 120-121, 123, 142
Banebdjed 81, 104-105
Bastet 70, 109-110, 142, 147
Bes 30
Duamutef 26-27, 51, 117, 142
Four Sons of Horus 9, 26, 117, 120, 125, 128, 130, 142
Geb 59, 65, 67, 78, 81-82, 92, 99, 118, 120, 123, 142, 145
Hapi 102, 117, 120, 142
Hapy 26-27, 51, 117, 142
Hathor 58, 65, 67, 90-92, 99, 100-101, 103, 109-110, 135-137, 139, 141-142, 144-147
Hathor-nebet-hetepet 120
Heh 143
Hehet 143
Heka 94
Henut-wat 97
Heqet 136-137
Heryshef 104
Hor-Khenty(-en)-irty 117, 141-142
Hor-Khenty-khety 74, 143
Hor-nedj-it-ef 117, 136, 141-142
Hor-sa-aset 77, 102, 110, 143, 147
Hor-sema-tawy 143-144
Horakhty 120
Hormerty 74
Horus 24, 26, 29-31, 34, 39, 51-53, 56, 91-92, 97, 111-114, 116-117, 119-127, 130-134, 137-138, 141-144
Imsety 26-27, 51, 117, 142
Iremawa 89, 94
Isden 82
Isdes 32, 123-124, 130
Isis 9, 24-25, 28, 30-31, 51-52, 56, 65, 75-76, 84-85, 93, 98-99, 102, 104-105, 107, 110, 112-113, 116-120, 122, 125-128, 130-131, 136-137, 141-143, 146
Iunmutef 94
Keket 143
Keku 38, 143
Kem-wer 61, 82, 85, 110-111, 147
Khentyamentiu 76-77
Khepri 142
Khnum 56, 103-104
Khonsu 97, 143
Khonsu-Horus 110
Khonsu-Neferhotep 97
Maat 40, 42, 54, 66, 120, 124, 134, 142-143
Mahes 143
Merkhetes 102
Min 55-56, 88, 91, 93, 104, 110
Min-Amun 93
Min-Ra 97
Montu 33, 53, 75, 99, 123, 126
Montu-Ra 33, 92, 97, 123
Mut 97, 121
Nebet-hetepet 74, 84, 142
Neith 49, 56, 61, 66, 68-69, 75, 77-78, 143
Nekhbet 26, 73, 117, 125, 146
Neper 99
Nephthys 9, 28, 38-39, 52, 54, 84, 99, 102, 104, 107, 112-113, 118-119, 122, 124, 126, 128, 131, 134, 136-137, 141-143
Nun 39, 143
Nunet 143
Nut 65, 118, 123, 142, 145
Opet 91, 93, 104
Osiris *passim*
Osiris-Andjety 73-75, 108
Osiris *djed* 143
Osiris 'Great Saw' (*ỉtfꜣ wr*) 28-29, 50, 52, 118-122
Osiris Hemag 7, 11, 27, 49, 57, 85, 87-93, 95-99, 102-105, 107, 109-110, 112-113, 116-117, 120-122, 125-126, 134-139, 144-145, 147
Osiris-Khenty-khety 74
Osiris 'lord of Abydos' 78, 111
Osiris 'lord of Djedu/Busiris' 28, 52, 92, 121-122
Osiris 'lord of eternity' 75-77, 145
Osiris 'lord of Ra-setjau' 28, 29, 49, 52, 118, 121-122
Osiris Merty 57, 85, 107, 110-111, 125, 144-145, 147
Osiris-Neferhotep 104
Osiris *pꜣ-mry=s* 75

Osiris-Sokar 90, 98
Osiris Wennefer 76, 119
Osiris Wennefer Neb-djefau 75
Ptah 55, 61-62, 66, 68, 70, 75, 90, 95, 99, 142
Ptah-Sokar 77, 89, 94, 104-105
Ptah-Sokar-Osiris 136
Ptah-Tatenen 98
Qebehsenuef 26-27, 51, 88, 117, 142
Ra 22-23, 39, 59, 67-69, 81-82, 93, 112-113, 120
Ra-Atum 120
Ra-Horakhty 77, 123, 142, 147
Rayt-tawy 92
Satet 56
Sekhmet 59, 74, 80-81, 90, 95, 108
Sepa 120
Sesheta-weret 146
Seth 77
Sha 34, 134
Shentayt 94, 102, 143
Shesmetet 65, 145
Shesmu 89, 94
Shu 32-33, 53, 58-59, 67, 81-82, 102, 112, 120, 123-124, 126, 130, 142
Sobek 38, 104
Sokar 90, 92, 95, 99-101, 104, 142-143, 147
Sokar-Osiris 88, 92, 99, 101-102, 104-105, 136
Sopdu 66, 143
Tatenen 62, 91, 98-99
Tefnet 32-33, 53, 99, 104, 112, 120, 123-124, 126, 130, 142
Thoth 74, 117, 119, 130-131, 136, 141-142
Tutu 109-110
Wadj-wer 117, 142
Wadjet 56, 62, 65, 73, 143, 145
Wepwawet 78, 114

2. Deities (in transliteration)

ꜣḫ 31, 122
ꜣsb ('Radiant one') 30-31, 52, 122, 126-127
ꜣkr 82
ỉwꜤ nṯr ('Heir of the god') 23-25, 51, 115-116, 128
ỉf ('Flesh') 46-47
ỉn-ḥr ('He who brings the face' ?) 30-31, 49-50, 52, 122, 126-127
ỉr-rn=f-ḏs=f ('He who makes his own name') 43-45, 54, 125, 127
ỉsbt-ỉm(y)-ḥtpwy 43
ỉsdn 33
ỉsds 33
ỉty 119
Ꜥꜣ-ḫrw 35-37, 53, 124, 126-127
Ꜥbwy ('He with two horns') 40-41, 54, 124
Ꜥnn-Ꜥbwy ('He who averts the horns') 41
Ꜥnḫ-m-fnṯw 30-31, 47, 123, 126-127
Ꜥnḫ-m-fdt 30, 47, 52, 122, 126-127
wnm-ḥwꜣt-nt-pḥwy.fy / *wnm-ḥwꜣt* 35-37, 53, 124, 126-128
wr-nrw 25
pḫrr 38-39, 54, 124-125
bnty 46
mꜣꜣ-ỉt=f ('He who sees his father') 24-25, 44-45, 51, 94, 116-117
mwyt 26-27, 51, 117, 125, 142
mnḫt-ḥbt ('Festive cloth') 84-85
mnḫt-štꜣt ('Secret cloth') 82, 84-85
mrt mḥw 143
mrt šmꜤw 143
mḥwnt 39
mds 43-44, 54
nꜤw wr ('Great serpent') 84
nb-rḫn 84
nb ḥḥ ('Lord of million') 84
nfr-nfrw 35-37, 53, 124, 126
nrw 45
nḥmmt 37, 43, 124
nḫbt 27, 51, 142
nḫt ('Strong one') 84
rꜣ-wꜣḥ ('The one with an enduring mouth') 84
rs-wrt 42
ḥꜣḳw ('Plunderer') 45
ḥwnt ('Young one') 40
ḥr=f-m-ḫꜣḫ ('His face is in haste') 39-40, 43, 54, 124
ḥr-m-ḥwrt ('Face as a poor woman') 40
ḥr-m-ḥwnt ('Face as a young girl') 38-40, 47, 54, 124
ḥḏ wr ('Great White') 82
ḫꜣbs 39-40, 42-43, 54, 124
ḫnfꜣ-ḥr / *ḫnfꜣ* 45
ḫsf-m-tp-Ꜥ ('He who repels at the beginning') 29-30, 52, 122, 126, 128
ḫssỉỉ ('Fish-man') 38, 54, 124
smt 36-37
snfy ('Bloody one') 84
sḥr-ḏw ('He who drives away evil') 24-25, 51, 115-116
sḫm 24, 26, 51, 116, 128
sḫm-ḥr ('Powerful of face') 44-45
sḫd-ḥr ('He with an upside down face') 31, 46-47
sḳd-ḥr ('Watchful of face') 30-32, 37, 52, 122, 126-127
šꜤ ('He who cuts to pieces') 34, 53
šꜤ-tb/šꜤ-bṯw 35, 124, 130, 134
šbtyt 142, 147
ḳmꜣ-ỉrw ('He who creates the form') 85
kkw ('Darkness') 39, 41, 54, 124
tm-ḥꜤw ('Complete of limbs') 84
db-ḥr-k 46
dwn-ḥr ('Extended of face') 24-26, 51, 116

3. Royal names

Amasis 7, 9-10, 14-15, 21-29, 33, 37, 41, 43, 45, 47, 49-50, 55-70, 72-82, 85, 87, 105, 107-118, 123, 125, 132-135, 138-141, 144-147
Amenhotep III 119
Apries 21, 33, 64, 67, 69-70, 72-77, 82, 107-109
Cambyses 69
Darius I 84
Djer 77
Domitian 70, 109-110
Horemheb 127
Merenptah 24, 29, 35, 39, 41-42, 115, 122, 124, 126, 128, 132, 134, 138
Nekau II 70, 73-74, 107
Nekhthorheb 21, 70, 72, 84-85, 107, 110-111, 121-122, 141
Nekhtnebef 21, 33, 70, 72, 88, 107, 110, 123
Niuserra 114, 117
Osorkon II 109, 129
Pepy II 114
Psamtek I 73, 82, 109-110
Psamtek II 73-75
Psamtek III 75
Psusennes I 24, 26, 29-32, 35-44, 46, 115-116, 122-124, 126, 128-129, 132-135
Ptolemy II Philadelphus 110
Ptolemy III Euergetes I 92
Ptolemy IV Philopator 91
Ptolemy VIII Euergetes II 91
Ramses I 127
Ramses II 39, 41-43, 62, 69, 111, 119, 124, 130
Ramses III 116, 120, 127-128
Ramses IV 127
Ramses VI 38-43, 46, 130-131
Ramses IX 127, 130-131
Ramses X 127
Sahura 117-118
Senusret I 69, 109, 114
Sety I 35, 37-43, 46, 77, 89, 94, 104-105, 123-124, 127, 130, 135, 137
Shabaka 69, 75, 109-110
Sheshonq III 35, 37-43, 46, 123, 130, 135
Taharqa 130
Tanutamun 130-132
Thutmose III 119
Tutankhamun 30-32, 36, 119, 122

4. Egyptian personal names

Ahaneferamun 119
Amunmes 87, 89, 95-96, 105
Amunemhotep 100
Ani 124
Ankhefenkhonsu 29, 44, 46, 123, 129
Ankhhapi (son of Ta-net-ba-anepet) 29, 35-36, 42, 129
Ankhhapi (son of Tefnakht) 24-25, 29, 32, 35-36, 41, 44, 46, 115, 129
Ankhnesneferibra 34, 39
Ankhwennefer 89
Anlamani 34, 124
Aspelta 34, 82, 124
Basa 89-90, 95
Djedhor (son of Iahmes) 24-26, 29, 32, 35-36, 41, 44, 116, 129
Djedkhonsuiuefankh 36, 81, 105, 147
Djehutymes 119
(Dua-)Tentopet 127
Gatseshen 119
Harkhebi 87, 89
Hetepimen 88, 97
Horaawesheb 129
Horemheb 30, 34, 44
Hornakht 129
Horpakhepesh 88
Iahmes (son of king Amasis) 24-26, 29, 31, 34-39, 41-42, 44-46, 69, 115-116, 123-124, 129, 132-134
Iahtesnacht 121
Ikherneferet 111
Imeneminet 105
Iufankh 121
Iuia 119
Iyrey 119
Kha 119
Khaemwaset 127
Khaf 25, 29, 31-32, 34-46, 117, 123, 129, 132, 134
Kheruef 119
Montuemhat 24-26, 29, 44-45, 129
Muthetepti 128
Mutirdis 24-25, 29, 32, 34-43, 45-46, 114-115, 117, 123-124, 129-131, 133-134
Naes 88, 97
Nakhtamun 119
Nakhtmin 119
Neferi 119
Nefertari 32, 37
Nekhtbastetru 24, 69
Nesnephthys 49
Nodjmet 119
Nu 119
Pabasa 130
Padikhonsu 119
Padimahes 143
Padipep 120-121
Paennestitaui 119
Pakhar 119
Panehemisis 30-31, 34-35, 37, 41, 44, 129
Pareherwenemef 127
Paser 119
Pasherientaihet 121
Pasherihoraawasheb 45
Pediamenopet 49, 87, 90, 109, 121, 129-130
Peftjawyneith 76-78, 110
Ptahmes 119
Qalhata 130-132
Ra 119
Ramose 129-130, 133
Senenmut 119

Sethherkhepshef 127
Sewer 120
Sitra 127
Tameret 119
Tayuheryt 119
Tjahorpta 26
Tyti 127
Userhat 119
Wennefer 35-36, 45, 129
Yewerhen 89

5. Names of buildings and places

Abu Simbel 69
Abusir 84
Abydos 39, 41-43, 64, 67-68, 70, 73-78, 89, 94-95, 104-105, 110-111, 113, 119, 121, 123-124, 130, 135-137
Agurmi 56
Alexandria 12-14, 16
Armant 99
Athribis 28, 33, 55, 61, 66, 68, 70, 72-75, 82-85, 89, 107, 109, 138-139, 141, 147
Avaris 90
Ayn el-Muftella 56, 81, 105, 147
Behbeit el-Hagar 88, 90, 96-97, 102-103, 107, 135
Behdet 91
Biggeh 56
Biket 142, 147
Bubastis 56, 68, 70, 72, 88, 90, 107, 110, 119, 121, 141
Busiris (Djedu) 28, 52, 73-75, 92, 108, 111, 121-122, 136-137
Buto 55
Cairo 13, 18, 60-61, 64, 67-68, 70, 72
Coptos 56, 76, 88, 90-93, 110, 143-144, 147
Deir el-Bersha 119
Dendera (Iunet) 25, 29, 32, 34-36, 38, 42, 45-46, 65, 88-95, 98-105, 107, 109, 121, 135-137, 146
Edfu 32, 34, 36, 56, 65, 91-93, 98-99, 101, 104, 111, 121, 136-137, 142, 146
El-Baqlieh 72, 74, 109
El-Kharga 98
El-Kurru 130
El-Lahun 89, 96
El-Nahhariya 56, 78, 107
Elephantine 56, 67-68
Elkab 56, 136
Esna 69, 75, 110
Fayum 38
Fekat 57, 138, 144
Giza 24, 69, 119
Heliopolis (Iunu) 56, 73-74, 87, 90, 107, 110, 120-123, 126, 136, 144, 147
Hermopolis (Khenemu) 41, 56, 99, 117, 131, 141-144
Hibis 38, 98-99, 102-104, 107, 109, 131, 142
Hierakonpolis 113
Horbeit (Shedenu) 74, 108
House of gold 89-90, 92-95, 103, 105
House of *hemag* 88, 90-95, 104, 135
House of Sekhmet 59, 74, 80-81
Ipet 87
Karnak 15, 36, 62, 69, 75, 87, 89-90, 92-93, 95-96, 102, 104-105, 114, 121
Kher-Aha 90, 120, 122
Kom Abu Billo 138-139
Kom el-Ahmar 11, 13-16, 20, 28, 33, 37, 41, 45, 47, 57-58, 65, 67-70, 72-73, 75, 85, 90, 107, 109, 111, 113, 117, 123, 125, 138-141, 145-147
Kom el-Heitan 119
Kom el-Nawa 55
Kom el-Qal'a 55
Kom el-Sultan 77-78
Kom Firin 56
Kus 110
Leontopolis 143
Letopolis 141, 143-144
Medamud 91, 93, 137
Medinet Habu 38, 120
Mefekat 138-139, 142-147
Memphis 47, 50, 55, 60-61, 66, 68-70, 73, 75, 87, 89-90, 92, 94-95, 99, 107, 114, 122, 136, 142-144, 147
Mendes 55, 58-59, 67-68, 70, 73-75, 81, 90, 141
Mensha (Ptolemais) 77, 139
Mit Gharita 72
Mit Rahina 55
Naukratis 56
Nekhen 78, 82
Nub-Taha 73
Philae 56, 102, 104
Qantir 119
Qaw el-Kebir 70
Rosetta 56, 78, 107
Sa el-Hagar 49, 56, 59, 78, 80, 96-97, 107
Saft el-Henna 33, 72, 107, 110, 123
Sais 11, 49, 56, 59, 66-68, 70, 72-75, 78, 80-81, 88-90, 96, 103, 107-108, 139, 143-144, 147
Sakhebu 143-144
Saqqara 55, 66, 88, 97, 114, 119, 129, 132
Sehel 56
Shen-Qebeh 119-120
Sohag 78
Tanis 31, 56, 69, 88, 90, 97, 107, 128-130, 135
Tanta 56
Tebtunis 117, 121
Tell Defenneh 56, 68
Tell el-Maskhuta 56, 68-69
Tell Nabasha 7, 55-56, 62-63, 66-67, 70, 73
Tell Tebilla 141
Thebes 56, 62, 68, 70, 73, 87, 90, 105, 116, 120-121, 123, 126, 128-131, 145

Tjepehet-djat 98-99
Tod 38
Umm el-Qaab 77
Wadi Hammamat 56

6. Museum collections

Alexandria, Archaeology Museum
JE 25774 33, 123
Athens, Archaeological Museum,
A 112 24
Baltimore, Walters Art Gallery
22.122 80
Berlin, Ägyptisches Museum
- 3002 119
- 23729 45
Bologna, Museo Civico Archeologico
EG 347 26, 129
Boston, Museum of Fine Arts
23729 34, 124
Brooklyn Museum 64.146 143
Brussels, Musées royaux d'Art et d'Histoire
- E 5283 74
- E 5818 71-72, 74, 84, 109
- E 7429 84
Cairo, Egyptian Museum
- CG 1747 114
- CG 17029 77, 139
- CG 23110 139
- CG 23144 120
- CG 29301 29, 31, 35-37, 42, 44, 129
- CG 29303 24-25, 29, 31-32, 34-38, 41, 44-46, 116, 123, 129
- CG 29304 24-26, 29, 31-32, 34-38, 41, 44, 116, 123, 129
- CG 29306 26
- CG 29310 35-37, 45, 129
- CG 29319 37, 44
- CG 29394 45
- CG 38274 29
- CG 38424 108
- CG 41001bis 29, 31, 36-37, 44-46, 123, 129
- CG 42211 36
- CG 48483 119
- CG 51189 119
- CG 61030 122
- CG 70001a 109-110
- CG 70003 69
- CG 70004 69
- CG 70005 69
- CG 70006 109
- CG 70007 69, 75, 109-110
- CG 70008 21, 33, 72, 74, 82, 107, 109
- CG 70009 73-74
- CG 70010 60-61, 66-68, 70, 74, 150
- CG 70011 28, 33, 60-61, 67, 109-111
- CG 70013 21
- CG 70018 70
- CG 70019 21, 110
- CG 70021 33, 72, 107, 110, 123, 142
- CG 70022 21
- CG 70040 123
- CG 88205 70, 74
- JE 25774 33, 123
- JE 29670 119
- JE 32020 100
- JE 36997bis 87, 89, 95-96
- JE 42276 114
- JE 43281 70, 73-75, 108
- JE 43285 74
- JE 45936 139
- JE 47276 69, 114
- JE 47580 73, 109-110
- JE 48887 74
- JE 61946 122
- JE 87297 24, 26, 29, 32, 35-37
- JE 92591 120
- JE 95838 119
- TR 2/2/21/14 109-110
- TR 21/11/14/6 44
- TR 22/11/55/1 72, 74, 109
- TR 30/5/24/5 72, 74, 109
Chicago, Oriental Institute Museum
- 9787 121
- 10729 89-90
Cologne, Seminar fur Ägyptologie
Aeg. 10207 87, 121
Delos, Archaeological Museum
A 379 49
Florence, Museo Egizio
- 1522 49
- 8691 74
Khartum, Sudan National Museum
1868 34, 124
Leiden, Rijksmuseum van Oudheden
- AM 107 *passim*
- I 383 98
- T 3 119
- T 7 119
London, British Museum
- EA 32 34, 39
- EA 94 80
- EA 610 77
- EA 957 82
- EA 1079 107
- EA 1106 70
- EA 2018 127
- EA 6666 45, 129
- EA 10009 119
- EA 10010 128
- EA 10064 119
- EA 10477 119
- EA 50698 127
- EA 50699 127
- EA 50702 127
- EA 50703 127
- EA 50704 127
- EA 61283 127
- EA 68169 66
London, Petrie Museum
UC 14468 76, 151

Memphis Tennessee, Institute of Egyptian Art 50, 55
Montgeron, Musée Municipal 2007.4 145
Naples, Museo Archeologico Nazionale 237 87
New Haven, Yale Peabody Museum ANT 264191 88
New York, Metropolitan Museum of Art 35.9.21 36
Paris, Louvre
- A 93 76
- C 119 120
- C 318 88, 97, 102
- D 29 14-15, 21, 27-28, 33, 37, 41, 47-48, 57, 65-68, 72, 109-111, 113-114, 117, 123, 125, 138-145, 147
- D 37 33, 123
- E 5534 105-106
- E 6258 119
- I 3079 120
- N 504 66
Rome, Musei Capitolini
- MC 0035 68, 79-80
- MC 2156 88, 90
Rome, Museo del Vicino Oriente, La Sapienza 1000 35, 129
St. Petersburg, Hermitage 766 24-26, 31-32, 34, 38, 42, 115, 129, 132
Toronto, Royal Ontario Museum 969.137.2 66
Turin, Museo Egizio
- 1791 121
- 8438 119
- 22055 84-85
Vatican, Museo Gregoriano Egizio
- 38603 87
- 48832 121
Verona, Museo Archeologico 30297 72, 143
Vienna, Kunsthistorisches Museum
- ÄS 4 30, 129
- 213 82
Yverdon-les-Bains, Musée d'Yverdon 83.2.1 145